THE INNOVATOR'S PARADOX 2.0

Harnessing AI to Disrupt Before You're Disrupted.

By Moe Nawaz

©2023 Moe Nawaz

All rights reserved. No part of this publication may be reproduced, stored, or transmitted in any form or by any means, whether electronic, mechanical, photocopying, recording, or otherwise, without prior written permission from the publisher. Printed in the United Kingdom.

Publishers details

Duke Brothers Ltd
30th Floor
Leadenhall Building
122 Leadenhall Street
London. EC3V 4AB
United Kingdom

Tel. 0207 5161 001

www.moenawaz.com

Legal Disclaimer

This Book Does Not Constitute Legal or Business Advice

The information provided in this book is intended for educational purposes only and should not be construed as legal or business advice. Reading this book does not establish a consultant–client relationship between you and Moe Nawaz or Duke Brothers Ltd.

To receive tailored advice specific to your circumstances, you must formally engage my services as a consultant. This requires signing a written engagement agreement, which will outline the terms of our relationship, including the scope of work and associated fees.

Until such an agreement is signed, the content of this book is offered solely as a resource to help you expand your understanding of leadership, innovation, and business growth strategies.

For personalized guidance or to discuss engaging my consultancy services, please contact my office using the details provided above.

About the Author

Moe Nawaz – The 10X Mentor

Moe Nawaz, widely known as *The 10X Mentor*, is a trusted strategic advisor to FTSE 100 and Fortune 500 companies, and the confidential mentor behind some of the world's most ambitious business transformations. With over four decades of front-line experience scaling companies, navigating post-acquisition complexity, and disrupting stagnation at the board level, Moe has become a go-to ally for high-stakes leaders seeking clarity, accountability, and exponential growth.

What sets Moe apart isn't theory, it's results.

From building his own companies to advising multi-billion-pound enterprises, Moe's hands-on insights have shaped a legacy of transformation. His proprietary **Five Strategic Pillars Methodology**—Systemization, Staffability, Scalability, Sustainability, and Sellability—has been the foundation for helping leaders collapse five-year goals into three-year realities. This framework underpins his work and continues to be adopted by scale-stage businesses looking to make their growth not just bigger, but smarter.

Moe is the author of several best-selling books that have redefined how CEOs and founders think about leadership, scale, and strategy:

- **The 7 Habits of Highly Successful Leaders**: A field manual for the personal disciplines and leadership habits that separate high achievers from hopefuls.
- **The 10X Mentor**: A high-stakes guide to unlocking exponential growth through vision, accountability, and the

Five Strategic Pillars.

Mastermind Groups: The Fastest & Safest Way To Grow Your Business (*Directors WarRoom Edition*): A behind-the-scenes look at the exclusive peer environments Moe curates for 8- and 9-figure leaders.

In *The Innovator's Paradox 2.0,* Moe turns his lens toward a new battlefield: the collision between internal stagnation and external disruption. He challenges readers not just to adap, but to lead the charge. With his trademark clarity, candor, and strategic pressure, Moe pushes leaders to see further, act faster, and build companies that don't just survive disruption, but initiate it.

Known for his fearless advice and no-excuses style, Moe is the advisor boards bring in when they're ready to move from performance to legacy. His clients don't hire him for comfort—they hire him for results.

In addition to his private advisory work, Moe speaks regularly at global business forums, facilitates elite mastermind groups, and mentors emerging leaders committed to building impact-driven companies. His work is as much about reshaping industries as it is about reshaping the minds leading them.

To learn more, join his network, or apply for private mentorship, visit **www.MoeNawaz.com** or connect with him on LinkedIn and share what *The Innovator's Paradox 2.0* changed for you.

Table of Contents

About the Author iv
    Moe Nawaz – The 10X Mentor iv
PART I: THE TRAP OF SUCCESS 14
Introduction: The Inescapable Truth of Disruption 15
    My Own Blind Spots 18
    The Innovator's Paradox Defined 21
    A Call to Radical Self-Assessment (Not Denial) 24
    What You'll Discover 27
Chapter 1: The Innovator's Blind Spot: Why Success Can Be Your Greatest Obstacle 29
    The Disruption I Didn't Want to See 31
    What I Learned About the Illusion of Winning 34
    The Comfort Trap 36
    The Empire of Inertia 38
    Metrics vs. Momentum 40
    From Operator to Architect 41
    The AI Whisper 43
    The New Moat Isn't Money, It's Intelligence 45
    The Innovator's Paradox in the AI Age 47
    So Why Don't They Act? 49
    Blind Spot Diagnostic: 7 Strategic Questions 51
    Legacy vs. Leverage: What Are You Actually Building? 55
    The Founder's Dilemma: If You Left Today, What Breaks? 57
    Your First Disruption Sprint: What to Kill, Reinvent, or Rewire? .. 60

Chapter 2: Beyond Adaptation: Mastering the Art of Offensive AI Strategy 63

SECTION 1: The AI Advantage Playbook 63

AI as a Strategy Layer, Not Just a Toolset 65

Why Most CEOs Underuse AI (Even the "Smart" Ones) 67

4. From Automation to Augmentation to Advantage 68

Reinvent Value Propositions 70

Enter New Verticals 72

Case 1: The SaaS Company in San Francisco That Tripled ARR With AI-Powered Onboarding 77

Case 2: The Ecom Brand in Dubai That Created a New Category Using AI Market Insights 80

The Challenge: Competing in a Saturated Market 81

The Insight: Predictive Demand > Trend Following 81

The Execution: AI as Brand Strategist 82

The Outcome: A New Category, Not Just a Product 83

Industry Takeaways for E-Commerce Founders 83

Case 3: The Accountancy Firm in Poland That Scaled with an AI Engine Instead of Hiring 84

The Challenge: Growth Without Complexity 84

The Pivot: AI as Diagnostic and Delivery Engine 85

The Impact: Revenue per Consultant Up 3.5x 86

Industry Questions: What Service Firms Must Now Ask 87

Final Word: The New Smart Firm Isn't Bigger, It's Faster 87

Case 4: The 9-Figure Company That Used AI to Enter a New Industry in 6 Months 88

The Challenge: Expansion Without Guesswork 88

The Move: AI That Models, Maps, and Simulates Outcomes 89

The Execution: Rapid GTM, No Bureaucracy 90

The Impact: 12% New Revenue in Less Than a Year 91

Industry Takeaways: Lessons for CEOs of Mature Companies 91

AI Offense Audit: 12-Point Assessment 92

Where Are You Still Playing Defense? 95

Your AI Battlefield Map: Who's Already Coming for You?........................... 99

Offensive Playbook Builder: What Will You Reinvent, Replace, or Reposition in the Next 90 Days?... 102

Chapter 3: The Systemic Innovator: Empowering Your Team to Drive Transformation 107

1: Building a Culture of Experimentation 107

The Permissionless Principle 109

Rewarding Failure vs. Celebrating Learning 111

Rapid Cycles, Safe Boundaries 113

2: Decentralizing Innovation.. 116

The Innovation Council Model 119

Empowerment Frameworks: When to Say Yes, When to Step Back 121

Accountability Without Micromanagement 123

3: The Innovation Operating System 125

The Four Pillars: Discovery, Design, Deploy, Debrief 127

Tech Stack and Tooling for Innovation Velocity 130

Creating Innovation Rhythm: Cadence, Reviews, Iteration Loops 133

4: Case Studies of Team-Led Disruption 135

5: Moe's Mirror 142

Chapter 4: The Strategic Cadence: Varying Your Reflection for Sustained Impact.. 147

Beyond the Mirror... 147

From Insight to Instrument 148

Guest Reflections 160

The Rationale for Variation 162

Why One Mode Is Never Enough 164

A Practical Parallel: The Military vs. the Studio.......................... 165

Closing the Loop 165

Preventing Reflection Fatigue... 166

The Illusion of Discipline 166

The Neuroscience of Engagement... 167

The Discipline of Variation... 167

The Cadence of Change 168

Reflection Is Not a Solo Sport 169

Designing for Surprise 169

Closing Reflection 170

Building a Holistic Innovation Muscle 173

The Future-Proofing Mirror: Your Business in 5 Years 178

The Legacy Mirror: What Will You Leave Behind? 181

The Action Integration Mirror: Bridging Thought and Execution 185

CHAPTER 5: The Post-Book Blueprint: From Insight to Unstoppable Momentum 189

SECTION 1: The 90-Day Innovation Sprint Template 189

SECTION 2: Building Your Disruption Council 199

SECTION 3: The Digital Toolkit 209

3. Strategic Solitude Practices: Where Clarity Begins 215

Moe's Mirror 226

CHAPTER 6: The Market's Roar: External Pressures and Competitive Disruption 231

SECTION 1: The Unseen Attackers: Who's Eating Your Lunch (and How)? 231

The Incumbent's Dilemma: Defend, Adapt, or Transform? 233

SECTION 2: The Speed of the Market 239

Shifting Sands: Consumer Behavior & Expectations 241

SECTION 3: Competitive Intelligence in the Age of AI 247

SECTION 4: Moe's Mirror 255

CHAPTER 7: The Disruptor's Blueprint: Building Your Legacy as an Industry Shaper 265

SECTION 1: The Offensive Mindset 265

The Psychology of the Offensive Leader 266

"Playing Not to Lose" vs. "Playing to Win Big" 266

The Hidden Cost of Playing It Safe 267

You're Already Qualified 268

First Principles Thinking: Deconstructing Your Industry 269

The Cost of Default Thinking 269
How to Deconstruct Your Industry with First Principles Thinking 270
Why Most Leaders Resist This (and Why You Can't) 272
The Visionary's Edge: Seeing What Others Miss 273
The Two Lenses: Intuition and Data 273
How Visionaries Train Their Senses 274
Vision Is Not Enough, You Must Act on It 276
SECTION 2: Category Creation Strategies 276
What Is White Space, Really? 277
Where White Space Hides 277
How to Hunt for White Space 279
Leveraging AI for Demand Sensing and Trend Discovery 280
White Space Is Only Valuable If You Own It Fast 281
The 'Blue Ocean' Playbook: Creating New Demand 282
What Is a Blue Ocean? 282
Four Strategic Levers of Blue Ocean Creation 283
Case Study: The Silent Headphones Company That Beat Bose 285
The Methodology Behind the Move 286
If You're Not Creating Demand, You're Competing for It 286
Naming & Framing Your New Category 287
Why Language is Your Trojan Horse 287
How to Name Your Category 288
Category Framing: The Story You Must Own 289
Evangelizing the Vision 290
You're Not Just Competing for Market Share, You're Competing for Mindshare
.... 291
SECTION 3: The 'Musk' Mentality 292
Elon Musk: The Grand Vision & Relentless Execution 292
The 'Impossible Problems' Filter 292
First Principles Thinking at Scale 293
Vertical Integration as a Strategic Weapon 294
Speed Over Perfection 295

Long-Term Thinking With Tactical Obsession 296
Adopt the Mindset, Not the Persona 296
Jeff Bezos: Customer Obsession & Day 1 Mentality 297
The Day 1 Philosophy 297
The Relentless Customer Flywheel 298
Long-Term Thinking as a Competitive Weapon 299
The Power of Frictionless Thinking 300
Innovation Anchored in Principles 301
How to Apply the Bezos Playbook Today 302
Other Industry Shapers: Diverse Paths to Disruption 303
Steve Jobs: Obsessive Design and Narrative Control 303
Reed Hastings: Reinventing Models, Not Just Products 304
Sara Blakely: Scrappiness, Simplicity, and Underdog Momentum 305
Common Threads of Disruptive Leaders 306
Final Thought: Diverse Playbooks, Shared Psychology 306
SECTION 4: Building an Ecosystem of Disruption 307
Strategic Partnerships for Exponential Growth 307
Why Partnerships Accelerate Innovation 308
Who Should You Partner With? 308
The Co-Creation Model: From Supplier to Partner 309
A Final Litmus Test 310
Attracting & Retaining Disruptive Talent 310
What They're Really Interviewing For 312
Designing for Talent Density 313
Funding Your Future: Beyond Traditional Capital 313
The Limitations of Traditional Capital 314
Funding Is a Signal 316
SECTION 5: Moe's Mirror 316
Step Into the Future, Now 317
The Trap of Realism 318
The First Domino: Identifying Your Initial Action 319

What's Your First Domino? 319
Why This Step Matters More Than Any Other 320
A Challenge for You 320
Committing to the Uncomfortable 321
The Anatomy of Discomfort in Innovation 321
From Tolerance to Commitment 322
The Final Commitment 323

Conclusion: The Continuous Innovation Journey 325

Innovation Is Not a Destination 325
You're Not "Done" After This Book 325
The Cost of Success Is Complacency 326
Innovation Is Not an Act. It's a System. 327
You're Now the Architect 327
One Final Truth 328
The Innovation Flywheel: How to Keep Momentum After the Book 329
What Is the Innovation Flywheel? 329
Step 1: Build a Culture That Senses 330
Step 2: Reflect with Strategic Cadence 330
Step 3: Take Fast, Focused Action 331
Step 4: Learn Relentlessly 331
Step 5: Adapt with Precision 332
From One Flywheel to Many 332
Ritualizing the Habit of Innovation 333
The Innovation Flywheel Is Not Optional 333
The Strategic Disruption Circle: Who You Surround Yourself With Shapes How Boldly You Move 334
Why Isolation Is the Silent Killer 334
The Role of Strategic Confrontation 335
A Mirror, a Model, a Multiplier 336
Why This Is Personal 336
An Invitation 337

Moe's Final Mirror: Your Legacy, Designed Today 339

    You Don't Need More Ideas. You Need Momentum. 339

    Innovation Is Personal..340

    Why I Want to Hear From You...340

    Never Be Shy About Reaching Out 341

    Visit My Website, Explore Further 342

    Leave a Public Footprint..342

    Your Legacy Doesn't Start Later. It Starts Now. 343

PART I:
THE TRAP OF SUCCESS

Introduction:
The Inescapable Truth of Disruption

Let me tell you a story, one I don't share often, but it's stuck with me because it captures everything this book is really about.

I was sitting across from the CEO of a well-known luxury department store chain here in the UK. Family-owned for generations. £300 million in turnover. Loyal customer base. Eleven flagship stores. The kind of business that prides itself on heritage, reputation, and what they called "timeless taste."

They weren't in crisis, not visibly. In fact, they were celebrating a strong Q4. Footfall was returning after the pandemic, and their VIP loyalty program had crossed 1.2 million active members. From the outside, everything looked stable, even promising.

That was the problem.

During our meeting, he smiled as he handed me their latest report. Solid margins, strong inventory position, positive forecasts. And I asked him one question:

"Who's your biggest competitor right now?"

He leaned back. Named a few other high-end chains. Some overseas players trying to get a slice of their market. All logical answers. All wrong.

I asked again, but slower this time.

"No, not your competitors from the last five years. Who's coming for you in the next five?"

The Innovator's Paradox 2.0

That changed the mood.

You see, while they were focused on protecting what they'd built, disruption had already entered their world, and it didn't knock on the front door. It crept in through the customer's phone.

What they didn't know was that their most affluent, trend-sensitive customers, young professionals, fashion-forward Gen Z, high-earning millennials, were spending more time buying curated AI-personalised "luxury boxes" through TikTok live-streams and Instagram boutiques than stepping foot in their stores. These boxes weren't just stylish, they were algorithmically precise. Styles were tracked in real-time from Seoul, São Paulo, and Stockholm. Micro-trends updated daily. Product recommendations learned your tastes faster than any in-store stylist ever could.

And while the CEO's buyers were still doing annual European buying trips to Milan and Paris, a small AI startup had quietly onboarded several of their suppliers, offering predictive fashion demand models that shaved 28% off lead times.

Then there was logistics. They'd just spent millions upgrading a regional distribution centre, but a rival was testing drone-based last-mile delivery with 24-hour cycles from click to door. In other words, the game had changed. And they were still perfecting the old one.

That CEO wasn't foolish. He was smart, proud, and experienced. He'd spent decades mastering his market. But he was looking in the wrong direction, just like so many others.

It's easy to feel safe when the numbers are steady and the people around you are nodding. That's when the blind spot forms. Not from ignorance, but from experience. The longer you've been successful, the harder it becomes to spot the thing that will undo you. That's the paradox. Your success gives you confidence. That confidence hardens into certainty. And that certainty makes you miss what's quietly changing underneath.

I call it the Innovator's Blind Spot.

And it's not just a retail story. I've seen it play out across every sector I work in.

In healthcare, I worked with a diagnostics firm whose radiologists were being quietly outperformed by AI in detecting cancer patterns. Not because the doctors weren't brilliant, but because the machines were learning faster.

In manufacturing, one client believed their speed was unbeatable, until a three-person AI-enhanced team at a rival firm undercut their unit economics by 40%.

In legal, senior partners scoffed when I warned that contract reviews wouldn't take three days forever. Now it's done in 12 minutes, with better accuracy, and the clients know it.

This isn't about technology replacing humans. It's about a fundamental shift in *where* disruption begins. It used to start with a loud noise, a new entrant, a drop in market share, a scandal. Now, it begins with silence. A small shift in customer behaviour. A subtle change in expectation. A whisper in the data that no one listens to, until it's too late.

I know this is uncomfortable to hear. But this book wasn't written to make you comfortable. It was written to wake you up, not out of fear, but out of clarity.

If you're reading this and thinking, *"We're doing well, this doesn't apply to us,"* I need you to understand something: that's exactly who it applies to. The companies most at risk aren't the weak ones, they're the ones who think they're still winning the last game, while the rules have already changed.

This isn't a lecture. It's a conversation between leaders. I've sat in enough boardrooms and private strategy sessions to know this: the threat isn't failure. It's relevance. Staying relevant to your market, your people, your future. And if you're not watching closely, you'll find yourself investing in efficiency while someone else invests in reinvention.

That's why this book begins with a warning. Not a dramatic one. A surgical one.

I'm not asking you to panic. I'm asking you to look up.

What if the real disruption isn't coming, it's already here?

What if it's not loud, but silent?

What if you're not falling behind, but *blind to what's already passed you by*?

That's what we're going to explore together. Not as a consultant and a client. But as two people who've built, broken, and rebuilt. As leaders who want to leave behind more than profit. As architects of what's next.

Because the tsunami isn't on the horizon. It's already underneath your feet.

And the question now is this: will you ride it, or drown in it?

My Own Blind Spots

You know, it's easy to talk about blind spots when you're pointing them out in someone else's business. It's much harder when the finger is turned inward. And I'd be lying if I pretended I haven't been caught off guard myself.

There was a time, early in my advisory career, when I was riding high on momentum. I'd helped turn around a few major companies, one in logistics, another in manufacturing, and suddenly, doors that were once bolted shut began to open with ease. Strategy sessions at The Ritz. Last-minute calls from FTSE boardrooms. Even my waiting list for private clients had started to grow longer than I could handle.

I told myself I'd earned it. And I had. But what I didn't realise at the time was that I was slowly becoming the very thing I helped others escape from, comfortable.

It wasn't dramatic. I didn't lose everything or hit some crisis point. That's what makes blind spots so dangerous. They don't shout. They whisper. And mine whispered in the form of certainty, believing I already had the best model, the most effective methodology, the clearest answers.

Then something shifted.

I was advising a company in the telecoms sector that was under increasing pressure from more agile digital-first competitors. Midway through one of our strategic sessions, the COO politely interrupted me and said, "Moe, we love your frameworks, but our biggest challenge isn't covered in any of your slides."

That sentence hit me like a freight train.

Not because he was being rude, he wasn't. He was being honest. Brutally so. And it was exactly what I needed to hear.

He went on to explain that while my advice had helped them streamline and stabilise, it hadn't prepared them to reinvent. They didn't need polish. They needed provocation. They were trying to play offense in a game where I had only shown them how to defend better.

That's when I realised I'd been sharpening the wrong tools.

I'd built my reputation helping companies optimise, but the world was now demanding reinvention. AI wasn't just automating processes, it was reshaping customer expectations, redefining what value looked like, and compressing timelines in ways I hadn't fully accounted for. My strategies were still effective, yes, but they were no longer complete.

The Innovator's Paradox 2.0

I'd been focusing on speed, efficiency, and predictability. But what this client needed was unpredictability. They needed asymmetry. They needed to disrupt themselves before someone else did it for them.

So I went back to the drawing board, not just for them, but for myself. I started immersing myself in AI, not from a hype angle, but from a strategic lens. I worked with data scientists, joined think tanks, and sat with founders building AI-native companies. I started studying not just the big players like Musk or Bezos, but the lesser-known founders who were quietly redefining entire categories with ten people and a machine learning model.

And more importantly, I began asking myself the same uncomfortable questions I usually ask my clients.

Where am I still relying on old wins to justify current decisions?

What mental models am I clinging to, just because they've worked before?

What would it look like to outgrow my own expertise?

These weren't rhetorical questions. They were real. And they forced me to evolve, not just my strategy work, but how I show up as a mentor, an author, and a thinker.

Even now, with everything I know, I still have to guard against the comfort that comes with competence. It's easy to coast when the accolades come in. When the inbox stays full. When your last book did well. But comfort doesn't care about your past, it only delays your fall.

That's why I wrote this book, not just for CEOs and founders navigating massive change, but for myself too. Because the paradox of innovation is universal. It's not reserved for big corporations or old industries. It sneaks into any space where yesterday's thinking is left unchallenged.

And if I can miss it, you can too. That's not a weakness, it's a reality. The goal here isn't perfection. It's pattern recognition. It's building the habit of questioning what we're most confident about. That's where growth lives. That's where relevance is born.

So if you've ever caught yourself thinking, *"I already know this,"* pause. That thought right there, that's the beginning of the blind spot.

Now that we've both admitted we've been caught off guard before, let's talk about the things we *don't* see, and why they often matter more than what we do.

The Innovator's Paradox Defined

You know what still surprises me after all these years? It's how often the very thing that made someone successful becomes the very thing that holds them back.

I've seen it happen to companies, to leaders, even to myself. And not just once. Repeatedly. Like a pattern that keeps playing out, quietly, subtly, until the damage is already done.

That's the paradox.

The innovator's paradox isn't a slogan. It's a trap. A silent one. And it tends to ensnare the best of us, the seasoned leaders, the high-performers, the companies who once *were* the disruptors. The paradox is this:

What got you here won't get you there. And worse, it may be the very reason you never arrive.

Let me put it plainly. The strategies, beliefs, and systems that powered your past success start to calcify. You come to trust them, even revere them. You protect them, teach them to others, scale them across your business. And without meaning to, they become sacred. Untouchable.

Until one day, the world shifts, and your sacred becomes your ceiling.

You see, innovation has a peculiar rhythm. It doesn't just reward new ideas. It punishes attachment to old ones. Especially the ideas that once worked brilliantly.

One of the most painful conversations I've ever had was with the founder of a tech company in the security space. Their software had revolutionized on-premise data protection for corporate clients. For ten years, they dominated the market. Fortune 500 contracts. Press coverage. They were the standard.

But when cloud computing started to redefine the category, they hesitated. They had good reasons, too. Their current product was still performing. Their clients weren't demanding change. The market still looked "stable."

By the time they realized stability was a lie, their competitors had already built leaner, cloud-native platforms, and had eaten half their enterprise pipeline.

When I asked the founder what stopped him from moving earlier, he didn't say money. He didn't say talent. He said this:

> *"We were too proud of what we'd built."*

That stuck with me.

You don't often hear leaders admit that. But that's the paradox in action. Past innovation creates present pride, and present pride creates future blindness.

And here's the part that stings the most: the more successful you've been, the more at risk you are. Because success builds momentum, yes, but it also builds assumptions. And assumptions, left unchallenged, turn into blind spots.

You begin to assume the customer still values what they used to value.

You assume the competitor won't move faster than last time.

You assume what worked before will keep working, maybe just with a few tweaks.

But disruption doesn't tweak. It rewrites. It doesn't ask for permission. It doesn't care about your track record. It simply moves. And if you're still polishing what got you here, you won't even notice it's passed you by.

I remember once walking into a board meeting for a professional services firm, think legal, finance, the kind of business that thrives on relationships and legacy. They were worried about market share decline, client attrition, and younger firms undercutting them with tech.

But as we dug deeper, the issue wasn't external. It was internal.

They couldn't innovate because they were still worshipping what had worked 15 years ago. Their org chart. Their pricing model. Their "client-first" approach that, frankly, was now lagging behind client expectations.

When I gently suggested that their most experienced partners were the bottleneck, I was met with polite smiles, and quiet panic.

It's not that they didn't care. It's that they were caught in the paradox.

Their strength had become their ceiling.

And unless they rewired the way they thought about growth, they would keep trying to solve a new problem with an old blueprint.

So let me ask you this, just between us:

What are you still holding on to, because it once worked?

Is it a product line? A belief about your customer? A way of running meetings or making decisions? Something in your culture you tell yourself is a strength, but deep down, you suspect it might now be holding you back?

You're not alone. I've seen billion-pound businesses cling to models they *know* are outdated, because those models are familiar. They feel safe. But the truth is, they're dangerous.

Comfort is rarely obvious. It hides behind competence. Behind numbers that still look "fine." Behind the success stories we tell ourselves to avoid facing the new questions we don't want to ask.

But this book will ask them. Gently, at first. Then surgically.

Because if we're going to lead the next era, we need to be willing to let go of what made us kings of the last one.

The paradox is real. But it's also the beginning of something else.

Once you see it, once you *name* the tension between past wins and future relevance, something shifts. You start to feel your grip loosening. You begin to unlearn, to question, to move again.

And that's where real innovation starts, not with a whiteboard or a brainstorm, but with a willingness to challenge the very things you've built your success on.

So, as we move forward together, I want you to remember this:

Your greatest strength may still be your greatest obstacle.

But only if you let it stay unchallenged.

A Call to Radical Self-Assessment (Not Denial)

Before we go any further, let me make something very clear: this book isn't here to scare you.

The Innovator's Paradox 2.0

I'm not writing to join the noise of sensational headlines, apocalyptic predictions, or empty futurism. If you're expecting doom and drama, you're in the wrong room.

This is about clarity. Precision. Seeing your world, your business, your industry, your leadership, with sharper eyes and a cleaner lens.

And that starts with something simple but rare in the executive world: radical self-assessment.

Not judgment. Not shame. Just an unfiltered look in the mirror.

Because before we dive into AI strategies or innovation models, we have to pause. Just for a moment. And ask a few honest questions.

Not about *what's happening out there*, we'll get to that. But about *what's happening in here*.

You see, most disruption isn't technical. It's psychological.

It begins when we lie to ourselves. When we convince ourselves that "things are different in our industry." Or that "our customers aren't asking for that yet." Or worse, "we've always managed to adapt in the past."

But past adaptation doesn't guarantee future readiness. In fact, it often delays it. Because success has a way of numbing urgency.

And so, I want to invite you, right now, before we move into frameworks and case studies, to take a quick internal scan. Not as a public declaration, not even with your team. Just you and the truth.

I call it a *Disruption Readiness Scan*. Think of it like a health check, not to point fingers, but to establish a baseline. A diagnostic. Something to come back to as the book progresses.

Let's try a few sample questions, shall we?

- When was the last time you made a strategic decision that felt deeply uncomfortable, but necessary?

- If your industry's most unconventional startup acquired your company tomorrow, what would they shut down first?
- Are your most experienced people also your most resistant to change?
- Where are you still investing time and capital into systems that no longer produce compounding value?
- If AI could do 30% of what your business delivers now, better, faster, and cheaper, what happens to your pricing model?

You don't need to answer these out loud. But I encourage you to sit with them. Let the tension surface. That discomfort? That's not a threat. It's a signal.

You might be thinking, *"But Moe, we're not asleep at the wheel. We're making changes. We're exploring new tech. We've even got an AI task force."*

Good. That means you're in motion.

But motion and momentum aren't the same thing. You can spin in place for years and call it innovation. What we're looking for is trajectory. Strategic offense. And above all, honesty.

That's why I'll be introducing a full Disruption Readiness Scorecard later in the book, one you can use with your board, your leadership team, or just for yourself. Not to impress anyone. But to surface blind spots before they become real-world risks.

I've worked with companies that waited too long. I've also worked with those that moved just in time. The difference was never funding or talent or luck. It was self-awareness. The leaders who moved early were the ones who admitted they didn't have all the answers.

So let's agree, right now, that this book is a space for truth.

You don't need to have it all figured out. You just need to be willing to see clearly.

Because once you do, the rest gets easier.

Ready?

What You'll Discover

So, what exactly are we setting out to do here?

This book isn't just a cautionary tale. And it's not just theory either. It's a playbook, for leaders who want to build companies that don't just *survive* disruption, but drive it.

You'll learn how to spot disruption before your competitors do. How to build teams that aren't afraid of the unknown. How to make AI work for you, not as a gimmick, but as a growth engine.

And above all, you'll learn how to become the kind of leader who builds a company that reinvents itself before anyone else gets the chance.

The journey is broken into four distinct parts.

In **Part I: The Trap of Success**, we'll explore how today's strengths become tomorrow's liabilities. We'll unpack the hidden dangers of legacy thinking and walk through real stories, from Kodak and Blockbuster to lesser-known examples inside AI-driven industries like logistics, law, and fashion. You'll see how the paradox shows up not just in boardrooms, but in everyday decisions.

Part II: The Enemies of Innovation will dive into the silent friction inside most companies, culture, internal politics, resistance, fear of cannibalization. We'll explore how AI intensifies that friction and what you can do to neutralize it. This isn't just about tools, it's about rewiring how decisions get made and who gets to make them.

Then in **Part III: The New Architecture of Innovation**, we'll move into building mode. You'll learn the strategic infrastructure behind self-disruptive businesses, from how to run innovation labs that don't die within 12 months, to how to audit your own business model for fragility. We'll also explore how to layer AI into your operations without losing your soul.

And finally, **Part IV: The Future and the Final Challenge** will shift the focus inward. This is where we move from company strategy to leadership identity. Because to truly lead in the age of disruption, you have to think like a designer of systems, not just an operator. You'll learn how to build scenario maps, how to scale legacy beyond your own presence, and how to ensure that your vision outlives your role.

Throughout the book, you'll find tools, questions, frameworks, and yes, more of my Moe's Mirror reflections, designed to slow you down just enough to see what you might be missing. Not to punish you. To protect you.

You'll also meet clients I've worked with who've faced this head-on. Their stories are from industries you'll recognize, so you can see how this plays out in the real world, not just in theory.

And one final promise: I will never ask you to think smaller. Every section is designed to stretch your imagination, your strategy, and your confidence, not with hype, but with precision.

So let's begin.

Not with fear. Not with regret. But with the belief that disruption is not your enemy, it's your invitation.

Let's make sure you're ready to answer it.

Chapter 1:
The Innovator's Blind Spot: Why Success Can Be Your Greatest Obstacle

The Day I Faced My Own Blind Spot
The Boardroom That Changed Me

It was meant to be a routine session. A half-day strategy review with the board of a client I'd worked with for nearly four years, one of the UK's better-known logistics groups. Consistent revenue, disciplined ops, predictable leadership. On paper, they were doing everything right.

We were in one of those sleek glass-walled boardrooms, perched high above the city skyline. The kind with panoramic views and catered lunches that make everyone feel important. I'd just walked them through a refined roadmap for optimizing their regional expansion, complete with operational benchmarks, supply chain forecasts, and a modest AI integration proposal to streamline warehouse scheduling.

They nodded, took notes, even complimented the clarity of the deck.

Then one of the quieter board members, head of product, I believe, leaned in and asked a question that hit me like a punch to the gut.

"Is this your best thinking, Moe? Or is this what you thought we wanted to hear?"

Silence.

He wasn't being confrontational. He was calm, almost surgical. But that one question sliced through the polished strategy I had just spent weeks crafting. And deep down, I knew exactly what he meant.

I had played it safe.

Not because I lacked insight. But because I'd been working with them long enough to know what ideas they'd likely resist. Where they were still fragile. What would cause friction. And without even realising it, I'd started shaping my recommendations to fit within the comfort zones I had once been brought in to challenge.

It hit me hard. Not just because he was right, but because I hadn't seen it myself.

That boardroom was the mirror I didn't know I needed.

As I stood there, re-evaluating the very frameworks I'd laid out, I had to confront a sobering truth: even the disruptors, especially the disruptors, are vulnerable to the slow creep of comfort. Mine had arrived wrapped in the language of "client alignment" and "strategic timing," but underneath, it was the same old fear, what if I push too hard and lose the room?

That was my blind spot.

I had fallen into the exact trap I've spent my career helping others avoid. I was protecting my past work. Defending what had worked before. Overvaluing harmony at the expense of honesty. And I had dressed it up as strategy.

After the meeting, I walked alone through the lobby, head still spinning. I found a quiet corner in a nearby café, opened my notebook, and scribbled six words in capital letters:

"WHEN DID I START PLAYING DEFENSE?"

Because that's what it was. Subtle, yes. But real. I had moved from provocateur to protector. From designing for change to preserving comfort. And if I, someone who lives and breathes this work, could fall into that trap, what chance did a founder buried in operations or a CEO managing twelve crises at once have?

That was the moment I decided to tear it all down, my own process, my own assumptions, even the way I framed problems in client sessions. I started asking different questions. I stopped giving answers too quickly. I went back to studying what made self-disruptors *actually* different, not just in vision but in behavior, structure, psychology. And I gave myself permission to be uncomfortable again.

That boardroom didn't just challenge me, it changed me. Not in theory, but in muscle memory. It reminded me that relevance isn't something you earn once. It's something you fight to re-earn every day. Especially now, in an age where AI can outpace human insight in weeks, where industries morph before you've finished your annual plan, and where playing it safe is the riskiest move of all.

We'll dive into frameworks, tools, and real case studies soon. But I wanted to start here, not with a theory, but a confession.

Because this book isn't written from a pedestal. It's written from the trenches. I'm not just here to teach. I'm here to walk alongside you.

And if you've ever found yourself wondering whether your smartest moves have quietly become your safest ones, then you're exactly where you need to be.

The Disruption I Didn't Want to See

There's something strangely comforting about being the one who spots the storm before others do. When you're the advisor in the room pointing out where the cracks will form before anyone else notices, it's easy to start believing you're immune to missing them yourself.

But I wasn't. Not even close.

Years ago, I was working with a mid-sized firm in the professional services sector, compliance and corporate governance, to be specific. They were sharp, profitable, respected. And like many in that space, their value lay in intellectual capital, high-trust relationships, legacy knowledge, and manual expertise.

They were starting to ask the right questions about tech, "Should we be investing in automation?" "How do we use data more intelligently?", but nothing felt urgent. Their biggest clients weren't asking for AI-powered reports or predictive compliance tools. And when I brought up some early examples of how AI was being tested in risk management, the CEO waved it off.

"Interesting," he said, "but our clients don't trust black boxes. They want human eyes on every report."

I nodded. And here's the truth: I let it go. I didn't challenge him as hard as I should have. I had enough respect for his intuition, and enough respect for the fees I was earning, not to push. That was my mistake.

Fast forward eighteen months.

A tech-first competitor entered the market. Lean team, AI-enhanced services, real-time dashboards, automated risk assessments with predictive flagging. Their pitch wasn't cheaper. It was faster, clearer, and data-backed. Their first two clients? Both former accounts of my client.

It wasn't a mass exodus, but the shift had begun. Quiet, slow, and irreversible.

When the board called me back in to help "solve the client leakage issue," I had to look the CEO in the eye and say, "This isn't a retention problem. It's a relevance problem."

And I knew, painfully, that I had seen it coming. I just hadn't *wanted* to see it.

That's the worst kind of blind spot. The one you *suspect* is there, but you bury it. You ignore the signs. You tell yourself there's still time. You downplay the early indicators because the status quo is still delivering dividends.

Personally, that was one of the hardest professional moments for me. Not because the client was disappointed. But because I had let my own judgment dull. I had made the subtle shift from truth-teller to consensus-keeper.

Looking back, I can see how it happened. I had grown too comfortable being right. Too used to the feeling of delivering value without resistance. But disruption doesn't care about your past accuracy. It only cares about your present clarity.

And clarity, I've learned, demands confrontation, with reality, with your clients, and most importantly, with yourself.

We all have disruptions we'd rather not acknowledge. Maybe it's a new competitor you pretend isn't serious. A technology you don't fully understand but claim "isn't relevant yet." Or maybe it's a part of your business that no longer deserves to exist, but still gets your protection out of habit or fear.

In my case, the disruption wasn't just in the market. It was in my mindset. The moment I stopped challenging the people I was there to help, that was the moment I stopped doing my real job.

That lesson cost my client millions.

It cost me a bit of my own credibility.

But it also gave me the sharpest lens I've ever used.

And I'll hand that lens to you, if you're willing to look through it.

What I Learned About the Illusion of Winning

It took me longer than I care to admit to realise that success can be one of the most dangerous things that happens to a business leader. Not failure. Success.

We're trained to fear losing. We monitor losses, we analyse shortfalls, we obsess over risk. But success? Success we celebrate. We wear it. We point to it as proof that we've earned our place in the room.

But here's what I've learned, both painfully and personally: **Success has a way of seducing us into irrelevance.**

Not instantly. Not dramatically. Slowly. Quietly. Like water dripping onto stone.

In the years after my early wins, when I started mentoring board-level executives and consulting with multi-million-pound businesses, I noticed a pattern. The companies that were most difficult to shift weren't the ones that were struggling. They were the ones that were winning, on paper.

They had the revenue. The clients. The reputation. They were the market leaders. But when we dug deeper, their internal systems were rigid. Their innovation budgets were performative. Their culture was cautious. And most dangerously, their leaders were convinced they still had time.

Comfort had crept in. And comfort, I've come to realise, is a master of disguise. It doesn't show up wearing slippers. It shows up wearing KPIs. Growth graphs. Awards. Familiar faces who don't challenge assumptions because everyone's still getting paid.

But underneath that surface, something corrosive starts to take root, **the illusion that what's working today will keep working tomorrow.**

That's what nearly caught me out. I was delivering results, yes. Clients were referring me, yes. But I wasn't seeing the next curve. I wasn't listening for the whispers of change because the volume of approval was drowning them out.

Disruption doesn't knock politely. It doesn't wait for permission. And it doesn't just attack weaknesses, it exposes where we've gotten comfortable.

One of my private clients in the retail sector said something to me during a strategy session that I'll never forget. She'd just finished reviewing her five-year growth plan and stopped mid-sentence. Looked up. Then said, "I think we're about to be punished for winning."

It was a strange thing to say in a room full of charts showing double-digit growth.

But she was right.

Their systems were optimised for yesterday's demand, not tomorrow's agility. Their top people were rewarded for preserving efficiency, not questioning assumptions. And their entire business model, once celebrated as the gold standard, was vulnerable to a single tech-led competitor that didn't even exist five years ago.

Winning had created a forcefield around their thinking. A comfort zone disguised as a best practice.

That's the real danger of the Innovator's Blind Spot. It doesn't just make us miss the threat, it convinces us there isn't one. Because we're still winning. Until we're not.

So let me ask you, when was the last time you challenged the very thing that's made you successful?

Not because it's broken. But because it might be quietly expiring.

It's not an easy question. But it's the question that defines whether you lead the next wave or get caught in the last one.

And if this book does nothing else, I hope it reawakens that hunger. That discomfort. That willingness to unlearn, even when the world is still applauding you.

Because the applause fades. But irrelevance? That tends to linger.

Let's make sure you're not there when it arrives.

The Comfort Trap

What Success Actually Does to the Brain

Let's get honest about something few leaders like to admit: success doesn't just change your lifestyle, it rewires your brain.

We like to think that the more we win, the sharper we become. That experience is the ultimate strategic advantage. But neuroscience, and experience, tell a different story.

The truth is, success creates comfort. And comfort creates blind spots.

When we succeed, our brains release dopamine, a chemical that rewards us for getting things "right." Over time, that reward system creates a loop. We start to crave that feeling of being right. Of being respected. Of being in control. And gradually, we begin filtering new information through one quiet, unspoken question: *"Does this validate what I already believe?"*

This is where it gets dangerous.

Because once that loop is established, your brain starts protecting your past decisions rather than questioning them. You start seeing your strategy not as a hypothesis to be tested, but as a legacy to be defended. And that's when pattern blindness sets in.

You miss the anomalies. You ignore the whispers. You downplay early signals of disruption because they don't match the script that got you here.

I've sat with leaders running nine-figure companies who couldn't see the threat sitting right in front of them, not because they weren't smart, but because they were successful. They were emotionally invested in their own patterns. The story they had told themselves, about their industry, their customers, their team, was too deeply woven to let in a conflicting truth.

And it's not just pride. It's biology.

Loss aversion kicks in. Suddenly, you're not playing to win anymore, you're playing not to lose. You avoid risks that might challenge the status quo. You default to safer bets, even if the payoff is shrinking.

Then comes the sunk-cost fallacy.

You've spent years building this team, this model, this brand. It can't just be wrong now, can it? You look at the money, the effort, the years of sacrifice, and your brain tells you, *"Protect it."*

But in protecting what you've built, you might be blind to what needs to be dismantled.

And that's the paradox again, isn't it?

The very mindset that got you to the top, focus, consistency, pattern recognition, is now the same mindset that can stop you from seeing what's changed.

I'm not pointing fingers. I've been there myself. More than once.

That's why this chapter isn't a warning shot. It's a mirror.

Because until we understand how success silently conditions us, we'll keep building castles on shifting sand, convinced we're on solid ground.

And when the storm comes, we won't just be surprised, we'll be stunned.

The Empire of Inertia

I once worked with a multinational in the food and beverage sector, household name, billion-pound revenue, legacy brand recognition across Europe. When I was brought in, it wasn't for a crisis. Quite the opposite. They were on a three-year winning streak. Margins were strong, distribution was expanding, and their flagship product lines were growing steadily.

But underneath the glossy performance reports, something was beginning to rot.

They had been sitting on a new health-conscious product concept that had tested well in early trials. The research was clear, consumers were shifting habits, especially the under-30 demographic. But the internal conversation kept circling the same drain:

> *"If we launch this now, won't we cannibalize our hero products?"*

The phrase "cannibalize our success" came up in nearly every meeting. It wasn't a financial concern, it was emotional. The brand's identity was so tied to its traditional SKUs that even discussing a new category felt like betrayal.

So, they waited. Delayed. Repackaged the same offering with healthier language but without a real product shift.

Eighteen months later, a newer competitor launched a near-identical product to the shelved concept, and took 12% of their market share in under a year. Twelve percent.

And you know what hurt the most?

They didn't lose because of bad execution. They lost because of **inertia disguised as strategy**.

Inertia is seductive like that. It looks like discipline. It feels like loyalty. But it's often fear in a tailored suit.

The same story plays out across industries.

A client in the insurance sector refused to automate their claims process because they "didn't want to upset loyal brokers." A retail chain dragged its feet on mobile-first e-commerce because "footfall was still strong." A construction firm delayed digital project management tools because "the old way still worked."

Each time, the logic sounded defensible.

But in every case, the real driver wasn't logic. It was fear.

Fear of letting go of what had worked. Fear of disrupting internal harmony. Fear of proving that the old way, the one they built their careers on, might no longer be the best way.

That fear builds an empire of inertia. An invisible fortress around your current success. And like all fortresses, it gives you the illusion of security, right up until it crumbles.

So let me ask you:

Where in your business are you defending yesterday's empire at the cost of tomorrow's relevance?

It's a hard question. But if you don't ask it now, the market will answer it for you.

And it won't be polite about it.

Metrics vs. Momentum

I remember sitting with a CEO who ran one of the most dominant logistics networks in the UK. Ten-year compound growth. Consistent EBITDA performance. Operational efficiency that would make a German engineer blush.

As he clicked through the quarterly slide deck, his pride was evident, and to be fair, well earned.

But something wasn't sitting right with me.

Every chart showed success, except the one that wasn't there.

No slide for momentum.

Because here's what most high-level operators don't realise: **great metrics can mask stale momentum.**

And over time, that's how relevance erodes. Quietly. Logically. In spreadsheets full of confidence.

Legacy KPIs, revenue, margin, customer retention, are designed to measure how well you're managing the *present*. But disruption lives in the *future*. And your P&L, as clean and satisfying as it may look, won't warn you when momentum is slipping away.

I call this *momentum blindness*.

It happens when your internal dashboards show green, but your external relevance is already yellow, or worse, blinking red.

You start mistaking *efficiency* for *advancement*. You see profitability as proof that strategy doesn't need to change. You chase incremental optimisation instead of exponential reinvention.

And here's the dangerous part:
Momentum rarely leaves with a bang. It fades.

Slowly. Silently. Then suddenly.

One of my retail clients watched year-on-year revenue climb 6%. On paper, things looked stable. But when we did a deeper dive, their new customer acquisition had dropped 22% over two years. Their top-line growth was coasting on historic loyalty. Momentum was decaying beneath the surface.

Another example, a mid-cap financial services firm was celebrating record profits. But they hadn't launched a new product in 26 months. Their innovation pipeline? Empty. Their tech stack? Two years behind. They were winning yesterday's game without realising today's had already changed.

Here's the hard truth:
KPIs are comfort food. Momentum is oxygen.

If you're not measuring where your relevance is going, you might be walking into irrelevance with your numbers still in the green.

So ask yourself:

- Are you tracking the pace of new ideas?

- Are your best people still growing, or just repeating?

- Is your strategic plan a reflection of today's opportunity or last year's logic?
  Because the market doesn't care how good your numbers look today.

It cares whether you'll still matter tomorrow.

And that's what momentum is really about.

From Operator to Architect

When I look back at the leaders who made the leap, those who didn't just weather disruption but *led* it, there's one shift they all had in common.

They stopped thinking like operators.
And started thinking like architects.

At first glance, that might sound like semantics. But it's not. It's a redefinition of identity. One that changes how you see your role, your company, and the future you're building.

Operators focus on execution.
They optimise, manage, troubleshoot. They make today work better than yesterday.

Architects, on the other hand, design systems that *survive without them*.
They don't just fix problems, they build frameworks that prevent them. They don't just manage teams, they craft cultures. They don't ask, "How do we grow revenue this quarter?"
They ask, "What kind of company would make this question irrelevant?"

The trap, of course, is that most of us were rewarded for being world-class operators. That's how we rose through the ranks. That's how we built trust. We got good at solving problems, executing under pressure, delivering results.

But in a world where AI can execute faster than any team and automation can optimise operations without blinking, being an elite operator is no longer enough.

The leader who wins in the next decade is the one who designs the game, not just plays it better.

I had to go through this shift myself.

Early in my advisory career, I prided myself on being the guy who could step into chaos and bring order. Fix broken systems. Reignite stalled teams. Deliver fast wins. It felt good to be the one who knew what to do when everyone else was stuck.

But over time, I realised I was solving the *same problems* over and over. Not because the world wasn't changing, but because my clients weren't. Not fundamentally. Not structurally.

And that's when I understood: I had to stop acting like the chief firefighter.
And start acting like the city planner.

Because the real work isn't just putting out fires, it's designing a place where fires don't break out in the first place. Or if they do, they're contained before they spread.

So let me ask you:

Are you spending more energy managing what exists, or designing what's next?

Are you building structures that will evolve without your direct input, or ones that require you to constantly push?

If your answer leans toward the former, congratulations, you're still running a strong business.

But if your answer leans toward the latter, then good.

Because that means you're ready to become the architect your business actually needs.

And from this point forward, that's who this book is written for.

The AI Whisper

It Doesn't Shout, It Compounds

There's something deceptive about how real disruption happens. We like to imagine it crashing through the wall with sirens, headlines, and panic. But AI didn't arrive like that. It didn't barge in with fireworks. It whispered.

And most leaders didn't hear it.

The thing about AI is this: it doesn't come to take over in one bold sweep. It compounds. Quietly. Incrementally. Relentlessly. One marginal gain after another. One inefficiency removed, one process sped up, one insight surfaced that a human would've missed.

It doesn't feel like a revolution at first. It feels like... convenience.

I worked with a mid-sized manufacturer in the precision components industry, high-spec parts for aerospace and defense. Legacy contracts. Skilled workforce. Old-school pride. The CEO, a man who'd built the company from nothing, prided himself on quality, discipline, and handshake reliability.

One of their lesser-known competitors, a firm less than half their size, began experimenting with AI-enhanced predictive maintenance and workflow scheduling. They didn't announce it. They didn't even publicise it. But over 18 months, their output increased by 23%. Scrap rate dropped. Machine downtime halved. Lead times improved without extra hiring.

When I mentioned this during a strategy review, the CEO scoffed. "Yeah, but are they profitable?"

They were. In fact, they were beating his margins by 6% without lowering prices.

You see, while he was measuring success by the same ruler he'd always used, on-time delivery, quality assurance, gross margin, the game had shifted underneath him. Not dramatically. Subtly.

The competitor wasn't playing harder.
They were playing smarter.
And AI was their compound interest engine.

That's what makes AI different from the tech waves we've seen before. It doesn't replace, it *rewires*. It doesn't disrupt in headlines, it disrupts in hidden efficiencies.

It's the back-end system that detects a bottleneck before your team even sees the delay.

It's the customer insight that tells you which clients are likely to churn, before they even call to cancel.

It's the pricing algorithm that adjusts in real time while your commercial team is still stuck in quarterly reviews.

The threat isn't that AI will suddenly overtake you.
The threat is that it already has, and you didn't notice because everything *still felt normal.*

That's what keeps me up at night when I sit with traditional businesses still debating whether they're "ready for AI."

Because readiness is no longer the question.
Relevance is.

And the companies that are pulling away aren't the loud ones. They're the quiet ones. The ones that listened early. The ones who didn't wait for the shout, but tuned into the whisper.

The New Moat Isn't Money, It's Intelligence

There was a time when money was the moat. The bigger your war chest, the stronger your position. You could outspend competitors, lock up supply chains, flood the market with marketing muscle, and wait for smaller players to run out of oxygen.

That era is ending. Quietly, but definitively.

Today, the most dangerous competitor isn't the one with more cash. It's the one with a smarter feedback loop.

The new moat is intelligence.

Let me explain.

I was mentoring a founder in the SaaS space, mid-eight figures, bootstrapped, lean team. His competitor was a publicly funded firm with ten times the headcount and a much bigger runway.

But there was one difference.

My client's product team was integrating AI into their data flow, not to automate customer service or write code faster, but to *learn faster*. They built adaptive pricing models that recalibrated based on user behavior in real time. They tested onboarding flows and features using micro-adjustments guided by live data, not quarterly reports. Their AI stack didn't just automate, it *learned*, *adapted*, and *redirected* before a human could even flag a trend.

Meanwhile, the Goliath competitor was still making decisions the old-fashioned way: executive offsites, consultant slide decks, and the ever-faithful "gut feel."

Within a year, David had doubled his average revenue per user.

That's the power of smarter, faster learning loops. That's the new unfair advantage.

AI gives birth to a kind of intelligence that doesn't sleep, doesn't defend egos, and doesn't need to be convinced. It just observes, adapts, and compounds.

So when I talk to CEOs still bragging about headcount, or market share, or how much capital they've raised, I always ask:

"But how fast does your company learn?"

Not how fast it operates. How fast it *learns*.

Because in this new game, scale without intelligence is just weight. And weight, in a volatile market, doesn't anchor you, it drowns you.

The companies that win now aren't necessarily the biggest. They're the ones with *tighter feedback loops*.

They learn what works faster. They test faster. They recover faster. And most importantly, they *let go* of what no longer works faster.

AI is not just a tool. It's an amplifier of learning. A compass that recalibrates itself every second. And if your competitor's compass is updating in real time while yours updates every quarter, guess what?

You're not just behind. You're out of the race, you just don't know it yet.

So ask yourself:

Are you building your moat with money?
Or with intelligence?

Because only one of those compounds.
And only one of those will still matter five years from now.

The Innovator's Paradox in the AI Age

The original paradox is still true:
The more successful you are, the harder it becomes to change.

But in the age of AI, that paradox has evolved, and sharpened.

Now, success doesn't just slow your ability to change.
It can actively **amplify your resistance** to it.
And AI, for all its power, is a force multiplier for both sides of the equation.

Let me explain.

I've worked with legacy businesses whose scale, reach, and reputation are beyond question. On paper, they're bulletproof. But inside, they're brittle.

Their processes are refined to a point of rigidity. Their metrics are optimised for yesterday's world. Their culture celebrates precision and punishes improvisation.

And now here comes AI, fast, adaptive, unpredictable.

You'd think these organisations would jump at the chance to harness it. But instead, they stall. Not because they don't believe in the potential, but because **the very systems that made them strong now make them slow.**

I remember sitting across from the CFO of a global logistics firm. He said, "Moe, we know AI could save us tens of millions... but if we implement it, we'll expose how much of our org chart is redundant."

And there it was.

AI doesn't just offer efficiency, it threatens comfort. It doesn't just challenge your tech, it challenges your *structure*. Your *incentives*. Your *identity*.

This is the paradox in full view:
The more there is to protect, the harder it becomes to evolve.

And yet, there's another side.

Because when legacy companies *do* embrace AI, intelligently, deliberately, structurally, they gain access to advantages that younger startups can't touch.

They have the data.
They have the customer base.
They have the operational scale.

AI, in their hands, becomes a superpower.

But that superpower has to be **unlocked**.
And unlocking it requires something rare in successful leaders:
The humility to question the very system that made you successful.

That's the hard part.

Because AI doesn't care how long you've been winning. It doesn't pause for respect. It doesn't give you extra time to adjust because you built a strong brand.

It simply shows up, and rewards the companies that learn faster and let go sooner.

So the paradox in the AI age is sharper, but also clearer:

If you can let go of what made you successful, AI will multiply your edge.
If you can't, AI will multiply your fragility.

There is no middle ground.

And that's why this chapter, and this book, matters.

Because the real risk isn't that AI will disrupt your business.
The real risk is that *you* won't.

So Why Don't They Act?

I've sat in enough boardrooms to know most CEOs aren't stupid.

They see the headlines.
They've been pitched the AI demos.
They know something is shifting, fast.

And yet, they stall.

They build committees.
They hire a "Head of Innovation."
They ask for one more workshop.
They say, *"Let's review again next quarter."*

What they're really saying is: **"Not yet."**

And I've heard that whisper, **"not yet"**, more times than I can count.

It's rarely said aloud. You don't hear it in strategy slides or quarterly earnings calls. It lives in the quiet moments, between meetings, in risk registers, in polite nods to disruptive ideas followed by… inaction.

So what's behind it?

Fear.
Ego.
And the illusion of readiness.

Let's take them one by one.

Fear says:
"If we change too fast, we'll break what's already working."

Ego says:
"My decisions got us here, why should I question them now?"

And **illusion** whispers:
"We'll act when we're more prepared, more resourced, more sure."

But AI doesn't wait for readiness. It rewards momentum.
And the hard truth is, by the time you feel *ready*, it's already late.

One client, a healthcare CEO, told me his team needed "more time to assess the landscape" before making any strategic AI commitments.

Eighteen months later, one of their smaller competitors had deployed machine learning across diagnostics, scheduling, and patient communications, and was now winning contracts that used to be rubber-stamped for the bigger player.

The bigger player was still planning.
Still assessing.
Still "getting ready."

What they hadn't realised was that readiness is an illusion.
Action creates readiness. Not the other way around.

But it's uncomfortable.
Because acting now means confronting your own blind spots.
It means challenging the structures you've built.
It means admitting you don't fully know where it's heading, but you're going anyway.

And for most leaders, that level of vulnerability doesn't sit well.

So instead, they whisper *not yet*.

Not yet to rethinking the org chart.
Not yet to building that internal AI council.
Not yet to killing the product that's still profitable but slowly losing relevance.

But *not yet* is a story we tell ourselves to avoid the pain of transformation.

And every time we whisper it, the compounding curve of those who said *"right now"* pulls further ahead.

You don't need all the answers. You never will.

But if you're still whispering *not yet*, ask yourself this:

What, exactly, are you waiting for?
And when will the cost of waiting become louder than your comfort?

Because by the time you say *"now"*, the market may have already moved on.

Blind Spot Diagnostic: 7 Strategic Questions

Let's strip away the noise for a moment.

You've read the stories. You've seen how AI doesn't shout, it whispers. And now, before we go any further, it's time to hold up the mirror.

This part isn't theoretical. It's not inspirational either. It's diagnostic. Designed to give you clarity you might not like, but can't afford to ignore.

What follows are seven questions I ask my private clients, the CEOs, the founders, the boardroom veterans, when they feel stuck but can't quite put their finger on why.

I don't want quick answers. I want honest ones.

Let's begin.

1. What are you protecting that no longer serves your future?
Every leader has sacred cows. Products, processes, even people they defend because of past performance.

But the market doesn't care about your history. It rewards your relevance.

A global retail client once clung to an in-house legacy software platform they'd invested millions into. It was slow, clunky, and impossible to scale, but they stayed loyal out of pride. Meanwhile, a more agile competitor built on modern SaaS tools and overtook them in 18 months.

Ask yourself: *What am I preserving out of sentiment or sunk cost, rather than strategic sense?*

2. Where are you confusing efficiency with innovation?
Being operationally tight feels like progress. But squeezing cost out of an outdated system isn't the same as redesigning the system itself.

One logistics firm I advised was proud of reducing delivery costs by 2%. But they hadn't realised a startup in their space was deploying AI to eliminate entire delivery routes altogether through dynamic warehousing.

Optimisation is not innovation.
Where are you polishing a dying model?

3. If your top three competitors used AI brilliantly, where would they hit you first?

This is a painful but essential thought experiment.
If someone were to attack your core value proposition using intelligent systems, data, prediction, automation, where would the damage show up first?

Pricing? Personalisation? Speed? Experience?

A professional services firm I worked with never saw it coming when a small AI-enabled consultancy began offering strategic roadmaps at one-tenth the cost, delivered in days not weeks. Same insights. Faster delivery. More margin.

Don't wait to be blindsided. Imagine the hit now, while you still have time to move.

4. What do you personally resist that your organisation needs?

This is the ego trap.
Maybe it's adopting tech you don't fully understand.
Maybe it's empowering younger voices with sharper instincts.
Maybe it's killing a pet project you created.

One of the hardest decisions I made in my own business was to delegate keynote decisions to a junior strategist. I was reluctant, until I saw our pitch conversion triple.

Where are *you* the bottleneck?

5. How fast can your organisation learn, really?

Learning is the new competitive advantage.
But most companies confuse motion with feedback.
They hold meetings, gather data, but resist actually applying it.

Ask: How quickly can a new insight from the front lines reshape your customer experience? Your product roadmap? Your pricing model?

If the answer is longer than a week, you're already behind.

6. What's the one thing you'd do if you had no fear of failure or judgment?
Now we're getting into the real tension.

Most CEOs I mentor already *know* what needs to change.
They've seen the cracks. They've had the idea. But they're waiting, for buy-in, for proof, for the "right" time.

That time rarely arrives.

Your instinct isn't the problem.
Your delay is.

7. Where are you telling yourself "not yet"?
Let's bring it full circle.

Are you waiting to hire that AI lead?
To test that bold new model?
To phase out that low-margin offering that just "keeps things stable"?

The phrase *not yet* is often a disguise for *never*.

Look at your strategy deck. What's been deferred for more than one quarter? More than one year?

Those are the whispers you've been ignoring.

And whispers don't go away. They grow.

Take a pause here. Reread your answers. Don't edit them.

This isn't an exercise in polish, it's a confrontation with truth.

Because once you see your blind spots clearly, the rest of this book becomes less about theory, and more about what you're going to do next.

Legacy vs. Leverage: What Are You Actually Building?

Let me ask you something I rarely hear spoken in boardrooms, but often feel just beneath the surface:

Are you building a legacy, or are you just maintaining one?

It's an uncomfortable distinction. And one many CEOs avoid confronting because they're surrounded by praise, tradition, and performance metrics that say they're still doing well.

But *well* is not the same as *right*.

And "still doing" is not the same as *moving forward*.

I had a private session with a founder of a £300M company in the financial services industry. On paper, everything looked golden. Steady growth. Great EBITDA. No major issues. But under the surface, the real story was starting to show. Product innovation had flatlined. The team was over-reliant on a single revenue engine. And worst of all, the founder, brilliant, intuitive, respected, was no longer building.

He was *protecting*.

Protecting the structure. Protecting the process. Protecting his place in it all.

He looked me in the eye and said, "Moe, I've built something great. I just don't want to be the one who breaks it."

And that's when I told him the truth:

The Innovator's Paradox 2.0

You don't have to break it.
But if you're not evolving it, the market will.

That's the choice leaders face when disruption comes whispering.
Do you use your legacy to create leverage?
Or do you use your leverage to cling to your legacy?

Because the companies that win in this next chapter, the AI-led, speed-dominant, insight-advantaged era, aren't the ones with the longest track record.
They're the ones who ask, *"What part of our success can be reengineered to create our next edge?"*

And they act on the answer.

Let's get personal for a second.

What are you maintaining right now that once made you proud... but no longer moves you forward?

It might be a flagship product you built your reputation on.
A business model you mastered.
A role you still hold onto, not because it suits you, but because it feels too risky to hand over.

But maintenance isn't momentum.
It's inertia dressed in respectability.

The market doesn't care how much you *had* to build to get here.
It only cares how fast you can re-leverage it into what's next.

Take AI, for example. Most leaders I speak to think about it as something to layer *on top* of the business. A feature. A bolt-on.

That's maintenance thinking.

The ones who win think, *"How do I use AI to rethink the foundation?"*

To streamline their customer insight loop.
To shift from human-dependent ops to intelligence-led systems.
To identify new markets, models, even missions.

They don't ask, *"What can AI help me preserve?"*
They ask, *"What can it help me unlock?"*

That's leverage.

So I'll ask again, as plainly as I can:

What are you actually building right now?

A structure that will stand as long as no one questions it?
Or a system designed to evolve, without needing your constant control?

Are you building a legacy that's stuck in time?
Or a lever that lifts your business into a new era?

One path feels safer.
The other builds something that survives you.

Choose well. Because whether you act or not, the market has already made its choice.

The Founder's Dilemma: If You Left Today, What Breaks?

Let's cut through the noise.

If you stepped away today, just walked out of the office and didn't return for six months, what would break?

Not what would *slow down*, or *shift*, or *get handled differently*.

What would actually *break*?

This is one of the hardest questions I ask founders and CEOs. And most of them smile at first. Then pause. Then the colour drains from their face.

Because the truth, if we're being honest, is that many businesses are still too dependent on one person: **you**.

Even if you've scaled.
Even if you have teams.
Even if you've "delegated."

There's a difference between *people executing your instructions* and *a company that knows how to win without you watching over it.*

I've seen it with an 8-figure founder in the B2B software space. On paper, his systems looked automated. Sales, marketing, operations, all humming. But when he got COVID and had to step back for three weeks, the entire pipeline stalled. Decisions froze. The team hesitated. Clients sensed it.

The business had grown.
But it hadn't evolved.

It was still running on *him*.

He didn't build a company.
He built a control system.

And here's the gut-punch:
That's not leadership. That's dependency.

You see, ego doesn't always show up as arrogance.
Sometimes, it disguises itself as *duty*.
"I have to be involved. Only I can make the final call. They're not ready yet."

But if you've been saying "they're not ready" for more than a year… that's not on them. That's on you.

Because the founder's real job is not to control everything.
It's to **design something that works when you're not in the room.**

And if that scares you, good.

Because here's the truth few will say aloud:
Your real legacy isn't what you built, it's what still thrives when you're gone.

So let me give you a short exercise. Not for show. For truth.

Grab a sheet of paper, just one.
Divide it into three columns.

1. **Gains** – What systems, decisions, or growth strategies *only exist* because of your direct involvement?

2. **Gaps** – What stops when you're not around? What decisions get deferred until you're back?

3. **Ghosts** – What old habits, fears, or unspoken rules still shape your team's thinking, even though you've "moved on"?

Now look at that sheet.
That's your real succession plan.
That's your mirror.

If you want to build a company that lasts, not just one that runs...
You have to design yourself *out of the machine.*

Not tomorrow.
Not once it's all "perfect."
Now.

Because one day, whether by choice, illness, acquisition, or simply fatigue, you'll have to let go.

And the question won't be, *"Did you build it big?"*
It will be, *"Did you build it to outlive you?"*

Your First Disruption Sprint: What to Kill, Reinvent, or Rewire?

We've talked enough about blind spots.
Now it's time to do something about them.

This isn't theory. This is your first move.

I call it the **30-Day Disruption Sprint**, a focused, uncomfortable, and absolutely necessary challenge to start shaking the foundation *before* the market does it for you.

Why 30 days?
Because momentum doesn't come from insight. It comes from action.
And 30 days is long enough to create clarity, short enough to remove excuses.

Let's get to work.

Here's what I want you to identify:

1. Three Sacred Cows to Kill
Every organisation has them. Products, services, processes, or people that no longer add value, but are protected like heirlooms.

One of my clients in the telecoms sector had an entire division dedicated to legacy infrastructure support. It was unprofitable, unscalable, and draining resources. But "it's what built the company," they told me.

Exactly. And that's the problem.

The past deserves respect.
But it should never dictate the future.

In the next 30 days, I want you to name three things your team would *never dare question*, and put them on the table.

Ask: *If we killed this today, what would we actually lose? And what might we gain?*

2. Three Fragile Wins to Reinvent
These are the wins you're proud of, but if you're honest, they're brittle.

Maybe it's a big client who's overly dependent on one relationship.
Maybe it's a service offering that still delivers revenue, but only because of brute-force operations.
Maybe it's a market edge that isn't as sharp as it once was.

These fragile wins create false confidence. You celebrate them, but deep down, you know they're vulnerable.

I worked with a logistics CEO who was proud of their high client retention. But when we dug deeper, 40% of their top clients were tied to one sales director. One departure could bring the whole house down.

Your task: list three wins that *look solid* but are one disruption away from falling apart.

Then ask: *How do we reinvent these before someone else does?*

3. Three Blind Spots to Hunt Down
This is the tough one. Because by definition, you can't see your blind spots.

But your team can.
Your customers can.
Your competitors already have.

In the next leadership meeting, ask this:

"Where do you think we're winning, but I'm missing something?"

Then shut up and let them talk.

Listen for patterns. For hesitations. For nervous laughter. That's where the real signal lives.

Then take those insights and schedule three deep-dive reviews with cross-functional teams, not to defend your position, but to interrogate it.

This isn't a critique. It's a hunt.
And what you find may just be the crack that saves your company later.

Now, here's your full **30-Day Disruption Sprint**:

- **Week 1**: Identify and frame your Sacred Cows
- **Week 2**: Deconstruct your Fragile Wins
- **Week 3**: Hunt your Blind Spots
- **Week 4**: Decide: What will you kill, reinvent, or rewire?

If you commit to this sprint, I guarantee you'll walk away with clearer priorities, faster decisions, and the kind of discomfort that leads to real movement.

But if you read this and nod, then do nothing, then we both know what happens.

Comfort wins.
Ego survives.
And the whispers of disruption grow louder… just out of sight.

So here's my final question to close this mirror:

What's going to change in the next 30 days, because of you, not in spite of you?

Write it down.
Make the call.
Start the sprint.

Chapter 2:
Beyond Adaptation:
Mastering the Art of Offensive AI Strategy

SECTION 1: The AI Advantage Playbook

The Three Levers – Velocity, Intelligence, Margin

Let's make one thing clear from the outset:
AI is not a gadget. It's not a dashboard. It's not a trend.

It's a new lever of value creation, and if you're still thinking of it as just another efficiency tool, you're already playing catch-up.

AI is offensive strategy.

And like any strategy that matters, it doesn't win by doing what everyone else is doing, it wins by shifting the game.

In every industry I work with, manufacturing, finance, healthcare, SaaS, logistics, the same pattern appears: AI becomes lethal when it's used not to defend market share, but to **amplify three specific levers**.

Let's break them down.

1. Velocity – Learn faster, decide quicker, move earlier.
You've probably sat through your share of AI presentations promising automation and time savings. But that's surface-level.

The real value is velocity, not just doing things faster, but **learning faster than your competition can keep up**.

Take a B2B SaaS company I advised. Instead of spending months debating new features, they trained a machine learning model to analyse real-time usage data and surface emerging client behaviours. Within days, they had product insights their competitors didn't even know to look for.

Velocity isn't about speed for the sake of it.
It's about decision advantage.
And AI shortens the time between signal and response.

In markets moving this fast, **that's everything**.

2. Intelligence – See what others can't.
AI isn't about replacing human thinking, it's about expanding what you're able to see and interpret.

Most companies are blind in places they don't realise. They have oceans of data, customer behaviours, operational anomalies, market shifts, but no real visibility.

AI turns that chaos into clarity.

I worked with a food logistics company that used AI to detect subtle demand signals based on weather, local events, and historical purchasing data. It sounds niche, but that foresight allowed them to reroute supply chains *before* competitors even adjusted their forecasts.

That's not automation. That's prediction.
And prediction beats reaction every time.

When you have better visibility into what's coming, **you stop following the market, and start shaping it**.

3. Margin – Operate leaner, smarter, and at scale.
The third lever is financial, AI improves margin, not just by cutting cost, but by eliminating friction.

One of the UK's top private healthcare providers used AI to optimise patient intake and treatment matching. The result? 30% fewer missed appointments, smoother scheduling, and better utilisation of specialist consultants. Same infrastructure. Higher throughput. Better care.

That's not a marginal gain. That's a structural leap.

Margins matter. Especially in industries where inflation, talent shortages, and regulatory shifts compress profitability.
AI creates **asymmetric returns**, doing more with less, more often.

Put these three together, velocity, intelligence, margin, and you've got more than a toolset. You've got a new **operating philosophy**.

The companies who wield AI offensively don't ask:
"Where can we make this slightly better?"
They ask:
"Where can we play a completely different game?"

And the answer is often hiding in plain sight.

AI as a Strategy Layer, Not Just a Toolset

Let me tell you the mistake most smart CEOs make.

They look at AI the same way they looked at cloud computing or CRM systems.
As an upgrade. A feature. A thing to bolt on to the business once "we're ready."

It's not.

AI is not something you *adopt* like new software.
It's something you *absorb*, into your strategy, your thinking, your cadence.

It's not a department. It's a **design layer**.

When I sit down with leadership teams, I don't ask, *"Where are you using AI?"*
I ask, *"Where should intelligence be driving this business, and why isn't it yet?"*

That changes everything.

You stop thinking in silos, *"Let's use ChatGPT in marketing,"* or *"Let's automate support."*
You start thinking in systems, *"How do we create a business that learns faster than it operates?"*

And that's the real shift.

One of my manufacturing clients made this leap. Instead of asking their CTO to "bring in some AI tools," they reframed the challenge: *"What would our operations look like if our machines, logistics, and finance team could learn from each other in real time?"*

The result wasn't just a new platform. It was a new business rhythm.

Lead times shrank.
Forecasts sharpened.
Margin improved, because they didn't just *use* AI. They *redesigned* around it.

This is what most companies miss:
AI is not a tech stack. It's a thinking stack.

It forces you to question your assumptions about speed, visibility, and decision-making.

It changes how you resource teams.
How you measure progress.
How you respond to change.

And most importantly, it changes *who wins*.

The Innovator's Paradox 2.0

The ones who treat AI as a tool will get some lift.
The ones who treat it as a new way of seeing the game will change the game entirely.

That's where you need to be.

Not asking, *"Where can we add AI?"*
But, *"If intelligence was the foundation of how we operate, what would we do differently, right now?"*

That's the real playbook.
And it starts at the top, with you.

Why Most CEOs Underuse AI (Even the "Smart" Ones)

Let me say something you won't hear in your average AI keynote:
The problem isn't that CEOs don't understand AI.
It's that they **delegate it too quickly**, and too far down.

You'd be surprised how many "visionary" leaders I speak with who nod along in boardrooms, talk about ChatGPT at dinner parties, then quietly hand off the AI brief to their CTO or innovation lead without ever engaging in what it really means for the business model.

Why? Three reasons.

First, fear.
AI threatens the things you've mastered. The meetings you run. The decisions you control. It confronts your relevance. So the instinct is to posture as interested, but remain distant. Safe.

Second, ego.
No one wants to admit they don't fully grasp it. That maybe their 30 years of experience aren't enough to lead this next chapter. That the intern with the Python notebook might be seeing more of the future than the seasoned MD.

Third, silos.
AI experiments get trapped. A pilot in marketing. A tool in operations. A chatbot in customer service. Each team tinkers, but no one rewires the actual system. The sum stays unchanged.

That's how you end up with "AI transformation programs" that produce dashboards… and not much else.

Let me be blunt: **AI is too important to outsource.**

Not in execution. In ownership.

You don't need to write code. But you do need to own the questions.

- Where can intelligence create new value, not just save time?
- What assumptions about how we serve, scale, and price need to be rethought?
- What would this company look like if speed and foresight were built-in?

If you're not asking these, you're not leading this.

The CEOs who get this wrong will still be "informed."
But the ones who get it right? They'll be *transformed*.

4. From Automation to Augmentation to Advantage

AI has stages. And how you approach each one defines whether you stay relevant, or get quietly replaced.

Stage 1: Automation
This is where most companies start.
Use AI to cut costs, eliminate routine, boost efficiency. Nothing wrong with it. But it's the floor, not the ceiling.

You'll hear phrases like, "We've automated X hours per week."
Good. But if that's all you're doing, you're already behind.

Stage 2: Augmentation
Now you're using AI to enhance human decision-making.
Surfacing insights faster. Highlighting patterns. Guiding priorities.

In finance, this could mean predicting client churn based on micro-behaviours. In healthcare, it's matching patients to treatment protocols based on historical success data.

Here, AI doesn't replace the expert. It *amplifies* them.

Stage 3: Advantage
This is where the magic happens.
You've built a business model that is now *learning-enabled*.
It adapts faster. Personalises better. Prices smarter.

And it does this **at scale**, without needing you to manually drive each initiative.

Few companies get here. But those who do become the new incumbents, because their system gets sharper with every transaction, every user, every click.

As a CEO, your job isn't just to fund AI.
It's to **lead the leap**, from automating tasks to transforming capability.

So ask yourself:
Which stage are you really in?
And more importantly...
What's your plan to move to the next one?

Reinvent Value Propositions

When I sit with CEOs and we start talking about AI, most of the early conversation stays around tools and tasks, faster service, quicker operations, better margins.

But then I ask a different question.

"What happens to your value proposition when intelligence becomes expected, not exceptional?"

That's when the room goes quiet.

Because AI doesn't just change *how* we deliver value.
It changes *what value even means*.

Let's unpack that.

1. AI-Enhanced Outcomes vs. Traditional Benefits

There was a time when having access to smart professionals, accountants, lawyers, advisors, *was* the value. Expertise was scarce. Insight was expensive.

Now? Not so much.

Take financial planning.
Two firms, both serving affluent clients. One offers static, human-led advice based on quarterly reviews. The other uses predictive AI to adjust portfolios weekly based on live risk assessments, spending habits, and even geopolitical shifts.

Guess which one grows faster?

It's not that the second firm is "smarter." It's that they've shifted the **value anchor** from advice to outcomes.

Old model: "Pay for what we know."
New model: "Pay for how we help you *adapt*."

This shift shows up everywhere.
Healthcare: From appointments to proactive health management.
Retail: From transactions to predictive styling.
Education: From curriculum to adaptive learning journeys.

AI reframes the question from *"What do we offer?"* to *"How intelligently do we help clients succeed?"*

That's a different league.

2. Dynamic Personalization at Scale

This is where AI becomes not just helpful, but impossible to compete with.

Most businesses have one-size-fits-most products. Segmentation, if it exists, is broad. Campaigns are batch. Customer journeys are linear.

But AI allows you to shift that entirely, **in real time**.

Imagine a fitness app that adapts its entire interface based on your mood, weather, sleep data, and how hard you trained yesterday.

Or a B2B sales platform that changes pricing and payment terms dynamically, based on customer signals, not generic personas.

I helped a client in the direct-to-consumer wellness space build this. We used AI to adjust their subscription model every 30 days, based on customer engagement and retention signals. Their churn dropped by 42%, without lowering prices.

Why?
Because **value wasn't fixed anymore. It moved with the user.**

And once your customer experiences that kind of responsiveness… Everything else feels rigid.

This is the power of dynamic value:
It creates emotional loyalty because the product feels alive, *and aligned.*

Enter New Verticals

When most companies talk about expansion, the conversation is usually cautious, months of market research, hiring experts, and dipping toes into adjacent sectors.

But AI doesn't just make you better at what you do.
It gives you **unfair access** to markets that once looked off-limits.

And here's the thing:
Your competitors are still playing by the old rules, headcount, hierarchy, and heritage.

You don't have to.

1. Barrier Bypass: Using AI to Skip Legacy Constraints

Let's talk about legacy constraints, those invisible handcuffs that stop great companies from entering new industries.

In logistics, it's regulatory complexity.
In finance, it's compliance and insight latency.
In healthcare, it's data integration and risk prediction.

Now enter AI.

I worked with a mid-sized logistics firm that wanted to expand into the pharmaceutical delivery space. On paper, it was a terrible fit, high regulation, sensitive cargo, compliance minefields.

But they didn't try to fight legacy with legacy.

Instead, they built an AI-powered compliance engine that could model delivery variables, predict delays, and auto-generate documentation for local regulations, all at scale.

They bypassed the barriers that kept bigger, slower players stuck.

Another client, a SaaS platform in the B2B marketing world, used embedded finance data to pivot into SME lending. Not by hiring bankers, but by training a machine learning model to assess real-time customer creditworthiness better than the banks.

The legacy gatekeepers didn't see it coming.

That's the game AI enables:
Jump the queue. Rethink the rules. Move where others can't.

2. Speed to Competence: How AI Reduces Ramp-Up Time in New Markets

In the old world, entering a new vertical meant one thing:
Build the bench.
Hire experts. Train the team. Study the space. Wait 12–18 months for relevance.

AI compresses that timeline, radically.

Because now, competence doesn't rely solely on human expertise. It's built through *predictive modeling, natural language processing,* and *contextual feedback loops.*

Let me give you an example. A SaaS analytics firm I advised wanted to enter the property tech space. Instead of hiring a room full of real estate analysts, they trained their AI to scan thousands of property transaction records, zoning regulations, customer reviews, and utility data.

Within weeks, they were advising clients more accurately than some traditional firms that had been in the industry for decades.

It's not that the machine knew more, it just *learned faster*.

This is what CEOs often miss:
AI doesn't just help you grow.
It helps you **arrive ready**.

It lowers the cost, and risk, of entry.
And that makes adjacent markets not just possible, but *profitable*.

So next time you say, "We're not ready for that vertical"...
Ask yourself:
Or is it just that *we're not thinking with the right lens*?

Optimize for Hyper-Growth

I've spent enough time in boardrooms to know that everyone says they want scale.
But when you peel back the layers, most leaders are still thinking in **linear terms**.

More sales? Hire more reps.
More leads? Spend more on ads.
More complexity? Hire consultants.

That's not scale. That's **expansion by friction**.

True hyper-growth, the kind that bends industries, doesn't come from doing more of the same.
It comes from **compounding capability without compounding cost**.

And that's where AI changes everything.

1. AI-Driven Demand Gen and Sales Precision

Let's start with the top of the funnel.
In the old world, you built demand through brute force, cold emails, generic ads, rinse and repeat.

But AI flips the funnel.

Now, your messaging adapts in real time to intent signals. Your campaigns write themselves based on past performance. Your sales pipeline isn't just ranked, it's *predicted*.

I advised a SaaS founder recently who'd built a custom AI layer into their CRM. The system scored leads not just on behaviour, but on timing, sentiment, and interaction heat.
His team wasn't guessing who to call.
They knew exactly when and *why* a prospect was ready to convert.

We saw conversion rates increase by 38%, with the *same team, same budget*.

Another client used AI to generate thousands of micro-targeted ad variants weekly, each adjusted based on audience psychographics. The result? Their cost per acquisition dropped by over 50% in 60 days.

This isn't smarter marketing.
It's **weaponized precision**.

And it scales with zero human fatigue.

2. Scaling Without Headcount, Or With Lean Teams

Here's the uncomfortable truth:
The future of growth is *less about hiring*, and more about **orchestrating systems**.

We're seeing 7- and even 8-figure businesses run by teams of five to ten people, with AI handling everything from lead gen to customer service to operations.

I've worked with e-commerce founders who built entire logistics chains using AI to forecast demand, auto-negotiate with suppliers, and optimise delivery routes, without needing a back office.

One media brand I mentor creates hundreds of pieces of content a month across platforms using an AI editorial engine that writes, edits, and even schedules based on engagement patterns.

They scaled to 2 million monthly impressions, with a content team of two.

These aren't unicorns. These are **early adopters** of what the next decade will make standard.

AI doesn't just reduce the need for people.
It redefines **what people are needed for**.

Your job as CEO isn't to resist that shift.
t's to *design around it*.

3. From Startup to Market Leader: Compounding Speed as Strategy

Let me leave you with this:

Speed isn't just a byproduct of AI.
It's a *strategy*, especially when that speed is **compounding**.

When your models learn faster, your ops run leaner, and your decisions sharpen over time, you start to play a different game.

I've seen startups go from idea to category leader in under 24 months, not because they raised more, but because they **moved with intelligence** the market couldn't match.

They built momentum loops.
They learned faster than competitors could react.
They turned speed into a moat.

This is what's available to you, if you're willing to abandon the "hire and hope" model of scale.

Because the next market leader in your space?
They're not hiring more people.
They're building more **learning systems**.

Case 1: The SaaS Company in San Francisco That Tripled ARR With AI-Powered Onboarding

Industry: B2B SaaS – Workforce Automation
City: San Francisco, USA
Key Figures: Adam Clarke (CEO), Fiona Reyes (Chief Product Officer)

I met Adam Clarke at a tech summit in Toronto.
Young, driven, and clearly exhausted. Over lunch, he laid it out with brutal honesty:

> "We're acquiring users, Moe. Thousands. But our churn is killing us. They sign up... and vanish. We don't even get the chance to sell."

Adam was the CEO of **TaskLayer**, a B2B SaaS startup based in San Francisco, focused on streamlining workforce scheduling for mid-sized logistics companies.
He had raised a healthy $8.5 million in Series A and had built a rock-solid platform.

But they were stuck.

Their product was good, their CAC was under control, and they were signing contracts, yet the user base wasn't growing fast enough to satisfy investors.
And when I looked closer, the problem was obvious:

They had no intelligent onboarding.

People didn't leave because the product was weak.
They left because they didn't understand how to win with it, fast enough.

The Challenge: Turn Onboarding Into a Competitive Advantage

The Innovator's Paradox 2.0

I flew to San Francisco to meet the team. Fiona Reyes, the Chief Product Officer, walked me through their current user journey.

A typical fleet manager from Birmingham or Manchester would sign up, click through a five-step setup, then get lost in a dashboard built for a tech-savvy operations analyst.

No context. No nudge.
No sign of success within the first hour.

I asked Fiona a simple question:

> "If your ideal user only had 15 minutes to try your product, what would you show them?"

She hesitated.

That silence cost them millions.

The Fix: AI That Feels Like a Human Guide, But Learns Like a Machine

We began by building what I call an *intelligent activation layer*, a machine learning system trained on historical user data that could adapt onboarding flows in real time.

If the user was a logistics director from Leeds, the system emphasised compliance tools, cross-depot tracking, and audit-readiness.

If the user was an operations assistant in Toronto, it guided them through task automation templates first, *exactly* what made their day easier.

The AI adjusted email cadence, pop-up help content, even the tone of in-app messaging, based on usage patterns, company size, and decision-making behavior.

Here's one key move:
Previously, TaskLayer showed all features on day one.

After the AI was introduced, the system *withheld* advanced modules until a user demonstrated engagement with core tasks.

The impact?

- **47% reduction in onboarding abandonment**
- **61% drop in first-month churn**

And critically, **they expanded into the UK, Canada, and India without hiring local onboarding or sales teams.**

Everything scaled through automation.

The Impact: ARR Tripled in 14 Months

Six months after rollout, Adam messaged me from Lisbon.

> "We just crossed $12.3M ARR. Same team. Same platform. Just smarter onboarding."

They'd entered three new markets.
Retention was up.
Customer lifetime value (LTV) had increased by 44%.
And the entire growth engine was run by a lean team of 18 people.

They weren't winning because of headcount.
They were winning because of **intelligent activation**.

Industry Insight: Questions CEOs in SaaS Must Ask

- *Are your onboarding flows customised by user type, region, or role?*
- *Do you track time-to-first-value, and is it under 15 minutes?*
- *How many users leave before they hit the 'aha' moment, and why?*

If you're in SaaS and still using generic walkthroughs, you're gambling with your growth.
AI isn't just a tool, it's how your product can learn to *sell itself*.

Final Word: Product Alone Won't Win

You can build a great solution.
But if customers don't feel the result, fast, it doesn't matter.

TaskLayer didn't hire more sales reps.
They built a system that learned faster than any rep could.

That's how they turned onboarding from a friction point into a strategic weapon.

And that's how you scale globally, without scaling overhead.

Case 2: The Ecom Brand in Dubai That Created a New Category Using AI Market Insights

Industry: Direct-to-Consumer (DTC) E-Commerce – Skincare & Wellness
City: Dubai, United Arab Emirates
Key Figures: Leila Mansoor (Founder), Jamal Qureshi (Chief Data Officer)

I first met Leila Mansoor at a founder's roundtable in Abu Dhabi. She had just launched **Desert Bloom**, a Dubai-based direct-to-consumer skincare brand focused on hydration and resilience in arid climates.

But what she said next caught my attention.

> "We're not here to compete in skincare. We're going to create a new category: *climate-adaptive wellness*. And AI is going to show us where to strike."

That wasn't founder bravado.
That was the beginning of a brand that would grow from zero to eight figures in under 18 months, **not by copying trends, but by predicting them.**

The Challenge: Competing in a Saturated Market

The DTC wellness space is brutally crowded, especially in the Middle East where international players dominate and local consumer trust can be hard to earn.

Leila wasn't trying to outspend these giants.
She wanted to out-learn them.

Her co-founder, Jamal Qureshi, was a former AI engineer who had built real-time recommendation engines for ride-share platforms. Together, they approached brand-building like a data science problem.

> "Why guess what the market wants," Jamal told me, "when we can **see it forming before it peaks**?"

So we worked together to build an AI market intelligence engine, trained to detect early demand signals from consumer behavior across Instagram, TikTok, Shopify, Reddit, and regional e-commerce sites like Noon and Namshi.

What it revealed wasn't just surprising, it was category-defining.

The Insight: Predictive Demand > Trend Following

The AI system picked up an unusual pattern:
Women in Gulf countries were complaining not about sun damage, but about *humidity fluctuation* and the way conventional skincare made it worse.

Thousands of micro-comments across platforms revealed a pain point no mainstream product was targeting. The keywords?
"Sticky."
"Not breathable."
"Clogs in humidity."

But buried in that noise was a goldmine.

Leila moved fast.

They launched **Desert Bloom Atmoskin**, a hybrid moisturiser that adjusted its absorption rate based on heat and humidity. The product was formulated in a Dubai-based lab and tested with a group of 500 beta users identified through AI segmentation.

Within six weeks of launch, they were backordered.
Not because of big ad spend, but because **they were first** to name and solve a growing problem, before it hit the mainstream.

The Execution: AI as Brand Strategist

Beyond product creation, AI powered their entire go-to-market strategy:

- **Pricing:** Adjusted dynamically based on inventory velocity and customer lifetime value forecasts.

- **Messaging:** A/B tested 60 taglines in 48 hours across social platforms, narrowing down the highest emotional engagement index.

- **Packaging:** AI analyzed Instagram Stories from target customers to guide visual design, optimising for shareability, not shelf presence.

They didn't just build a brand.
They built a **conversation engine** that evolved faster than competitors could copy.

I asked Leila how she made decisions with such speed.

> "We don't ask if the idea is safe," she said. "We ask if the signal is strong, and act."

The Outcome: A New Category, Not Just a Product

Today, Desert Bloom ships to 14 countries across the GCC, UK, and Southeast Asia.
Their flagship product spawned an entire line of AI-predicted formulations.

ARR crossed $10.4 million in under 18 months.
They operate with a team of 12, half of whom are data engineers.

And their latest round of funding?
It was oversubscribed in under 10 days.

Investors didn't just see a brand.
They saw a **system for sensing and shaping demand before anyone else could name it**.

Industry Takeaways for E-Commerce Founders

- *Are you reacting to trends, or reading them while they're still forming?*

- *Does your product development rely on focus groups, or live market signals?*

- *Is your customer feedback a database, or a decision-making engine?*

AI won't make you creative.
But it will **show you what your market is hungry for, before your competitors feel the rumble**.

Case 3: The Accountancy Firm in Poland That Scaled with an AI Engine Instead of Hiring

Industry: Professional Services – Accountancy & SME Advisory
City: Kraków, Poland
Key Figures: Tomasz Wójcik (Managing Partner), Anna Zielinska (AI Strategist)

I met Tomasz Wójcik through a mutual contact in Warsaw, another client I'd helped restructure post-pandemic. He was managing partner of **Wójcik & Partners**, a mid-sized accountancy and advisory firm in Kraków, serving fast-growing Polish SMEs in manufacturing, retail, and services.

He got right to the point.

> "We're drowning in client requests, but I refuse to scale by hiring bodies. I want to scale through brains, through systems."

At the time, his firm had 22 employees and over 300 active clients, ranging from Złoty 5M to Złoty 200M turnover. His advisory team was exhausted, his margins were thinning, and service quality was at risk.

The traditional route?
Hire more tax specialists, train junior consultants, and stretch capacity.

Tomasz wasn't interested.
He wanted something scalable, intelligent, and lean.

The Challenge: Growth Without Complexity

The problem wasn't client acquisition. In fact, Wójcik & Partners had more inbound leads than they could handle, particularly for their growing SME advisory packages.

But their services, especially financial diagnostics and business model analysis, were manually intensive. Every new client meant dozens of hours spent combing through financial statements, generating reports, preparing risk assessments, and mapping out growth plans.

> "I don't want my firm to become a sweatshop of spreadsheets," Tomasz said.
> "I want us to feel like a partner with superpowers."

That's where Anna Zielinska came in, a former machine learning engineer from Warsaw who had recently joined his team to explore AI capabilities.

Together, we mapped out a transformation roadmap that would replace bodies with brains, and **scale capacity without scaling payroll**.

The Pivot: AI as Diagnostic and Delivery Engine

The first phase was to build an AI-powered diagnostic tool.

We trained it on 1,200 past client files, feeding in balance sheets, income statements, market profiles, and performance benchmarks across Poland's SME ecosystem.

The result?

A virtual analyst we nicknamed **Klara**.

Klara could:

- Parse three years of financials in 17 seconds.
- Flag liquidity gaps, margin anomalies, and growth bottlenecks using predictive analytics.
- Generate a plain-English summary report for clients, ready for a strategy session, within minutes.

But we didn't stop there.

Next, we created **AI-led strategy sprints**. These were 30-day advisory programs where Klara would:

- Set growth priorities based on client segment and industry norms.
- Assign tasks to clients via automated prompts.
- Track behavioral data to adjust advice in real time.

And finally, we embedded **virtual delivery**: recorded explainer videos, chat-based AI advisors, and pre-emptive reporting, all branded under Wójcik & Partners, but run by Klara behind the scenes.

The Impact: Revenue per Consultant Up 3.5x

Here's what happened in the first six months:

- Client onboarding time dropped by 73%.
- Annual revenue per consultant rose from Złoty 148,000 to over Złoty 500,000.
- Staff workload fell by 41%, without cutting service depth or quality.

They were no longer billing for time.
They were billing for **insight and acceleration**.

And the clients?
They didn't care if a human or a system delivered the analysis, as long as it was right, fast, and actionable.

In fact, several began asking:

"Can we get access to Klara directly for our internal finance teams?"

Tomasz smiled.
He knew he was no longer running an accountancy firm.
He was building a **financial intelligence platform**, without ever writing a line of code himself.

Industry Questions: What Service Firms Must Now Ask

- *Where does 70% of your team's time go, and can AI replicate that thinking?*

- *Can you serve twice as many clients with half the staff?*

- *What if your best analyst never slept, never got tired, and never made a mistake?*

This isn't just about automation.
It's about creating **a new category of service delivery**, where insight is productized, scaled, and priced by value, not hours.

Final Word: The New Smart Firm Isn't Bigger, It's Faster

Tomasz didn't scale through bloat.
He scaled through boldness.

His firm didn't become more complex.
It became **more intelligent**.

In the end, the smartest firms won't be the ones with the biggest headcount.
They'll be the ones that learn fastest, adapt instantly, and deliver value **before the client asks for it**.

That's not consulting.
That's evolution.

Case 4: The 9-Figure Company That Used AI to Enter a New Industry in 6 Months

Industry: Industrial Equipment Manufacturing → Vertical Expansion into Smart Agriculture
City: Munich, Germany
Key Figures: Klaus Brenner (Group CEO), Sophia Neumann (Chief Innovation Officer)

I first met Klaus Brenner over a quiet lunch at the Mandarin Oriental in Munich.
He runs **Brenner Group**, a €180M industrial equipment manufacturer best known for building precision hydraulic components for German auto and aerospace firms.

But on that day, he wasn't interested in legacy.
He was fixated on something else entirely.

> "We've maxed out this sector, Moe. Our margins are flat, our growth is capped. I want to enter a new industry, but I can't wait 18 months to figure out where and how."

He wasn't asking for a market report.
He wanted a map, and he wanted it now.

That's when we brought in AI.

The Challenge: Expansion Without Guesswork

Sophia Neumann, his newly hired Chief Innovation Officer, laid it out clearly:

"We're sitting on a treasure trove of engineering talent, supply chain strength, and manufacturing precision. But we've never used it to go outside our core."

What they needed was clarity, not on *what* they could do, but on *where* and *how fast* they could win.

Traditionally, expansion into a new vertical would involve 6-12 months of consulting reports, whiteboarding sessions, and pilot fatigue.

We had no such luxury.

So, we built a live **AI Scouting Engine**, and we gave it one mission: **Find the most underserved, high-growth adjacent vertical where Brenner's assets gave them an unfair advantage.**

The Move: AI That Models, Maps, and Simulates Outcomes

The system ingested:

- Market data across 14 adjacent industries
- Product gaps based on patent filings and customer reviews
- Regulatory pathways for European expansion
- GTM costs, lead times, and pricing benchmarks

It didn't spit out a deck.
It built **real-time simulations**.

And it pointed to something surprising:
Smart agriculture.

There was a massive gap in Europe for ruggedized automation tools for large-scale, variable-climate farms, particularly in Spain, France, and Poland.

One key finding?
More than 70% of large farms in the EU lacked predictive irrigation and weather-adaptive machinery, despite rising climate volatility.

Klaus leaned in.

> "So you're saying we already build the parts... we're just aiming them in the wrong direction?"

Exactly.

The Execution: Rapid GTM, No Bureaucracy

Here's what happened next, fast and ruthless:

1. **A pilot product was scoped in 3 weeks**: repurposed actuator tech from aerospace lines for smart irrigation valves.

2. **GTM strategy was simulated using AI**: competitor responses, pricing wars, channel risks, all modeled in 48 hours.

3. **A "shadow launch" page went live** in Spanish and Polish, A/B testing messaging before they even had a product.

Within 60 days, they had 3 LOIs from large-scale agribusinesses. By month four, a limited beta rollout was underway across farms in Zaragoza and Lublin.

No guesswork. No endless planning.
Just **signal, simulation, strike**.

The Impact: 12% New Revenue in Less Than a Year

Brenner's agri-tech unit, now called **Brenner Terra**, accounted for 12% of group revenue by year-end, €21.5M from a standing start.

And it operated with only 8 dedicated staff, piggybacking on existing logistics and manufacturing lines.

The board?
They were stunned.

But Klaus wasn't.
He saw what most legacy CEOs miss.

> "It wasn't a moonshot. It was adjacent. But without AI, we'd have never seen it fast enough to win it."

Industry Takeaways: Lessons for CEOs of Mature Companies

- *What adjacent markets are you ignoring because they don't look like your past?*

- *What if your next €20M opportunity is one simulation away?*

- *Who on your team is tasked with creating, not just protecting, revenue?*

AI isn't just about automation.
It's about **expansion velocity**.
The winners won't just be efficient.
They'll be first.

AI Offense Audit: 12-Point Assessment

I was in Zurich, sitting across from the CEO of a €600 million logistics firm. Smart. Seasoned. Battle-tested. He leaned back, arms crossed, and said something I've heard a hundred times.

> "We're not ignoring AI, Moe. We're just not rushing into it."

It's always the same line, different accent, same trap.

So I told him a story.

Six months earlier, I'd worked with a much smaller player. A regional distribution company based in Valencia. Family-run. Tightly resourced. Not a drop of Silicon Valley in their DNA.

But they didn't wait.

They fed their historical route data into an AI model, layered in weather patterns, fuel costs, and driver fatigue stats. Then they let the machine propose a new logistics schedule.

Three months later, they had shaved 11% off delivery times, cut fuel costs by 18%, and doubled their customer retention rate.

The CEO looked at me and asked, "How did they know where to start?"

And that's when I pulled out what I'm about to walk you through now.

Not a spreadsheet.
Not a sexy framework.
Just a conversation, twelve questions I ask every leader in rooms like this, when the bluff of "we're already doing AI" starts to collapse.

First, I ask:
How fast is your R&D really learning?

The Innovator's Paradox 2.0

If your product or service development still depends on quarterly feedback, gut instinct, or analyst reviews, you're flying blind. One client in Tel Aviv built an AI model that forecasted user feature adoption three months ahead. They killed two failing features before a single complaint ever landed. That's not luck. That's leverage.

Then I ask:
Is your sales team still relying on spreadsheets and hunches?
In Johannesburg, I saw a company transform its B2B sales process using a simple AI model that tracked deal signals, email sentiment, meeting cadence, even silence patterns. They started closing 27% more deals with half the team. Not because they worked harder. Because they knew who to talk to, and when.

Next, we look at customers.
Do you actually know how they feel, right now?
Not in surveys. Not in NPS charts. I'm talking about real-time friction mapping. One retail chain in Manchester used AI to track drop-off points in their app flow and made three micro-adjustments that drove a £2.1M lift in conversions in 8 weeks.

I ask about marketing.
Are you still debating headlines in meetings?
Or are you letting the machine test 100 versions while your team sleeps?

In operations, the question shifts:
Are your teams making decisions, or cleaning up after them?
True AI in operations isn't about dashboards. It's when the system starts deciding. A manufacturer in Malmö removed three full-time schedulers after training their AI to dynamically re-route production based on supply volatility. Nobody was fired. The team just moved upstream, to strategy.

We get to people.
Is your hiring still based on CVs? Or contribution prediction?
In Kraków, Tomasz, whom you'll meet in a later chapter, built an internal AI model that mapped who was most likely to burn out

based on workload and personality dynamics. He didn't just prevent attrition. He built culture by acting before people collapsed.

Then I shift the lens forward.
Are you stress-testing your 3-year vision against real-world shifts?
Most leaders have a plan. Very few have a model that updates that plan daily, based on competitor moves, tech signals, or policy changes.

And speaking of competitors,
How often do you simulate what they might do next?
In Munich, Klaus didn't just enter a new market, he ran 18 AI-modeled GTM war games against legacy players before launch. He didn't hope to win. He out-planned the incumbents before they knew he was coming.

Let's go back to your customers.
Do you really know what they need next?
A client in Toronto built an AI sequence that tracked usage behavior and automatically triggered "next best offer" moments. Renewal rates? Up 36% in three months.

What about cost?
Do you cut waste in hindsight, or in real time?
In Singapore, a SaaS CFO used AI to flag duplicate tool subscriptions across departments. They found $1.2M in annual bloat before the next procurement cycle.

And finally, the question most CEOs flinch at:
Is your business actually getting smarter with every decision?
Not your people. Your system.
Does your business have a memory?
Does it learn, compound, evolve?

Or does it restart every quarter like a goldfish?

I didn't give the CEO in Zurich a score.
I gave him a mirror.

He sat there in silence. Then he exhaled.

> "We're playing defense. Quietly. And calling it strategy."

It wasn't judgment.
It was relief.

He could finally see the gap between ambition and architecture.

That's what this book, and this chapter, is really about.

Because AI isn't a checklist. It's a litmus test for leadership.

And in the next section, we'll dive deeper into the most dangerous illusion in business:

The belief that legacy is leverage. When, in reality, it may be your greatest anchor.

Where Are You Still Playing Defense?

There's a moment in every strategy session when the masks drop.

It usually happens just after the excitement, once the real risks are laid out. The numbers are up, the room quiets, and the CEO looks down for just a beat too long. That's when I know we're not talking about scale anymore, we're talking about safety.

You can hear it in the phrases:

> "Let's monitor first."
> "We'll revisit this next quarter."
> "The team's not quite ready."

I've said those same words myself.
They sound rational. Measured.
But more often than not, they're camouflage for fear. Fear of risk, fear of ego death, fear of becoming irrelevant.

We don't call it defense, of course.
We call it discipline. Focus. Prudence.

But here's what I've learned:
You can't scale from the back foot.

If you're leading from a place of preservation instead of creation, it's only a matter of time before someone else rewrites your market, and you're left defending a map that no longer matters.

Let me show you where defensive thinking hides, even in the minds of world-class operators.

1. You're measuring activity, not trajectory.

I once worked with an 8-figure media company in Birmingham. Their dashboard was a monument to movement, campaigns launched, content produced, meetings held. Impressive output.

But when I asked where the company was going, what "10X" looked like, the founder froze.

They weren't measuring velocity toward a vision. They were counting calories burned on the treadmill.

It's a subtle shift, but critical.

Ask yourself: Are your KPIs showing progress or just motion?

2. You're hiring to plug gaps, not to create breakthroughs.

I remember a CEO in Helsinki who said, "We need another operations lead before we can think about product innovation."

They didn't need more hands. They needed new thinking. But safety told them to hire familiarity, not difference.

Here's the truth: defensive hiring protects what's already working. Offensive hiring questions it.

If your newest team members look just like your current ones, you're reinforcing today, not building tomorrow.

3. You're investing in optimization instead of obsolescence.

This one hits hard.

I once challenged the CFO of a major engineering firm in Manchester to walk me through their AI spend. Ninety percent was going toward cost savings and efficiency improvements on legacy products.

Not one initiative was focused on creating something that might make their current portfolio irrelevant.

> "We don't want to cannibalize ourselves," he said.

I told him, "That's exactly why someone else will."

If your tech budget is only defending what you already do well, you're not playing offense, you're extending your shelf life.

4. You're stuck in pilot mode.

This is where courage hides behind complexity.

A London-based insurance firm I worked with had tested AI claims automation across three product lines, with promising results. But they'd spent 18 months stuck in pilot loops, afraid of rolling it out systemwide.

> "We're just not sure it's scalable yet."

No. They were afraid of what would happen if it worked, and made their middle management layer obsolete.

Defense dresses itself up as "due diligence."
But progress punished for being too successful is still fear.

5. You haven't fired a "winning" product in years.

One of the clearest signs of a defensive mindset is what you're still protecting.

I met with the founder of a successful B2B software platform in Dubai. They had one product that made 60% of their revenue, and hadn't changed in seven years.

When I asked when they last considered sunsetting it, the room went cold.

> "That's our golden goose."

Exactly. And that goose was about to be someone else's lunch.

If there isn't at least one product, one process, or one sacred cow you're actively considering replacing, you're defending your past, not designing your future.

So, where are you still playing defense?

Maybe it's in your hiring.
Maybe your roadmap.
Maybe the stories you tell your board to avoid scaring them.

Wherever it is, find it. Name it.
Because until you admit where you're leading with fear, you can't build from freedom.

And the irony?

The more successful you are, the more tempting it is to defend instead of disrupt.

That's the paradox.

Your past makes you powerful.
But only if you're willing to let parts of it die.

Otherwise, it becomes your cage.

Your AI Battlefield Map: Who's Already Coming for You?

A few months ago, I was consulting with the CEO of a mid-market construction firm in Leeds. Solid business. £80M in annual revenue. Strong reputation. Tight operations.

We were discussing growth strategy when I asked a simple question:

> "Who's your most dangerous competitor right now?"

He rattled off three names, familiar, direct players. Companies he's been sparring with for years. The usual suspects.

So I nodded, smiled, and pushed a little further.

> "And who's using AI to do what you do, but ten times faster, from outside your industry?"

He paused.

And in that pause, I could hear it.
The sound of an unmarked flank.

Because here's the truth most leaders miss:
Your next biggest threat probably isn't even on your radar yet.
It's not the company across the street.
It's the outsider, the startup, the AI-native team that doesn't think like you, because they've never had to.

They don't carry your legacy.
They don't play by your rules.
And they don't need your scale to steal your relevance.

They just need better data, sharper learning loops, and the courage to ignore tradition.

Let's make this real.

Imagine you run a chain of physical therapy clinics. You're watching local competition. You're monitoring marketing spend. Maybe you're tweaking prices or testing online booking systems.

Meanwhile, in Oslo, a wellness tech startup is training a generative AI model to deliver remote, motion-tracked therapy sessions with 91% patient satisfaction, and zero overhead.

They don't need clinics.
They don't need your customer base.
They need one influencer, a distribution channel, and a year.

And then your waiting rooms start to look a lot emptier.

That's the battlefield now.

And it's not fair.
It's not even level.

Which is why you need a different kind of map.

I want you to ask yourself five hard questions, really sit with them:

1. **Which industry adjacent to mine is scaling faster through AI?**

If you're in travel, look at fintech. If you're in retail, look at media. If you're in logistics, look at healthcare.
AI doesn't respect sector walls. It moves wherever insight, speed, and experience can be redefined.

2. **What would a digital-first, AI-native version of my company look like, and who's already building it?**

The Innovator's Paradox 2.0

In Toronto, I worked with a legacy accountancy firm watching a three-person AI startup eat their mid-tier clients. Why? The startup automated tax strategy proposals in 30 minutes, using generative modeling based on industry and local legislation. No charm. No handshakes. Just answers.

3. **Who's collecting the data I wish I had?**

If someone else owns the data, especially behavioral, predictive, or longitudinal data, they're holding the keys to the future of your industry. They can price better, launch faster, personalize deeper.

4. **If I had to launch a new business to disrupt mine, what would I do first?**

Would you go all-in on automation?
Would you price on outcome, not hours?
Would you ignore everything that made your current model stable?

This thought experiment isn't theoretical.
It's survival strategy.

5. **Whose tech stack already gives them 10x feedback speed compared to mine?**

Because if someone else is learning faster, about customers, about friction points, about ROI, your size won't save you.

In fact, it will slow you down.

When I ask these questions in private sessions, the reaction is usually quiet discomfort. And that's the point.

You don't need more strategy decks.
You need better visibility into the invisible war already underway.

Because AI is changing the rules of category power.
What looks like a moat today becomes a speed bump tomorrow.

The best defensive play?
Go on offense.

Start building your AI battlefield map now.
Plot the non-obvious players. Track their velocity. Watch their hires, their product releases, their capital raises.

Disruption doesn't announce itself with a press release.

It arrives quietly, in your blind spot, just before your board starts asking why growth has stalled.

Offensive Playbook Builder: What Will You Reinvent, Replace, or Reposition in the Next 90 Days?

Let me ask you something we don't ask enough at the top:

> "What are you prepared to burn down, intentionally, in the next 90 days?"

That's not a dramatic question.
It's a strategic one.

Because reinvention never begins with strategy decks or vision boards.
It starts with courage, specifically, the courage to dismantle what once worked.

You've made it this far in the book, which tells me something:
You're not just curious about AI, disruption, or competitive edges.
You're hungry for a reset.
Not in the motivational sense.
In the boardroom sense.

You want a practical, executable shift.

So let's build it. Together.

I want you to take out a sheet of paper, or pull up your notes app, and draw three columns. No headings yet.

Now ask yourself these three prompts, slowly and honestly:

1. What will I reinvent?

This is where you look at your existing offerings, experiences, or systems, and ask how AI could completely transform them.

Not incrementally improve. Reinvent.

I had a client in Glasgow, mid-sized legal tech. Their onboarding process for clients was filled with human touchpoints they thought were irreplaceable. After we rebuilt it using conversational AI and contextual intake logic, they shaved ten days off their sales cycle and saw 23% more conversions.

Same outcome. Different path.
Less friction. More freedom.

So what in your world needs to be reinvented, not just refreshed?

2. What will I replace?

Now we get bolder.

This is about identifying sacred cows. Processes or products that feel core, but are quietly becoming anchors.

One CEO I advised in Cape Town ran a long-standing consulting business. Brilliant model in 2015. But by 2023, the entire mid-tier market was flooded with AI-driven advisory platforms.

He kept saying, "Our clients need the human touch."
But the numbers didn't lie. They were bleeding margin.

So he made a decision.
He replaced his entry-level offerings with an AI-powered strategy simulator, something none of his competitors had yet built.

Within a quarter, his churn dropped. His team focused on premium engagements. And they began winning clients who never returned his calls before.

So, what's your equivalent?

What will you replace, not because it failed, but because it's finished?

3. What will I reposition?

Sometimes the product isn't the problem.
It's the promise around it.

I once worked with a fintech founder in Frankfurt who was selling real-time payment APIs to developers. Great tech. Terrible traction.

So we asked: what problem are you really solving?

With AI, we repositioned the messaging from "API access" to "cash flow confidence." We trained a model to show CFOs how our tool predicted liquidity swings days in advance, something they deeply cared about.

Same product. Different lens. Exponential growth.

So, what do you need to reposition?
Not change what it *is*, just change what it *means*.

Here's your 90-day challenge:

Before you turn another page, before your leadership team meets next, write down your answers.

- One thing to **reinvent**
- One thing to **replace**
- One thing to **reposition**

Don't wait for Q3 planning.
Don't wait for buy-in from everyone.
Don't wait until the competition forces your hand.

Do it now, while it's still your choice.

Because the companies that lead this next wave won't be the ones with the best AI engineers.

They'll be the ones with the clearest offensive plan, and the nerve to execute it early.

Take a deep breath.
You've just built the first layer of your offensive AI playbook.

In the next chapter, we'll shift gears and focus on your team, because without a culture of transformation, even the best AI playbook dies on arrival.

Chapter 3:
The Systemic Innovator: Empowering Your Team to Drive Transformation

1: Building a Culture of Experimentation

What Fear Kills Before It Begins

I remember sitting across from a COO in Manchester, sharp, structured, and absolutely paralysed.

Her team had just killed an internal idea that could have slashed 18% off their operating costs. Killed it in silence. Not because it was flawed, but because no one wanted to be the first to speak.

She said to me, "Moe, I don't get it. We're hiring smart people, paying them well. Why do they just... wait for orders?"

I leaned forward and said what most leaders don't want to hear.

"It's not intelligence that's missing. It's psychological permission."

You see, what fear kills isn't just ideas, it kills initiative *before* it's even conscious. It buries the impulse in silence. No one wants to be the one who sticks their head above the parapet, only to have it shot off with a passive-aggressive look, a dismissive remark, or worse, complete indifference.

Let me tell you what that feels like from the inside.

You're in a meeting. You've spotted a way to streamline a broken process, maybe even automate it. But you pause. You glance at the faces around the table. Will this make your boss look bad? Will it create more work? Will you be seen as stepping out of line?

So, you keep quiet. You file it away. Maybe later. Maybe never.

Multiply that moment by a hundred people in your business, every week. That's your cost of fear.

Now, don't mistake fear for incompetence. Some of the most capable teams I've worked with were also the most hesitant. Why? Because they'd been trained, sometimes subtly, sometimes bluntly, that challenging the status quo was dangerous.

That's what I call *invisible conformity*. No one says, "Don't innovate." They just reward compliance and punish discomfort.

I had a client in financial services in Edinburgh who ran one of the most impressive top-line operations I'd seen. But beneath it? Creative paralysis. I interviewed their middle managers. Nearly all of them confessed, off the record, that they had ideas they never voiced. One manager said, "I don't want to be the guy who suggests something and ends up on the restructuring list."

He wasn't joking.

Innovation dies not from lack of talent but from lack of safety.

And let's be clear, this isn't about ping-pong tables and trust falls. It's about real permission: the kind that says, "You won't be punished for being wrong. You'll be punished for playing small."

So, if you're serious about transformation, start by asking yourself this:

When was the last time someone in your company openly disagreed with you? Not politely. Openly.

If the answer is "I can't remember," you don't have alignment. You have quiet obedience.

And no amount of strategy will compensate for a team that's too afraid to think aloud.

The Permissionless Principle

One of the sharpest founders I've ever worked with wasn't the loudest voice in the room, he just created the conditions for others to speak louder.

Luca ran a robotics logistics company out of Rotterdam. I remember walking through his warehouse and noticing something odd: every team leader had a whiteboard mounted outside their zone, not inside. Scribbled on each was a list of "Running Tests." Not KPIs, not production metrics, just experiments.

I asked him, "What's this?"

He smiled, shrugged, and said, "I don't want them asking for permission. I want them breaking things that aren't working."

That's the Permissionless Principle in action.

Luca didn't just allow experimentation, he operationalized it. His people weren't reckless, but they were empowered. Every two weeks, teams were expected to run one new initiative: a software tweak, a layout change, an AI-driven routing variation. And they didn't have to fill out a form or book a slot with HR. They just had to follow the framework: small, fast, reversible.

What happened next surprised even him.

One of the pick-and-pack crews trialled a machine learning adjustment on route assignments that shaved four seconds per order. Four seconds. Not headline stuff. But across 100,000 orders a month? It bought them an extra full-time equivalent, without hiring.

No one told them to do it. They saw a problem, they tested a theory, they implemented it.

That's the point: high-performing teams don't wait for a memo. They act, because the architecture around them says, "Try it."

Let me give you the flip side.

A multinational I advised had innovation labs in three countries. Beautiful buildings, cutting-edge talent, healthy budgets. And yet, nothing meaningful had shipped in 18 months.

Why?

Every idea needed a 14-slide deck, a sponsor VP, a budget forecast, and legal clearance, *before* a single customer interaction. What began as innovation turned into admin theatre.

Ideas don't die in the lab. They die in the waiting room.

Here's the truth that most legacy CEOs don't want to hear: Your best people already have the answers. They're just too buried in process, risk management, or fear to act on them.

Permissionless doesn't mean chaotic. It means governed freedom.

Think of it like a well-run Formula One team. The pit crew doesn't ask the team principal for approval during a tyre change. They've trained, practiced, and have clear parameters, but they're trusted to make real-time calls.

It's the same in innovation.

Give your people **frameworks**, not checklists. Offer **guardrails**, not gatekeepers. And measure them not just on outcomes, but on how often they try something new.

I once told a founder in Stockholm: "If no one in your team failed this month, you're not leading innovation. You're just managing consistency."

The Permissionless Principle is your insurance against inertia. It tells your team: "You don't need a permission slip to make things better."

And once that principle becomes embedded in your culture, don't be surprised when your company becomes unrecognisable, in the best way.

Rewarding Failure vs. Celebrating Learning

Let's get something straight.

I don't celebrate failure.

There's nothing noble about missing targets, blowing cash, or shipping a product nobody wants. The idea that a great innovation culture throws parties every time something breaks? That's not leadership. That's indulgence.

But I do celebrate *learning*. And there's a critical difference.

Several years ago, I worked with a fintech firm in Dublin. Bright team. Great culture, on paper. They had murals about risk-taking on the walls. Posters quoting Edison about "10,000 ways not to make a lightbulb." A budget for experimentation.

And yet, no one took risks.

When I dug deeper, I found out why. One of the engineers had launched a micro-lending feature in Latin America without full leadership signoff. It flopped. Cost them six figures. The CEO called it a "learning opportunity" in the press release, but internally, the engineer was benched, then transferred.

That's the hidden cost of performative failure culture. People hear the slogans, but watch the punishments. And they learn quickly: it's not safe to experiment here.

Compare that to a client I worked with in Leeds. A mid-size B2B SaaS company. They had a simple practice called "The Debrief Table." Every Friday, someone presented a failed initiative, not for blame, but for analysis. They walked through what the hypothesis was, what was tried, what went wrong, and what they'd do differently.

Sometimes, the person was the CEO himself.

And here's what changed: people started owning their decisions, not hiding them. The team began to take smarter risks because they weren't afraid of being wrong. They were only afraid of *not learning*.

One of their product leads, Maya, tried a bold onboarding sequence that cut customer activation time by 30%. On paper, it looked like a win. But two weeks later, churn spiked. She brought it to the Debrief Table herself.

"We got the activation," she said, "but we didn't earn the commitment. I rushed it."

That insight led to a new hybrid onboarding flow, and customer retention went up 11% the next quarter.

No punishment. No shame. Just iteration.

Here's the deeper truth: failure only teaches when reflection is institutionalised. That's your job as a leader, not to throw balloons when someone fails, but to build mechanisms that turn those failures into forward motion.

Ask yourself:

- Do your people know the *difference* between reckless decisions and intelligent risks?
- Have you created *structured opportunities* for teams to share what didn't work?
- When someone fails *with integrity*, do they feel safer afterward, or more exposed?

Rewarding failure doesn't mean tolerating incompetence. It means recognising the *right kind* of failure: calculated, data-informed, time-boxed, and done in the pursuit of progress.

And it means spotlighting the effort, the thinking, and the accountability that came with it.

You can't outsource innovation if people are punished for trying. But you *can* build an organisation where progress is made visible, even when it's ugly, raw, or incomplete.

That's not about being soft. That's about being smart.

So don't fall for the "fail fast" rhetoric. Replace it with this: *Learn faster than your competitors, and make your lessons count.*

Rapid Cycles, Safe Boundaries

One of the first things I tell executive teams when we talk innovation is this:

Speed doesn't come from chaos. It comes from structure.

But not the type of structure that strangles ideas with bureaucracy. I mean the kind that gives people just enough room to explore, without drifting into irrelevance or burning through resources.

I was mentoring a group of department heads at a manufacturing firm in Sheffield. Their CEO, Raj, had read every book on agile development and wanted to infuse the same speed into his ops team. He told his managers, "You have full permission to test new processes, however you want."

Sounds good in theory, right?

But within two months, things were falling apart. Productivity dipped, customers got inconsistent service, and his managers were at each other's throats.

Why?

Because he gave *freedom without focus*. No parameters. No clear objectives. Everyone was innovating in their own silo, without guardrails or shared definitions of success.

So we slowed it down, not to stop innovation, but to *make it safe*. We introduced a simple but powerful concept: **Rapid Cycles, Safe Boundaries.**

It worked like this:

1. **Set the boundary:** Every experiment had to align with one of three core objectives: increase throughput, reduce waste, or improve safety. That was the north star. If an idea didn't serve one of those, it didn't get airtime.

2. **Time-box the effort:** Each test was limited to a 14-day window. This kept risk small and feedback tight. No six-month projects disguised as innovation.

3. **Create shared debriefs:** Every team presented results, good or bad, on the same day, using the same format. This built institutional learning. It also stopped teams from reinventing the wheel.

One of the best experiments came from a junior team lead, Saira. She introduced AI vision cameras to monitor part defects in real time, without asking for permission. But because she knew the rules of the game, she scoped it tightly. Just one machine. One line. One week.

That single trial led to a full rollout, and a 9 percent reduction in waste.

No chaos. Just smart, fast feedback.

This is where most companies go wrong. They either:

The Innovator's Paradox 2.0

- Lock things down so tightly that nothing new survives a planning meeting, or

- Swing the other way and let every idea bloom unchecked, hoping something will work.

The answer is in the middle. Structure gives your teams the freedom to move fast *without spinning out*. Boundaries don't restrict creativity. They sharpen it.

I've seen similar models work across industries.

In a law firm in Toronto, the innovation team had a rule: no experiment could exceed 5 billable hours of client time without a clear case study in mind. It forced teams to get creative with scope and measure value early.

In a media agency in Cape Town, creative teams had one day a month to run "mad ideas" as long as they cost nothing and could be tested within 48 hours. One of those ideas? A TikTok filter that brought in three new client accounts.

The principle holds: **Speed without clarity creates anxiety. Speed with structure creates breakthroughs.**

So what does this look like in your company?

Ask yourself:

- What are the three most important outcomes we want experiments to drive?

- How short can we make the feedback loop without compromising quality?

- Where can we create micro-environments where teams are safe to try, fail, and learn?

When people know the rules of the game, and those rules are designed for learning, not control, they'll start playing to win.

And if you've built the right kind of boundaries?

They'll start winning faster than you ever expected.

2: Decentralizing Innovation

Command-and-Control Is the Real Bottleneck

I've lost count of how many times I've heard CEOs say, "I want innovation at every level." It sounds good, doesn't it? Inspirational even.

But here's the problem: most CEOs have no idea how their own structure is preventing innovation from even getting off the ground.

Let me explain.

A few years ago, I was working with a massive retail chain in Madrid. They had over 400 stores across Europe, an ambitious management team, and a leadership culture built around "top-down decision-making." The CEO, Enrique, was brilliant, sharp, charismatic, always thinking five steps ahead. But his innovation strategy? It was a bottleneck waiting to happen.

Every "innovative" idea had to pass through Enrique before it saw the light of day. Whether it was a new digital marketing campaign, a change in supplier relationships, or a new product design, it all went through him.

And this is what happened: every time Enrique got excited about an idea, he'd hold an internal meeting. He'd call up his VPs, his directors, and the head of every department. They'd have a brainstorming session. Ideas would flow. The team would get inspired.

And then... nothing.

It wasn't because the ideas weren't good. They were brilliant, often ahead of the market. But every single decision still relied on Enrique to make the call. He was so entrenched in the process that he didn't realize he had become the bottleneck.

This isn't unique.
This is **the** reality for most CEOs of larger businesses. They want innovation to happen everywhere, but their structure, their workflows, and most importantly, their mindset are still built on the old paradigm of "command-and-control."

This top-down approach doesn't scale. When everything flows up to the top, two things happen:

1. **It slows down decision-making**, everything takes longer. Innovation gets stuck in endless cycles of meetings, approvals, and red tape.

2. **It kills initiative**, the people on the ground, the ones closest to the customer and the front lines, stop taking risks. They wait for permission to act. And eventually, they stop proposing anything altogether.

But here's the twist: Most CEOs believe that bottleneck is just "part of the job." They think they need to be the final decision-maker on everything, that their perspective is the most valuable, or that they should ensure every idea aligns with their strategic vision.

The truth? **It's not the job of the CEO to decide everything**. It's the CEO's job to create the systems, frameworks, and environment that encourage everyone else to make decisions and take action.

When innovation is left solely to the top, the entire company becomes paralyzed. Employees stop thinking like entrepreneurs, and start thinking like employees. They wait for permission. They wait for direction.

Now let's flip the script.

When I worked with the team at a tech firm in Berlin, they took a completely different approach. Their CEO, Lukas, was determined to decentralize the innovation process. Instead of hoarding decisions at the top, Lukas created a culture where everyone, from junior engineers to department heads, had the power to experiment, test, and fail on their own.

The key to their success was simple: **empowerment without abandonment.**

Lukas gave his teams the tools, frameworks, and trust to take action, but he didn't leave them hanging. Teams were encouraged to set their own goals, experiment in rapid cycles, and make quick decisions. Importantly, they didn't have to clear every idea with Lukas first. They had **autonomy** to take risks, but there were boundaries: their experiments had to be aligned with company values and high-level strategic goals.

In this model, Lukas wasn't a bottleneck. He was a facilitator, constantly reinforcing the framework for innovation, while giving teams the freedom to act.

So when the product team came up with a completely new feature that used AI to predict customer behavior, something Lukas didn't even see coming, he didn't shut it down. Instead, he made sure the team had the resources, the backing, and the data to test it properly.

By the time the feature was launched, it increased customer retention by 20% in the first three months, and Lukas had hardly been involved in the day-to-day decisions.

The difference is clear:
Command-and-control leadership creates bottlenecks. Empowerment creates momentum.

In the past, it was common for CEOs to think they had to hold everything together. That their brilliance was needed to evaluate every new idea, make the final decision, and steer the ship.

Now, the best leaders know that the job is to create a culture of ownership and autonomy, one where decision-making is pushed to the front lines, to the people closest to the problems, closest to the customers, and closest to the real innovation.

That's the kind of company where **true systemic innovation** happens, not in top-down meetings, but in the work being done every day across teams. When your people are allowed to make decisions and test things for themselves, when they have the support to fail and learn, that's when innovation becomes embedded in your company's DNA.

The bottleneck is you.
The freedom to innovate is your people.

Are you creating that freedom? Or are you holding your company back?

The Innovation Council Model

Let me take you inside a meeting I had over tea at The Ritz in Mayfair. The setting was elegant, mahogany walls, impeccable service, and a CEO seated across from me who was anything but relaxed.

His name was Arvind, the second-generation owner of a leather shoe manufacturing business based in Kanpur, India. His company had been exporting premium handcrafted footwear across Europe for over two decades, with annual revenues hovering just under £90 million. Yet despite solid financials, something was gnawing at him.

"We've stopped reinventing," he said, glancing down at his tea. "My father built this company on innovation, but now everything feels... stuck. The factory runs well. The orders come in. But no one is questioning, pushing, experimenting."

He wasn't describing a lack of effort, he was describing cultural stagnation masked by operational efficiency.

So I asked him, "Who in your company is *allowed* to think outside the brief? And more importantly, who's empowered to act on it?"

That's when I introduced him to what I call **The Innovation Council Model**.

This isn't another committee. It's a practical tool to decentralize innovation without losing strategic oversight. You build **cross-functional micro-teams**, drawn from different levels and departments of the organization, and give them a defined challenge, a set budget, and the authority to act.

I explained to Arvind that the best Innovation Councils aren't made of the usual suspects. You don't just pull your VPs into a room and hope they think differently. You bring together a floor manager from the tannery, a data analyst from your supply chain team, a designer from product development, and someone from customer relations. People who live the friction points day to day.

He was intrigued but skeptical.

So we laid out a pilot together. Two councils. One would tackle raw material waste reduction using AI prediction models. The other? A customer experience overhaul for luxury buyers in the UAE, where expectations were shifting toward faster customisation and premium packaging.

Each team got a 90-day sprint window, a clear mandate, and £35,000 to execute small-scale experiments.

What came out of it?

The operations team discovered that by using an AI model to predict tannery input-output yield variations, they could cut waste by nearly 19%. On the customer side, the team prototyped a "design your own" microsite that integrated with WhatsApp for live customer consultations, something unheard of in their market. Within three weeks of launch, custom orders had increased 27%.

Here's the truth: neither of those breakthroughs came from Arvind's boardroom. They came from the edges of his company. From voices that had never been asked before.

People will surprise you when you stop hoarding the authority to innovate.

The Innovation Council worked because it gave permission, not just to think, but to act. And it did so within clear strategic boundaries: small, time-bound experiments tied to a real business objective.

Most leaders think innovation dies because of bad ideas. It doesn't. It dies because too few people are given the space to try.

Arvind went back to India not with a new product, but with a new playbook. Today, his factory still produces the same impeccable leather shoes. But behind the scenes, innovation no longer starts at the top. It starts everywhere.

And that's the point.

Empowerment Frameworks: When to Say Yes, When to Step Back

One of the biggest myths about leadership is that empowerment means stepping back completely. It doesn't. True empowerment is about clarity, being precise about when to say yes, when to challenge, and when to simply get out of the way.

I was sitting in a quiet corner of the Armani Hotel lounge in Dubai, meeting with Amina, the founder of a fast-rising luxury chocolate brand that had taken the GCC by storm. Her boutiques in Dubai and Doha were already thriving, and she was fielding offers to expand into Europe. The products were immaculate, handcrafted truffles, gold-dusted pralines, velvet-finished packaging. But the business was stalling in places she didn't expect.

The Innovator's Paradox 2.0

"They're waiting for me on everything," she said, frustration breaking through her otherwise poised tone. "Flavour testing, campaign ideas, even new ribbon colours for our Eid packaging. Nothing moves without my sign-off."

Then she leaned forward and said it, almost as a confession.

"I think I've made them too dependent on me."

I didn't nod. I didn't reassure. I pulled out my notebook and drew three rings.

"You haven't built the wrong team, Amina," I told her. "You've just never told them *how* to move."

I introduced her to what I call the **Empowerment Framework**, something I've used in boardrooms across industries, from aerospace in Germany to beauty retail in Singapore.

The first ring was the **Experimentation Zone**. Here, her marketing and product teams could run low-risk experiments, new flavour pairings, pop-up displays, localised Instagram reels, provided the budget stayed under a set threshold and they shared learnings weekly. It wasn't about control. It was about speed.

The second ring was the **Escalation Zone**. If an experiment spiked, like a dark chocolate and za'atar fusion that unexpectedly sold out in 36 hours, this was the moment to raise it in their next strategic call. Not to ask for permission, but to flag what might need resourcing or rollout.

The third ring was the **Execution Gate**. Here lived the heavy lifts: entering Harrods, signing regional distributors, or redesigning the flagship boutique. Anything that risked brand reputation or significant capital moved through her and the board.

Three rings. Shared understanding. Instant clarity.

Within six weeks, her packaging lead launched a limited Ramadan gift set, tested it in three outlets, and sold through inventory 40% faster than forecast. No waiting. No bottlenecks. Just trust, structure, and results.

Amina told me later, "I always thought I had to be in the centre of everything. But now I see, I just needed to define the edges."

That's the shift.

Empowerment isn't about letting go of control. It's about building a system where your people know how to move without asking.

So let me ask you:

- Where are your edges?

- Do your team members know the difference between a test and a transformation?

- Do they know when to act, when to report, and when to escalate?

Because innovation doesn't die in chaos. It dies in confusion.

And your job, as the architect of your business, is to make clarity your most scalable asset.

Accountability Without Micromanagement

One of the first things I tell CEOs when they ask about empowering their teams is this: *freedom without feedback isn't empowerment, it's abandonment.*

Not long ago, I was working with a fast-growing cybersecurity firm based in Tel Aviv. Bright minds, cutting-edge solutions, and a solid client base. But the leadership team was drowning in what I call "decision bottleneck syndrome." Nothing moved unless the CEO personally pushed it forward. The result? A culture of hesitation masked as diligence.

I couldn't fly to Israel at the time, visa issues made it too complicated, so Eli, the founder, flew into London with three of his senior team members. We met at my office in the Leadenhall Building on the 30th floor. I remember it clearly. Eli, always energetic, looked visibly worn down. During our session, he leaned back in his chair and admitted, "Moe, I feel like I'm doing everyone's job but my own."

He wasn't wrong. Like many founders who've built their companies from scratch, Eli had become both the engine and the brake. His team was competent, but cautious. Empowered on paper, hesitant in practice. Every decision ricocheted back to him.

So I laid out the truth: "Eli, you don't have a team problem. You have a feedback rhythm problem."

We rebuilt their accountability rhythm around three principles: **transparency, traction, and trust**. And we anchored it with a single rule, *we measure what matters, and we measure it together.*

The starting point? A hybrid OKR-Dashboard model. But we did it differently. Instead of cascading top-down objectives, we let teams define their own outcomes, anchored in real business impact. No more vanity metrics. No more spreadsheets collecting dust.

Each team had three to five key results they owned, visible to leadership but not micromanaged. And every two weeks, they ran focused, 45-minute huddles:

1. What moved?
2. What stalled?
3. Where are we stuck?

Simple. Direct. No fluff.

In one session, Maya, their engineering lead, shared a product delivery metric that had flatlined. No excuses, just clarity. "We missed the mark because our assumptions were wrong," she said. "We've already built the next test." That one sentence told me more about their new culture than any KPI could.

This is what real accountability looks like. Not fear. Not perfection. Just ownership in motion.

And the impact? Within six months, Eli sent me a message: *"For the first time in years, I don't feel like I'm the system. I feel like I've built one."*

That's the shift.

When you combine structure with trust, you stop being the bottleneck, and your team starts building momentum without needing your constant push.

So ask yourself:

- Are your dashboards a scoreboard, or a surveillance system?
- Are your team check-ins performance conversations, or permission requests?
- Is your role about oversight, or about unlocking others?

Because the best leaders I've worked with don't empower people by stepping back. They empower by building the system, then stepping aside, so their people can step up.

3: The Innovation Operating System

The Innovation Operating System

From Sporadic Genius to Repeatable Process

The Innovator's Paradox 2.0

A few years back, I was consulting with the CEO of a mid-sized fintech company in Manchester. Sharp guy, ambitious team. They had no shortage of ideas. In fact, they had *too many*. Every quarter, someone would come up with a game-changing concept, but nine times out of ten, it fizzled before it made it past the whiteboard.

During one of our sessions, I asked him, "What's your process for innovation?"

He smiled and said, "We don't believe in boxing in creativity. We like to keep it organic."

I nodded, but said nothing.

A few weeks later, after the third abandoned project in a row, he rang me. "Moe," he said, "I think we're *too* organic. Nothing's sticking."

Exactly.

Here's the paradox: we romanticize innovation as this wild, chaotic, creative genius at work. But the companies that innovate consistently don't rely on sporadic bursts of brilliance. They build **systems**. Structures. Operating rhythms. Just like they do for finance, sales, or ops.

In that same company, we eventually implemented what I call an **Innovation Operating System**, a repeatable, trackable process for moving ideas from spark to scale.

It wasn't glamorous. It wasn't complicated. But it worked.

We borrowed a cadence from product development, weekly sprints, monthly reviews, quarterly pivots. Every idea had to answer three questions before it got resourced:

1. Does it align with one of our core strategic bets?
2. Can we test it with less than £5,000?

3. Can we validate early traction in under 30 days?

If the answer was no, it went on the backlog.

This wasn't about killing ideas. It was about *respecting them enough to test them properly.*

And that's the heart of it.

Innovation doesn't die from a lack of creativity. It dies from a lack of structure. When everyone's throwing ideas into the air and no one's responsible for catching them, they don't land anywhere.

So I tell leaders: treat innovation like any other business function. Give it a system. Give it a rhythm. Give it accountability.

Because the truth is, most companies don't have an innovation problem, they have an *innovation discipline* problem.

The ones that win?

They've moved beyond chaos. They've built an engine.

The Four Pillars: Discovery, Design, Deploy, Debrief

I was once sitting across from Amira, the founder of a beauty tech startup based in Berlin. She'd flown into London for a half-day session after reading a couple of my earlier books. Her company had just raised €12 million, and she was terrified of wasting it.

"We've got 18 different initiatives floating around," she told me, half-laughing, half-panicking. "Some of them are great. Some... I honestly don't know. We're moving fast but I can't tell if we're moving *smart*."

I've heard this same confession from leaders running £200M businesses and those still clawing toward their first million. It's not about size. It's about structure. And without one, speed becomes a liability.

That's when I introduced her to the **Four Pillars**, a simple cycle that helps turn raw ideas into integrated solutions without losing momentum or burning resources.

Discovery. Design. Deploy. Debrief.

She raised an eyebrow. "Sounds like another framework."

I smiled. "Not if you actually use it."

Let me walk you through how we applied it to her team.

1. Discovery: The Idea Doesn't Have to Be Perfect, But It Has to Be Real

We started by forcing every new idea to earn its way into the light. Discovery isn't a brainstorming free-for-all. It's about defining the problem *first*, before proposing solutions.

With Amira's team, we set a rule: no new initiative gets attention until the problem it solves is clearly stated in one sentence. No fluff. No slides.

One of her engineers had pitched a new AR feature to try on makeup virtually. Great in theory. But in Discovery, we realized the actual issue wasn't customer engagement. It was that 30% of customers were returning products due to poor shade matching.

Now we had a problem worth solving. And the AR feature had a *real job* to do.

2. Design: What's the Smallest Version That Proves the Point?

Next, we tackled the Design phase. This is where a lot of innovation efforts die, because people try to build the final product instead of the *first signal*.

I challenged the team: "What would it look like to test this in a week, with less than €500?"

They hacked together a simple Instagram filter as a prototype. It wasn't polished, but it was usable. And it gave them real customer feedback in days, not months.

That's the essence of Design. Don't aim for perfect. Aim for proof.

3. Deploy: Fast, Public, and Measured

Deployment isn't a full launch, it's a *controlled release*. We picked a segment of their mobile user base and pushed the filter live, quietly. No big announcement. Just data collection.

We tracked interaction rates, bounce rates, return rates, and even added a simple emoji feedback option after each use.

Within 10 days, they saw a 17% drop in returns among users who tried the feature.

Suddenly, what was once just a "cool idea" became a proven asset. And because we'd kept it lean, the ROI was undeniable.

4. Debrief: What Worked, What Didn't, What Next?

This is the step most leaders skip. They move on to the next shiny object without harvesting the insights from what just happened.

We brought the team back into the room. Everyone involved had to answer three questions:

- What did we learn that we didn't know before?
- What assumptions did we validate, or kill?
- What would we change if we did it again?

The answers went straight into a shared learning doc. Not for compliance. For continuity.

Because innovation isn't just about the outcome. It's about what the *organization learns* in the process.

Amira texted me six months later.

"We've now run 11 ideas through the Four Pillars. We've killed 6, scaled 3, and pivoted 2. I finally feel like we have an engine."

That's the goal.

Not a pipeline of ideas.

A pipeline of *validated value*, on repeat.

Tech Stack and Tooling for Innovation Velocity

I'll never forget the day I walked into a boardroom in Birmingham, and before I'd even sat down, the CTO greeted me with a spreadsheet, titled "Innovation Stack – 2024."

Thirty-seven tools. Seven pages. Each with its own pricing, adoption status, and internal owner.

He looked proud.

I looked concerned.

"Out of curiosity," I asked, "how many of these are actually being used?"

He paused. "Actively? Maybe four."

That's the trap most well-meaning teams fall into. They confuse *stack* with *speed*. They think more tech means more innovation. But in reality, every additional platform you add without strategic intent is just another place for progress to get lost.

Innovation velocity isn't about how *many* tools you have. It's about whether your tools are making people faster, or just busier.

Let me share the setup I recommend to most of my clients, from a 12-person startup in Leeds to a £300M AI-driven media company in Dublin.

First, **every innovation system needs three layers**: Intelligence, Collaboration, and Execution.

Intelligence: Your Insight Engine

At the top, you need something that makes your organization smarter, daily. This is where AI becomes more than a buzzword.

I use a custom model we call "Sallay," our virtual insights manager. Sallay scrapes market signals, competitor updates, keyword shifts, internal performance metrics, and delivers a digestible dashboard every Monday at 8am.

One of my clients in the Middle East, a chocolate confectionery company in Dubai, now uses Sallay to detect social listening cues in real-time. If a flavor trend spikes in Brazil, it alerts their R&D team the same day. They don't wait for the market to move, they move with it.

That's the kind of edge AI can offer. But only if you treat it as a *team member*, not a gadget.

Collaboration: Fewer Tools, More Conversations

Here's a rule I live by: If your team is jumping between more than two platforms to work on an idea, they're already wasting time.

You don't need five project management tools. Pick one. I recommend Notion or ClickUp for most, simple, flexible, and designed to map ideas from inception to launch.

Pair it with a robust async tool like Loom or Slack for updates. Avoid the meeting swamp. Let people think in peace and update in bursts.

The Dubai confectionery team has a standing 20-minute weekly sprint call. Everything else? Logged as a Loom. Reviewed asynchronously. Commented on in Notion. They're shipping three prototypes a month with a team of six.

Execution: From Ideas to Outcomes

Finally, you need one clear system to track what's moving, and what's not. This is where your **insight dashboard** lives. Not buried in a spreadsheet. Front and center.

I build mine in Airtable or Coda, depending on the client's ecosystem. Each idea is scored on three factors: velocity (how fast it moved), impact (what it delivered), and learning (what it revealed).

Robert, our AI team lead in one of my portfolio companies, runs the whole idea pipeline through this dashboard. He updates metrics weekly, flags blockers, and automates reminders. He doesn't manage innovation, he *directs traffic.*

That's the secret.

Not the tool.

But how you use it to *focus effort* and *track momentum.*

The CTO in Birmingham later trimmed his list of 37 tools down to six. Within two quarters, his team shipped more in 60 days than they had in the previous 18 months.

So, before you shop for another shiny platform, ask yourself one question:

Is this tool removing friction, or just adding features?

Because at the speed innovation now demands, every click either compounds momentum… or kills it.

Creating Innovation Rhythm: Cadence, Reviews, Iteration Loops

I was in Doha, sitting across from a founder who ran a high-performing £90M industrial refrigeration company. We were tucked into a quiet corner of the Four Seasons, watching the skyline shimmer under the Qatari sun. He leaned forward, fingers tapping on the marble table, and said, "Moe, I've got smart people, good ideas, plenty of capital, but it always fizzles out. We'll have a strategy offsite, then nothing sticks. It's like we light the match, then forget we were supposed to build a fire."

I nodded. "That's because most companies treat innovation like a one-off spark," I said. "But without rhythm, there's no flame. Just smoke."

That's the issue. Innovation doesn't collapse because of bad ideas. It collapses because it doesn't have a **beat**.

Execution has a rhythm: financial reports, board meetings, sales cycles. But innovation? It requires its own **drumbeat**, not too loose, not too rigid, but consistent enough to create motion, pressure, and energy.

That's what we call the **Innovation Rhythm**, a structured cadence that turns sporadic creativity into sustained momentum.

Here's what we installed for that Qatari firm, and what's now being used in other parts of the world, from Dubai to Dublin.

Weekly: Signal Without Noise

Every Friday, one person from each innovation team records a 2-minute Loom video. One slide. That's it.

- What did we try?
- What did we learn?

- What's next?

No meetings, no approvals, no theatrics. Just momentum.

A Dubai-based chocolate confectionery company I work with calls this "Friday Flavour." Their R&D team logs every test run, flavour tweaks, packaging variations, shelf-life extensions. Some never make it past the kitchen. Others go live within a month.

What matters isn't the outcome. It's that every team is **moving**, and capturing the lessons.

It's the equivalent of innovation cardio. Fast, breathable, and impossible to fake.

Monthly: From Tactics to Traction

On the first Monday of each month, we run a 60-minute *Innovation Review Sprint*.

There's no performance theatre here. No PowerPoint wars. Just three brutal questions:

1. What moved last month?
2. What blocked it?
3. What deserves a second bet?

One client in Warsaw rotates leadership of the review each month. It could be HR one time, then marketing, then finance. This cross-pollination creates a unique dynamic: the finance director might ask why product timelines don't factor in supplier AI forecasts, or ops might challenge sales assumptions.

Innovation stops being the job of "that team over there." It becomes cultural oxygen.

Quarterly: Decide With Teeth

Every 90 days, we zoom out.

The Innovator's Paradox 2.0

This is not a 'celebrate progress' moment. It's a **strategic decision point**. What stays? What dies? What goes system-wide?

One Berlin-based manufacturer used this session to kill a £2M internal AI chatbot that had outlived its usefulness. Painful? Of course. But in the same 90-day window, they launched an AI-driven demand forecast platform and increased profit margin by 9.3%.

That's the power of cadence. You can't confuse activity with impact when you're forced to make decisions on a clock.

Quarterly reviews de-romanticise innovation. They stop teams from falling in love with dead horses. And they turn leadership from dreamers into scalers.

This isn't micromanagement. It's rhythm.

The jazz musician doesn't resent the beat, they rely on it. It gives structure to their brilliance. It's how you riff with meaning.

That's what innovation needs.

Not rules. Rhythm.

When a team knows it will report on Friday, reflect on Monday, and reset every quarter, they don't need chasing. They chase **themselves**.

So the next time someone in your business says, "We're innovating," ask them, "What's your rhythm?"

Because without cadence, innovation doesn't die loudly. It just... disappears.

4: Case Studies of Team-Led Disruption

Case 1: The Retail Ops Team in Washington DC That Reinvented Logistics with AI Forecasting

The Innovator's Paradox 2.0

I remember the call clearly. It was 6:00 a.m. in London when Marcus, the COO of a retail chain based out of Washington DC, rang. Not for a chat. His voice was low and sharp, like someone who'd just seen something he couldn't unsee. "We've got too much of the wrong stock in the wrong places, and too little of the right stock where customers are screaming for it," he said. "We're bleeding margin daily."

Marcus wasn't a reckless operator. His team had scaled from 8 stores to 94 across five states in just under six years. But with growth came complexity, and with complexity came chaos. Their logistics team had grown reactive. Forecasting relied on spreadsheets, instinct, and last year's demand patterns, none of which held up in the face of real-time customer behavior and unpredictable shipping delays.

What struck me was how self-aware Marcus was. He didn't call to be reassured. He called because he already knew: they had outgrown their system.

When I flew out to DC a week later, I sat with their regional managers, warehouse planners, even a few store leads. What I saw was talent, but siloed. Each function had its own "truth." Ops blamed marketing for surprise campaigns. Marketing blamed logistics for delays. And logistics blamed the forecast models, which hadn't been updated in two years.

Instead of launching a full systems overhaul, we started with one question:
"What if we could see the future five weeks ahead, and act on it today?"

That single question reframed the problem. Marcus's team didn't need more software. They needed intelligence.

We introduced a custom AI forecasting engine, built not to replace humans, but to enhance their judgment. It pulled live data from POS systems, weather feeds, social media sentiment, supplier lead times, and even local event calendars. It didn't shout. It whispered. Quiet signals became loud patterns.

One of the first test cases? A spike in online mentions of a particular hiking boot brand across the Mid-Atlantic. The AI flagged it. Within 24 hours, the system reallocated in-transit stock from slower-selling regions to the flagged stores, avoiding stockouts during a critical weekend and improving sell-through by 27%.

Marcus told me later, "The AI didn't make the decision for us. It just let us see what was actually happening, before it hit the P&L."

Six months in, inventory turns had improved by 32%. Delivery SLA failures dropped by 40%. And perhaps most importantly, the warehouse teams stopped fighting marketing, they started planning together, because they were now working off the same source of truth.

This wasn't just about forecasting. It was about restoring trust across functions by giving people tools that elevated their intelligence.

When I returned to DC months later for a WarRoom session, Marcus pulled me aside. "Funny," he said. "We always thought innovation was something tech companies did. Turns out it's what happens when you stop trying to control everything, and start trying to see everything."

Case 2: The B2B Service Firm in Germany That Created a New Product Line From the Frontline

It started over schnitzel and black coffee in Düsseldorf. I was meeting with Helena, the founder of a B2B compliance training firm that served financial institutions across Europe. Her tone was unusually flat that morning. "We're hitting our revenue targets," she said, "but it feels like we're just recycling the same content with different packaging. I don't think the frontline team believes in what we're selling anymore."

Helena built the business from scratch, a classic bootstrapped-to-seven-figures story. Their courses helped banks navigate everything from anti-money laundering to GDPR compliance. For years, they had been the safe choice. Reliable, compliant, and slightly boring. But something had shifted.

"We're not losing clients," she told me. "We're becoming invisible."

That's a dangerous place to be.

During my visit, I met with her client service leads, those on the frontlines of customer feedback. One comment from a junior associate stood out: "The clients don't want more modules. They want to sleep better at night." I paused. That wasn't just a customer insight, it was a strategic unlock.

That afternoon, I led a whiteboard session with ten of Helena's team. No executives. Just mid-level project managers, customer support, and even one of the newer sales interns. The challenge: "What do clients keep asking for that we keep saying no to, or pretending we didn't hear?"

Within minutes, the ideas poured in.

One recurring theme: predictive compliance. Banks wanted early-warning signals, alerts that would help them see what regulation risks were emerging before they became headline disasters.

The frontline team had been hearing this for months. But no one upstream had taken it seriously.

Over the next 60 days, Helena gave a small cross-functional team a clear mandate: "Build the MVP. No bureaucracy. No board reviews. Just solve the problem."

They built an AI-enabled dashboard that tracked real-time regulatory changes, social signals, and customer audit history. The tool, named "Sentinel," could flag potential issues days or even weeks before traditional compliance checks caught them.

What was remarkable wasn't just the tech, it was the confidence it created. For the first time, Helena's firm wasn't just helping clients pass audits. They were helping them *avoid* them.

When they launched the pilot with two longtime banking clients in Frankfurt and Zurich, the feedback was instant. "This is exactly what our internal teams have been missing," one risk officer said. "I don't want more e-learning. I want foresight."

Revenue from "Sentinel" surpassed the firm's original compliance training product within eight months. But more than that, it changed the way the team thought about their role.

Helena later told me, "The most uncomfortable truth? Our breakthrough came not from strategy retreats or consulting decks. It came from the service desk."

Innovation doesn't always roar in from the top. Sometimes it whispers from the bottom, if you're willing to listen.

When I visited again for a follow-up session, Helena had moved her product innovation meetings into the same room as customer support. No silos. No gatekeepers. Just signal, interpretation, and action.

The frontline had become the R&D lab. And the whole company was stronger for it.

Case 3: The $60M Cardboard Box Manufacturer in Philadelphia That Built a Customer Lab Without CEO Approval

It's not every day that a story about corrugated cardboard becomes a case study in frontline-led innovation. But that's exactly what happened at Carmichael Packaging, a $60 million family-owned manufacturer based in Philadelphia.

The Innovator's Paradox 2.0

I first met Darren, their Head of Regional Sales, at a supply chain conference in Chicago. Over dinner, he mentioned something that stuck with me: "Our CEO thinks innovation means buying faster printers. But our customers want something entirely different, they want fewer headaches."

That tension was at the heart of what came next.

Carmichael was known for their speed and reliability, boxes on time, as ordered, no drama. But Darren's team had started hearing the same frustrations from mid-size food distributors and e-commerce brands they served.

"We're drowning in packaging options," one buyer told him. "Just tell us what works best for our product and get it right the first time."

So Darren and a few others quietly pulled together a small internal team: one packaging engineer, a customer success manager, and two line supervisors. No titles, no approvals, just initiative.

They called it the "Customer Lab."

The premise was simple, invite key clients into the factory for short discovery sessions. Clients would walk the floor, watch their packaging run live, and troubleshoot in real time with the operations team. No PowerPoint. Just shared problem-solving.

The first client through the door was a mid-size organic snack brand based in Baltimore. They were struggling with breakage during shipping. Normally, this would have meant a blame game between ops and sales. But in the lab, standing side by side, the two teams iterated a new structural design with 11% less material, 22% fewer returns, and faster production.

Word spread.

Within six weeks, three more clients asked for their own lab sessions. And something strange began to happen, Carmichael's frontline teams started proactively *inviting* customer complaints.

Instead of seeing feedback as a fire to extinguish, they reframed it as data for innovation.

The lab concept evolved. They added a simple prototype station using a modified die cutter, two 3D printers, and AI-driven order history analysis. Engineers could now test five design options in a single afternoon.

By the time the CEO found out about the lab, it was already a hit. Not just with clients, but internally. Absenteeism on lab days dropped to zero. And for the first time in company history, sales, production, and logistics were collaborating without formal intervention.

When I visited Carmichael's Philadelphia facility a few months later, I saw something I rarely witness in traditional manufacturing: frontline employees asking clients, "What else can we do better?"

One plant supervisor, Esteban, put it best: "We stopped being box makers. We became problem solvers."

Financially, the shift was just as clear. Clients who went through the lab spent 19% more on average, renewed faster, and were less price-sensitive. But the biggest win wasn't margin. It was mindset.

I asked Darren why he never asked for CEO permission. He smiled and said, "Because it wasn't about approval. It was about accountability. We weren't waiting for innovation, we were living it."

To this day, Carmichael runs four Customer Lab sessions a month. Their backlog includes companies from New Jersey, Toronto, and as far as São Paulo.

And the CEO?

He now starts every board meeting with one slide: "Here's what our lab learned this quarter."

This wasn't a revolution from the top. It was quiet rebellion from the edge. No fanfare. Just cardboard, courage, and clarity.

5: Moe's Mirror

1: The Empowerment Scorecard – Who Really Has Decision Power?

Let's pause here and be brutally honest.

I've walked into more boardrooms than I can count, and I can tell you this with certainty: the problem is rarely innovation itself. It's power. Or more specifically, the illusion of who holds it.

You can talk all day about agility, experimentation, and team-led growth, but if every meaningful decision still funnels through your inbox, you're not empowering innovation, you're throttling it. Slowly. Quietly. Fatally.

So let's conduct a quick mirror exercise.

I call it the **Empowerment Scorecard**. No consultants. No jargon. Just truth.

Take a moment and think across the core functions of your business, sales, marketing, product, operations, finance, and HR. Now ask yourself one question for each:

If someone on that team had an idea tomorrow that could improve efficiency or drive growth, how far could they go without coming to me?

Be honest. Not how far *they think* they can go. Not how far your org chart *says* they can go. How far *you've actually allowed* them to go in the past.

Let's break this down:

- In **sales**, does your team have the autonomy to test new messaging or pricing strategies? Or do they need approval before touching a headline or changing a script?

- In **marketing**, can someone launch a microsite or ad campaign under £5,000 without clearance? Or are they stuck in two-week approval loops?

- In **product**, does the engineering lead have full authority to run an AI pilot on a low-risk feature? Or does every tool request end up in procurement limbo?

- In **ops**, when was the last time a frontline manager implemented a process change without it being run up the chain?

You get the idea.

What I'm asking you to do is score yourself. On a scale from 1 to 10, how much *real decision power* have you distributed? Not responsibility. Not accountability. Actual *authority* to act.

Now look at your lowest scores. That's where your business is most likely stagnating.

Because here's the paradox, your business will never scale beyond the boundaries of your permission.

Empowerment isn't about recklessness. It's about designing smart constraints. Giving your people enough room to move without needing your nod every time.

One CEO I mentored in Singapore implemented a "Two-Yes Rule", if any idea had two department heads in agreement, it could move forward without his approval. In six months, they'd launched three internal tools, slashed onboarding time by 40%, and uncovered a $1.2M process gap that had gone unnoticed for years.

Your scorecard isn't a judgment. It's a spotlight. Wherever decision-making is overly centralized, you're training your teams to wait, when what you actually need them to do is lead.

So here's your challenge: by the end of this week, have a meeting with your senior leadership. Show them the scorecard. And ask: "Where are we still acting like a bottleneck?"

You'll be amazed how fast innovation flows when you finally get out of your own way.

2: Challenge – Build an Innovation Sprint Without Involving You

Let's turn the mirror into a challenge.

Right now, I want you to choose a real opportunity inside your business. Something that's small enough to test in 30 days, but significant enough to learn from. Maybe it's a lagging customer experience issue. Maybe it's a bottleneck in delivery. Or a new revenue stream you've been meaning to explore but haven't had time for.

Now here's the catch:

You're not allowed to be involved. At all.

No steering. No approving. No peeking over shoulders.

This sprint belongs entirely to your team.

Write a one-paragraph brief, just enough direction to clarify the "what," not the "how." Then assign it to a small, cross-functional group. Give them a budget cap. Set a deadline. And give them full authority to execute, test, and report back without waiting for you to greenlight each step.

For example, I worked with a mid-sized SaaS firm in Dublin where the CEO launched a 30-day challenge to reduce customer onboarding friction. The brief was just two sentences: "Our first 14 days are too clunky. Fix it." The team overhauled the tutorial flow, tested three new AI-driven help features, and saw a 22% lift in trial-to-paid conversions. The CEO didn't see a single slide until day 30. That was the point.

This isn't just about process. It's about **trust, control, and identity**.

Because if you're the one who always makes things happen, you've built a business that needs you more than it should. And ironically, that dependency is what slows you down when it matters most.

So ask yourself:
Can your team run without you for a month?

If not, you don't have a team. You have a support staff. And no company scales on that.

This challenge isn't about perfection. It's about proof. Let your people surprise you.

And when they do, make sure the recognition is public, the lessons are captured, and the signal is clear:
Innovation isn't just allowed here, it's expected.

3: Final Question – Are You a Platform, or a Gatekeeper?

Let me leave you with a question that reshaped how I mentor founders and boards alike:

Are you a platform, or a gatekeeper?

Because you can't be both.

Gatekeepers slow things down. They protect what already exists. They decide who's allowed in, which ideas move forward, and what's deemed "good enough." At first, it feels like control. It feels like leadership. But it's not. It's friction dressed as order.

A platform, on the other hand, multiplies the possibilities. It's not about you anymore, it's about what others can build on top of what you've created. Platforms empower. They scale decisions. They invite experimentation, knowing not everything needs your fingerprint to succeed.

I sat with Hira, the CEO of a fast-growing fintech company in Kuala Lumpur, who told me bluntly, "I think I'm the bottleneck, but I also think I'm the glue." It took just two leadership diagnostics and a war-room sprint to prove otherwise. Her team wasn't waiting because they lacked ideas. They were waiting because Hira had become the gate they all had to pass through. Once she redesigned her role, from final approver to platform builder, her leadership team shipped more in 60 days than they had in the entire previous quarter.

And yes, it was uncomfortable.

Platforms still require boundaries, principles, and structure. But they start from trust, not fear. They expect good judgment, rather than micromanaging every move. And most importantly, they make themselves *less* essential over time, not more.

So here's your closing mirror for this chapter:

Are you still trying to control innovation? Or are you engineering a system where it happens without you?

If your business only moves when you push it, you're the gatekeeper.

If your team moves faster than you can track, and you're okay with that, you've become the platform.

That's when you know the transformation is real.

Chapter 4:
The Strategic Cadence: Varying Your Reflection for Sustained Impact

Beyond the Mirror

When Reflection Becomes Routine, It Stops Working

I remember sitting with a client, a £180M consumer tech CEO based in Dublin, who said to me, "I journal every week. I review my KPIs every month. I even do your 'Moe's Mirror' prompts religiously. But lately, it all feels... flat."

I nodded, because I've heard that more times than I can count. Reflection that once sparked fire becomes another checkbox. Another mental habit wrapped in the illusion of insight.

And that's the danger. Not the absence of reflection, but the *repetition* of it. The same questions. The same format. The same comfortable distance from the uncomfortable truth.

It's human. We crave rhythm, and when something works, we keep doing it. Until the work stops working.

This is the paradox of leadership reflection: the better you get at it, the more likely it is to become self-soothing rather than self-challenging.

Even the strongest leaders fall into this. You ask yourself the same question every Friday morning, "What did I miss this week?", and your brain starts delivering pre-packaged answers. Answers designed to look insightful, but not to sting. Because your subconscious has learned how to dodge the real discomfort.

Here's the hard truth: if your reflection no longer leaves a mark, it's not working.

This is why "Moe's Mirror" was never meant to be a static tool. It's not a ritual. It's a provocation. A mirror that evolves with you.

The questions must change.

The framing must shift.

The cadence must challenge your pattern of thinking.

When I first introduced the Mirror in private advisory sessions, it worked because it disrupted the leader's rhythm. It slowed them down. It cornered their certainty. But once they got used to it, the mirror needed to mutate.

And that's the lesson.

Your leadership lens must adapt, not just annually, but continuously. Especially now, in an era where AI is changing the speed of learning, the shape of risk, and the cost of delay.

So ask yourself:

Have your reflections become a safe haven?

Are you still disturbed by the answers?

Is your mirror evolving, or is it merely echoing?

The leaders who win in this new era are those who don't just build feedback loops around them, they change the questions *within* them.

From Insight to Instrument

The real power of reflection isn't in what it reveals, it's in what it changes.

I remember working with Fatima, a dynamic CEO running a luxury skincare brand out of Morocco. She was brilliant, methodical, and sharp in strategic review meetings. But six months into our work together, she said something that struck me:

"I've had a hundred insights, Moe. But I can't say I've changed a hundred behaviors."

That's the gap. And it's wider than most leaders admit.

Insight without instrumentation is like spotting a leak and doing nothing but admire the puddle.

Reflection only matters when it converts into motion, when it informs the next hire, the next kill-switch, the next quarter's risk budget. Yet most reflection models stall at the thought level. They stop just short of execution.

Why?

Because the mirror became a canvas for contemplation, not a springboard for action.

To turn insight into instrument, we need varied modalities, not just to think differently, but to *act* differently.

Sometimes that means converting a question into a dashboard. For example, "Where are we relying too much on human judgment?" becomes a prompt to audit decision points, and overlay AI models where appropriate. That's no longer a reflection. That's operational change.

Other times, it's about making the reflection visible. One of my clients in Singapore built a "Lead by Discomfort" wall, every senior leader posted one strategic initiative they'd been avoiding. Monthly, they had to report on it. It wasn't about shame. It was about *integrating* discomfort into the culture.

You see, real leadership reflection doesn't live in the mind. It leaves fingerprints, on calendars, on agendas, on hiring specs, on org charts.

It's the difference between asking, "Where am I playing it safe?" and scheduling a live debate at your next board meeting where someone is tasked to challenge your sacred cow business line.

It's the difference between wondering, "What am I not seeing?" and paying for a third-party teardown of your customer journey led by someone *outside* your industry.

Varied reflection styles create varied behavioral outcomes. That's why in my advisory work, I mix narrative journaling with scenario drills, KPI disruption challenges, and what I call "cognitive collisions", forcing two conflicting truths to fight it out in the open.

This isn't spiritual introspection. This is tactical rewiring.

And that's the challenge for you now.

If your reflection isn't driving you to *do* something different every quarter, it's a signal the mirror's become ornamental.

The goal is not to feel wiser.

The goal is to lead braver.

Cadence = Creativity = Change

I was having breakfast at The Ritz with Dinesh, the founder of a $120M packaging company in Mumbai. He leaned over, tapping his notebook, and said, "Moe, I've been reflecting every morning for years, but I don't feel any more strategic than I did five years ago."

That moment stuck with me. Because Dinesh wasn't the problem. His *pattern* was.

What most leaders don't realise is that reflection, like training, is only as effective as its *variation*.

You wouldn't train a world-class athlete using the same exercise on repeat. Why do we assume leadership reflection is any different?

Cadence drives creativity. And creativity drives change.

When a leader only reflects by writing in a journal, they sharpen introspection, but not communication. When they only talk it out with a coach, they improve articulation, but not necessarily decision-making. When they debate, they activate strategy. When they review data, they challenge assumptions. When they design experiments, they confront reality.

Each format triggers a different muscle group.

I've worked with CEOs who did quarterly "challenge sessions" where a trusted peer would take a single assumption, "our team is aligned," for example, and pick it apart ruthlessly. Others held "reverse reflections" where their executive team presented what *they* thought the CEO's blind spots were. One founder even ran quarterly "war games," role-playing their competitor's moves and asking: "If I were trying to destroy my own business, how would I do it?"

These aren't gimmicks. They're creative cadence at work.

Because when you vary how you reflect, you break out of mental grooves. You disrupt your own pattern-recognition. You create *momentum*.

And most importantly, you stop managing from the past, and start leading into the future.

So ask yourself: what's your current reflection style? Writing? Thinking in silence? Maybe you're a walker, a talker, a spreadsheet junkie?

Now ask: what haven't you tried?

Because the format you resist might be the one that reveals the breakthrough you need.

And if your leadership feels flat, stuck, or repetitive, it's not a motivational issue. It's a cadence issue.

Designing a Year of Strategic Reflection

Let's get tactical.

Imagine your year, not as four quarters of performance reporting, but four experiments in how you *reflect* as a leader.

Here's a rhythm I often recommend to my private advisory clients:

Q1: Questions
The year begins with clarity. Not on answers, but on *better questions*.
This is the quarter to go deep. Block out a full day and write down the 20 most important questions you can ask about your business.
Examples:
– "Where am I still central to operations?"
– "What do my competitors fear about me?"
– "What assumptions are no longer true?"
Use tools like the Disruption Readiness Scorecard here.
This is an inward-facing quarter, strategy via introspection.

Q2: Debates
Spring is for friction.
Host strategic debates with your execs. Choose themes: "Should we kill our flagship product?" or "Is our org chart designed for the past?"
Invite contradiction. Reward disagreement.
I once facilitated a session for a FinTech board in Berlin titled:
"How would an AI-native startup outcompete us in 12 months?"
The goal isn't consensus. It's combustion.

Q3: Experiments
Summer is for motion.
Run one live innovation sprint. Delegate it. Measure it. Learn from it.

This is your "kill-reinvent-rewire" quarter. Try an AI tool to replace a workflow. Test a new vertical. Cut a product line and see what breaks.

Leadership reflection becomes operational pressure testing.

Q4: Legacy

Autumn is for altitude.

Zoom out. Ask:

– "If I left tomorrow, what would endure?"
– "What culture am I unintentionally cementing?"
– "Which part of my strategy feels most like an echo chamber?"

Use this quarter to document lessons, train successors, codify your vision.

This is about scale through subtraction.

Across the year, you'll have exercised every leadership muscle, curiosity, conflict, creativity, and clarity.

And what you'll find, by year's end, is that you no longer *need* a mirror to ask the right questions.

You've become the mirror for others.

Field Exercises

I remember walking into a strategy session in Stockholm where the CEO had invited me not to present but to *be challenged*. He handed his executive team a simple brief: "Today, we're going to pressure-test three of my strategic decisions. Moe's here to moderate. Nothing is off-limits."

The room froze.

For the first 20 minutes, there was a lot of polite talk, surface-level questions, safe disagreements. Then one of the younger directors, a woman named Sofie, leaned forward and said, "With respect, I think our AI rollout was more about PR than performance. We're not ready."

Silence.

But that moment changed the culture of the company.

By the end of that afternoon, they'd identified blind spots that had gone unspoken for months. They didn't reverse the AI rollout, but they reinvented the process behind it. Not because the CEO lost control. Because he finally invited a challenge.

That's your first field exercise: **Run a Disruption Audit With Your Exec Team**.

Pick three recent decisions, big ones. Present them like a case study. Now invite your team to critique them as if they were your competitors.

Not to nitpick. But to probe. Ask:
– What did I miss?
– What assumptions did I protect?
– What would you have done instead?

Give them permission. Take nothing personally. What emerges will not just improve the decisions, but elevate the decision-makers.

Now for something harder.

A few years ago, during a personal retreat in Marrakech, I forced myself into 48 hours of silence. No phone. No team. No books. Just pen, paper, and the occasional mint tea.

It felt like withdrawal.

But somewhere in the middle of the second day, the noise in my head settled, and what was left were the *questions* I'd been avoiding for months. Big ones. Ugly ones. The ones I kept pushing to the bottom of my to-do list.

Silence has a way of confronting you with truths that busyness hides.

That's your second field exercise: **Go Silent for 48 Hours**.

No meetings. No email. No news. No social media. Just strategic thinking, reflection, and recovery.

If you lead a large organization, your mind is overstimulated. If you're like most high performers, even your "thinking time" is performative, filled with podcasts, note-taking, or planning. But real clarity requires *disconnection*, not just time.

Here's how to do it:
– Book two days off, not for leisure, but for vision.
– Tell your team you're unavailable and why.
– Bring only pen, paper, and your core questions.

And if that sounds indulgent, ask yourself: when was the last time your biggest breakthroughs came *during* a board meeting?

The kind of strategic insight that moves companies forward rarely arrives in noise. It arrives in stillness.

What these two exercises share is this: **tension**. The first invites it. The second removes everything but it.

Because growth doesn't just come from solving problems. It comes from creating environments where the right problems get *seen*.

And as a leader, your job is not just to reflect, but to model what reflection-in-action really looks like.

So, when will you schedule your audit?
And when will you be silent enough to hear what your gut's been trying to tell you all year?

CEO Debates/Dilemmas

Let me tell you about a conversation I had over dinner in Vienna with a seasoned CEO, we'll call him Mark. He ran a mid-sized industrial equipment firm that had one flagship product line, responsible for nearly 60% of their annual revenue. It had been a

The Innovator's Paradox 2.0

market leader for over a decade. The issue? It was no longer the future.

His head of innovation had just presented a new AI-driven maintenance platform that could render the legacy product nearly obsolete within three years.

Mark swirled the wine in his glass and asked me, "Would you kill your golden goose if you knew it was laying fewer eggs next year?"

That's the dilemma I want to put in front of you now.

The Legacy Product Dilemma

Imagine this: You run a highly successful SaaS platform. One feature, let's call it LegacySuite, brings in a third of your total revenue, but it's outdated. Your newer teams are constantly being slowed down by it. The market is shifting. Your competitors have leapfrogged your core offering with AI-native alternatives.

Your CTO wants to sunset LegacySuite within 18 months and reallocate all resources to a modular, AI-driven rebuild.

Your CFO is worried about revenue shock. Your board is split. Your team is hesitant.

What do you do?

Do you protect short-term revenue at the risk of long-term relevance? Or do you cut ties with your cash cow to chase the future?

There's no right answer, only a real one. The one you'd make, with your reputation, your team, and your capital on the line.

Now let's turn up the heat.

A few months ago, I was advising a CEO in Tel Aviv whose company was rolling out AI hiring software that could vet candidates in under 60 seconds using facial cues, tone, and language pattern analysis. It was fast. It was efficient. And it was dangerously close to being unethical.

They had no clear answer on data transparency. The algorithm was trained on datasets the company didn't fully control. Bias was a risk. But the clients loved the results.

She looked at me and asked, "Do I slow this down for the sake of principle, or double down while the competition sleeps?"

Here's your next boardroom dilemma:

The AI Ethics Tightrope

You've just deployed an AI system that's dramatically improving your fraud detection and client onboarding processes. It uses third-party data and pattern recognition to make risk assessments in real time.

Your compliance officer raises a red flag, there's a grey area in how user data is being collected. Nothing illegal. Just... questionable.

Meanwhile, your biggest client just asked if they can license your AI engine for their global operations. That's eight figures in ARR on the table.

So now the question becomes: How do you lead?

Do you slow down to investigate and risk losing the deal?
Do you push forward with disclaimers and policies, knowing others will exploit the same grey area anyway?

What does ethical leadership look like when the answers aren't black and white, but grey, and moving?

These aren't theoretical challenges. They're happening today, in boardrooms, Zoom calls, and strategy offsites around the world.

So, as you read this, ask yourself not just what you *would* do.
Ask what you're already tolerating.

Because leadership in the AI era won't be judged only by what you build, but also by what you choose to walk away from.

"What Would Moe Do?" Scenarios

There's a question I get asked in nearly every private boardroom I walk into:
Moe, what would you do in my situation?

So let me walk you through two real-world dilemmas, ones that might sound uncomfortably familiar. I'll show you how I think, not just in strategy, but in psychology, pace, and positioning.

Scenario 1: The Stagnant Market Entry

A few years ago, I was working with a £70 million manufacturing company in Birmingham that had hit a ceiling in the UK. They wanted to enter a new market, Germany, but every attempt felt like throwing darts in the dark. Different regulations, entrenched competitors, zero local brand recognition.

They were ready to invest heavily in a sales team and boots-on-the-ground presence. Classic playbook. But to me, that looked like expensive guessing.

So I asked:
"What do we *already* know, and what can AI tell us that we don't?"

We scraped and fed five years of German industry data into a market simulation engine. Not just sales data, but social sentiment, competitor campaigns, logistics costs, regional performance patterns. We ran 47 simulated go-to-market strategies across different cities, channels, and value props.

The AI didn't just suggest *where* to enter, it showed *how* to win faster than incumbents. It identified a regional cluster around Düsseldorf where no one was bundling service with product. We tailored our launch to that model, used hyper-personalized ABM outreach based on the data models, and landed five anchor clients within three months, without ever hiring a local team.

The lesson? Don't throw money at expansion. Throw intelligence at it first.

Scenario 2: The Internal Resistance to AI

I was flown to New York to advise a luxury hotel chain grappling with AI rollout. The CEO loved the vision, AI-powered guest experiences, predictive maintenance, dynamic pricing, but the senior managers weren't on board. The head of operations even called it "a fancy spreadsheet with a God complex."

I didn't argue.

I listened.

Then I booked a meeting room, invited the same senior managers, and gave them a challenge:
"Pick any recurring headache you deal with, guest no-shows, overbooking, staff scheduling, whatever. I'll come back in 48 hours with a working prototype that solves it. No slides. No sales. Just results."

They chose overbooking.

I pulled in my team and built a micro-AI tool that monitored booking behavior, weather patterns, and event traffic. It predicted overbooking spikes with 87% accuracy and gave staff two-day alerts to optimize occupancy.

When I showed it to the ops lead, he leaned back and said, "If AI is this... I'm in."

The resistance wasn't to *AI*.
It was to *irrelevance*, the fear of being replaced, misunderstood, or left behind.

That's why I always say: If you want your team to adopt AI, don't start with a pitch. Start with their pain. Solve something that *matters to them*. Let the machine prove its value.

In both scenarios, the strategy wasn't just technical. It was human. I didn't bulldoze through resistance or force belief. I created conditions where clarity could emerge, fast.

So next time you ask, *What would Moe do?*
Here's your answer:
I'd listen for the real friction.
I'd simplify the noise.
And I'd let data earn its place at the table, quietly but undeniably.

Guest Reflections

1. Reflection from a Tech Innovator

Ashwin Rao, Founder of QLogic AI, Bengaluru, India

"I don't trust certainty anymore. That's probably the most important mindset shift I've made in the past five years.

When I launched QLogic AI, we were building predictive analytics for small-to-mid-sized banks in Southeast Asia. At first, we built what they said they needed: reports, dashboards, the usual suspects. But nothing was sticking. We were right, technically. But we were wrong emotionally.

Then, one of our junior engineers, a 23-year-old named Meera, ignored protocol and launched a real-time loan fraud prototype without sign-off. She risked getting fired. But the client tested it anyway. Within 48 hours, the system had flagged three transactions their legacy systems had missed.

That changed everything. Meera's rogue idea exposed our blind spot: We were too polite, too 'client-first,' too committed to our roadmap. That failure-to-challenge was the real risk.

Disruption doesn't ask for permission, and neither should innovation inside your company. We now run an 'Open Rebellion Week' every quarter, any team member can break a rule, challenge a strategy, or test a product idea, as long as they document it and show potential upside. We've built features in five days that would've taken five months in the old structure.

For any CEO reading this: stop waiting for buy-in from everyone. You're not running a democracy, you're building a machine that evolves. Equip your people. Give them edges to push against. Then let go."

2. Reflection from a Traditional Industry Leader

Martina Vogel, CEO of Vogel Packaging GmbH, Stuttgart, Germany

"We make boxes. Cardboard ones. Not sexy, not high-margin, not the kind of thing people think of when they say 'innovation.'

But here's what I've learned: the more traditional your industry, the greater your risk of becoming invisible, and the greater your opportunity to lead, if you're bold enough to change first.

Five years ago, I would've laughed if someone told me we'd be using AI in a packaging plant. Today, our predictive maintenance system saves us €230,000 a year in downtime. Our custom-design configurator (powered by AI and customer purchase history) has doubled order conversion rates. None of this was in our five-year plan. It was sparked by a single workshop we ran with a visiting consultant who asked us a very simple question: 'What part of your process is dumb, but sacred?'

Turned out it was our quoting system. Thirty years old. Paper-based. Everyone respected it. Everyone hated it. Changing it meant disrupting our 'tribal knowledge', the exact kind of resistance Moe talks about in this book.

So we started small. Quietly. I didn't announce it on stage. I didn't create a task force. I just asked a team of two young engineers to see what was possible. Within eight weeks, we had an AI-powered estimator that outperformed the old system by 42% in both speed and accuracy.

The biggest threat isn't your competition. It's your comfort.

If you're leading a traditional company: don't wait for a Silicon Valley disruptor to show up. Invite one into your boardroom. Let them offend you. Then build from what you learn. Because in the end, disruption isn't about being futuristic, it's about being unafraid."

The Rationale for Variation

Engaging Different Cognitive Pathways

I remember sitting with a CEO in Mayfair who looked exhausted, not from the usual boardroom battles, but from trying to "think strategically" in the same way he had for years. His process was always the same: review a report, block time to reflect, write a note to himself... then wonder why nothing truly changed.

He was doing the right things, on the surface. But what he was really doing was rehearsing an old mental script. And his brain, highly trained, impressively efficient, had learned how to give him answers without ever asking deeper questions.

That's the hidden danger of reflection: the mind adapts too well. It builds shortcuts. Familiar tools lead to familiar answers. And that's why we need variation. Not for novelty. For neuroplasticity.

The Three Gears of Leadership Intelligence

Every strategic leader runs on three cognitive gears: analytical reasoning, creative exploration, and emotional intelligence. Most CEOs have overdeveloped one, tolerated another, and neglected the third. But innovation demands integration. Not just numbers. Not just vision. Not just intuition. All three, working together, in cadence.

Let's break that down:

1. Analytical Pathways: Precision and Pattern Recognition

These are your dashboards, OKRs, financial models, market analytics. It's where most CEOs are most comfortable. You ask, "What are the numbers telling me?" and your brain gets to work like a loyal analyst. This gear rewards discipline, comparison, and logic. It's why structured reflections like *Moe's Mirror* work so well for identifying blind spots, they're like mental audits.

But overreliance on this gear creates what I call *data paralysis*. You gather more and more evidence but shift less and less. You want certainty before action, forgetting that certainty is a luxury you rarely have when it matters most. Data becomes a safety blanket, not a decision catalyst.

Variation unlocks this. Try asking your team to interpret a dashboard without speaking, just drawing what it means. Or limit your weekly review to just one metric and ask, "If this were the only thing we knew, what would we do?"

Suddenly, the numbers provoke questions, not just conclusions.

2. Creative Pathways: Imagination, Reframing, and Possibility

This is the gear most underused in traditional leadership environments. It's not about being artistic, it's about breaking form. When I ask a CEO to imagine what their business would look like if Apple or Tesla ran it for a year, I'm not looking for fantasy. I'm shifting their lens.

Creative cognition lights up the brain's default mode network, the part responsible for associative thinking, lateral problem-solving, and risk ideation. This is the zone where disruption lives.

That's why I've included reflective exercises like "CEO Debates" or "What Would Moe Do?" scenarios. They force the reader to step into new shoes, imagine different outcomes, and test unfamiliar hypotheses.

Want to activate this further? Try journaling *as your competitor.* Ask your exec team to sketch a customer's day in pictures. Use metaphor, "What animal is our company right now? What animal should it be?" It may sound strange, but creativity doesn't respond to logic. It responds to permission.

3. Emotional Pathways: Empathy, Courage, and Conviction

No innovation survives long without emotional weight behind it. That's why I often say: "If your strategy doesn't make you feel something, excitement, fear, anticipation, it's not a strategy, it's a spreadsheet."

Emotional cognition is about more than vulnerability. It's about pattern recognition in relationships. It's about sensing where resistance lies, not in a process, but in a person. And it's about having the self-awareness to notice when your own fear is masquerading as due diligence.

Exercises like *The Legacy Mirror* or *Go Silent for 48 Hours* target this gear directly. They strip away noise. They remove the analyst, the manager, even the strategist, and leave just the human. The leader. The one who must make the call.

When you engage emotional cognition intentionally, you begin to notice how often your best decisions didn't come from a whiteboard, they came from a walk, a conversation, a gut instinct you had the courage to follow.

Why One Mode Is Never Enough

Here's what I've seen: CEOs who rely only on analysis tend to drift into stagnation. Those who lean only on creativity lose discipline and follow every shiny object. And those who operate solely from emotion burn out, or worse, become unpredictable.

The most dangerous thing isn't using the wrong cognitive gear. It's using the same one, every time, for every challenge.

Innovation requires toggling between them. That's why this book is structured the way it is, some sections provoke logic, others imagination, others introspection. It's not academic design. It's neurological strategy.

A Practical Parallel: The Military vs. the Studio

Think of it this way. The best organizations are like elite teams, part military, part artist's studio. The military brings cadence, discipline, SOPs. The studio brings messiness, play, divergence.

One without the other is useless. A studio without deadlines never ships. A military without reinvention gets blindsided.

Your reflection practices should reflect both. Some weeks, you need the Mirror. Other weeks, you need the Mess. You need to ask yourself hard questions one month. Debate with your team the next. Reframe your business in metaphor the month after. That's how cognitive flexibility becomes strategic strength.

Closing the Loop

So if you've ever felt like you're reflecting, but nothing's really changing, it's probably not about your effort. It's about your variation.

You don't need a new brain. You need new pathways.

That's what this section, and this chapter, is here to offer you. Not more thinking. Smarter wiring.

Preventing Reflection Fatigue

I once mentored a CEO of a successful manufacturing group who prided himself on his discipline. Every Friday, without fail, he blocked two hours to reflect. Same questions. Same notebook. Same quiet office. At first, it sharpened his focus. Then it flattened it.

By the sixth month, he confided in me: "I'm going through the motions. I write things down, but it feels like I'm repeating answers I've already given. I'm not getting new clarity, just new phrasing."

That's when it hit him, what was once strategic had become performative. What started as insight had decayed into ritual.

This is reflection fatigue.

It doesn't show up like burnout. You're not drained. You're dulled. Your insights lose their edge. Your curiosity dries up. You stop being surprised by your own thoughts. You're stuck, not because you're not thinking, but because you're thinking the same way, again and again.

The Illusion of Discipline

Repetition masquerades as rigor. When a leader gets comfortable with one method of reflection, be it journaling, reviewing KPIs, or using a self-assessment framework like *Moe's Mirror*, it becomes easy to confuse repetition with results.

But the brain is wired for efficiency. Once it learns the pattern, it automates the process. That's why your first time using *Moe's Mirror* feels revelatory. Your brain is fully engaged, challenged, even uncomfortable. But by the tenth or twentieth repetition, it can complete the exercise on autopilot, delivering safe, polished insights instead of real breakthroughs.

This is how comfort creeps in. And comfort is the enemy of transformation.

The Neuroscience of Engagement

To prevent reflection fatigue, you need to understand what engages the brain in the first place: novelty, difficulty, and emotional relevance.

Novelty activates dopamine pathways. New prompts, new environments, new formats all spark curiosity and increase attention.

Difficulty triggers cognitive strain, but in the right dosage, it leads to growth. It's the difference between lifting a weight that challenges you and one you can swing without effort.

Emotional relevance, the sense that what you're engaging with matters to your identity or your values, drives depth. Reflection must feel personal, not procedural.

When all three are absent, fatigue takes hold. The brain goes into power-saving mode. You might still look busy, but inside, you're recycling thoughts from last quarter.

The Discipline of Variation

Just as physical muscles plateau when you perform the same exercise repeatedly, cognitive muscles do the same. That's why athletes use cross-training, to keep the body adapting. Leaders must do the same with their minds.

Consider these examples:

- A CEO who always reflects solo switches to monthly peer interviews, recorded conversations where a trusted peer challenges their thinking aloud.
- Another swaps their journal for a quarterly internal podcast, speaking their reflections out loud to their team.

- A founder introduces sketchbooks instead of whiteboards, using visual storytelling to map strategy instead of bullet points.

These aren't gimmicks. They are rewiring tools. They introduce novelty, raise difficulty, and inject emotional stakes, because new formats feel riskier, more exposed.

This is the antidote to reflection fatigue: structured variety.

The Cadence of Change

In Chapter 4, we introduced the idea of varying your reflection style by quarter:

- **Q1: Questions.** Begin the year by asking better ones. Use challenge prompts, hypothetical scenarios, and "what if" models to reframe problems.

- **Q2: Debates.** Engage your team. Host formal debates around your assumptions. Let them challenge you, in public. Let the discomfort force clarity.

- **Q3: Experiments.** Don't just reflect, test. Turn your insights into live experiments. Make decisions on smaller bets. Then reflect on results, not just theories.

- **Q4: Legacy.** As the year closes, zoom out. Reflect on what you're building that will outlast you. These aren't weekly reflections. They're architectural blueprints.

Each quarter activates different mental muscles. You don't just reflect on strategy. You stress test it. You reimagine it. You live it.

Reflection Is Not a Solo Sport

Many leaders think of reflection as a solo practice. But some of the most powerful insights emerge in the presence of others. The real friction. The mirror you can't control.

In *The Directors WarRoom*, I've watched 9-figure CEOs break through walls they've hit for years, not because they journaled harder, but because another leader looked them in the eye and said, "You're still lying to yourself about this part of your business."

Sometimes, what prevents fatigue isn't a new tool. It's a new voice.

That's why one of the reflection formats I recommend is **The External Mirror**, a monthly session where someone you trust walks you through your assumptions, not your calendar. They ask, "Why haven't you done this yet?" "What would your biggest competitor say about this move?" "What truth are you pretending not to see?"

That's not repetition. That's revelation.

Designing for Surprise

The most effective reflection systems are designed to surprise you. They don't deliver comfort. They deliver confrontation. But that confrontation is what keeps the process alive.

Here's a simple test. If you know what your answer will be before you finish the question, you're not reflecting. You're recycling.

To avoid this, introduce **creative constraint**:

- **Limit time:** Set a five-minute cap for your answer. Force clarity.
- **Change format:** Don't write. Draw. Don't speak. Record a voice note.

- **Switch roles:** Reflect not as the CEO, but as your client, your competitor, your successor.

- **Change setting:** Step out of your office. Go somewhere that reminds you who you were before the success dulled your hunger.

Surprise is not about chaos. It's about shaking the system enough to let the truth slip through.

Closing Reflection

Reflection fatigue isn't failure. It's a sign of growth. It means you've mastered a form. But mastery of form is only useful when you use it to evolve function.

The goal isn't to throw away structure. It's to keep structure fresh. To re-engage your brain, your emotions, your imagination, so that every time you pause to think, it's not to preserve the past. It's to provoke the future.

You don't need more time to reflect. You need better tension.

That tension is where momentum lives.

Tailoring to Diverse Leadership Styles

No two leaders think exactly alike, and that's not a flaw in leadership development, it's the feature. Just as no two companies can scale on a one-size-fits-all operating system, no two CEOs extract insight from reflection in the same way. That's why effective strategic cadence demands not only structure, but adaptability. The moment your reflection routine begins to feel like someone else's prescription rather than your own exploration, its value diminishes. Worse, it risks becoming noise.

Over the years, I've sat across from leaders in boardrooms, off-sites, and even private suites at The Ritz, observing how differently they process the same strategic question. One might close their eyes and enter a deep monologue. Another scribbles a spider diagram across a flipchart, speaking only after connecting the dots visually. A third might ignore the question entirely, only to come back with a decision three days later after quiet contemplation. None of them are wrong. Each is operating from their unique zone of insight. The key is knowing which path brings clarity for you, and which path blocks it.

Some leaders are what I call "question processors." Give them a clean, focused question like, "What am I still protecting that should have been replaced last year?" and they'll go deep, often uncomfortable, but precise. These are the CEOs who write answers to themselves in email drafts they never send. For them, the act of sitting with a prompt, writing through it, then stepping away before returning to refine the answer, that's where the breakthroughs happen.

Others respond to pressure and provocation. These are "debate catalysts." Get them in a room with sharp peers, throw a strategic dilemma on the table, and they come alive. One founder I work with in Amsterdam won't move on a high-stakes decision until he's argued both sides out loud. His executive team knows the routine, someone has to play devil's advocate, and if no one volunteers, he'll assign roles. In that verbal tension, his clarity sharpens. For him, reflection isn't solitary. It's social, dialectical, and often uncomfortable by design.

Then there are the "story digesters." These leaders need examples, narratives, and parallels. Drop a case study on their desk, like how a manufacturing CEO in Poland used AI to enter new markets without hiring, and they'll mentally map the story to their own context. Their brain doesn't respond to questions. It responds to what's possible. These leaders often don't reflect by asking "What should I do?" but rather, "How did someone else solve this?" Their mirror is built from other people's pivots.

You'll also find the "system builders", those who need frameworks more than philosophies. When they reflect, they want scaffolding. Templates. Scorecards. Timelines. Their comfort zone is structured and measurable. They don't want to sit and meditate. They want a process to interrogate. For them, Moe's Mirror works best when paired with a tool like the Empowerment Scorecard or the AI Offense Audit. Their brains thrive on conversion, taking abstract thought and turning it into architecture.

Why does this matter?

Because when you, as a leader, force yourself to reflect in a style that doesn't match your wiring, you don't deepen your insight, you dilute it. It becomes a task, not a transformation.

This is also why the strategic cadence I teach and practice isn't just varied for the sake of novelty. It's intentional. Over the course of a year, we cycle through prompts, debates, stories, tools, and silence. We challenge pattern thinkers with chaotic creativity. We give systematizers moments of raw narrative. We balance questions with action briefs. And in doing so, we ensure that every type of leader gets their breakthrough, not just those who think like me.

One WarRoom member in Dubai, Aalia, a second-generation founder in the confectionery industry, once told me, "I don't do reflection. I do reaction." She meant it half-jokingly. But over the next few months, we designed a cadence around her style. Instead of weekly journaling, she recorded five-minute voice memos every Friday after her leadership meeting. Then we turned those voice memos into quarterly strategy debriefs. That was her mirror. And it worked.

Your mirror doesn't have to look like mine. It just has to be honest. And it has to challenge you.

As you continue through this book, notice which sections speak to you most. Is it the scenarios? The self-diagnostics? The stories? The templates? That's your natural reflection pattern. But don't stop there. The real growth happens when you test the others too. You might discover that your biggest blind spot wasn't strategic, it was stylistic.

Because the mirror you avoid might just be the one you need most.

Building a Holistic Innovation Muscle

How a varied approach contributes to a more well-rounded and adaptable leader

Leadership today is not a test of consistency. It's a test of elasticity.

In the past, a CEO could win by being exceptionally good at one style of thinking, operational execution, technical vision, or capital allocation. That was enough to anchor a career. But now? Markets shift in weeks, AI compresses business cycles, and disruption doesn't just arrive from your competitors, it comes from your own team, customers, and supply chain.

Which means the real edge belongs to those who are ambidextrous. Leaders who can reflect like a philosopher on Monday, decide like a tactician on Tuesday, and execute like a founder by Wednesday. That kind of agility doesn't come from reading more business books or attending another leadership summit. It comes from developing what I call your "innovation muscle", a set of mental, emotional, and strategic reflexes forged through varied, repeated, and intentional stretching.

Think of it like this. If you only ever lifted weights with your right arm, sure, it would grow. But the rest of your body would remain unbalanced, vulnerable, and unable to support you when it matters. The same is true with how you lead. If your only muscle is the "insight muscle", you'll be brilliant in conversation, but ineffective in execution. If you only flex your "decision muscle", you'll get things done fast, but you'll miss nuance, fail to listen, and leave opportunities unexplored.

The Innovator's Paradox 2.0

This is where the power of variation in your strategic cadence comes in.

Each form of reflection in this book has been designed not to suit a specific personality, but to stretch a specific part of your leadership muscle. When you write out your thoughts in response to Moe's Mirror, you're activating your introspective and emotional reasoning. When you run a Disruption Audit with your executive team, you're strengthening your group accountability and strategic pattern recognition. When you sit in silence for 48 hours, you're building mental resilience, detachment, and creative processing, skills no performance dashboard will ever measure but every crisis will demand.

One CEO I worked with, Thomas, ran a successful $80M manufacturing business in Sweden. Brilliant in execution, clear with KPIs, and admired by his team, but his strategic thinking plateaued. Not because he lacked ideas, but because he only reflected through spreadsheets and OKRs. Every insight had to convert into a number. So we designed a quarter where he couldn't use any numbers in his weekly reviews. Only narratives, metaphors, and team observations. At first, he struggled. Then, in week four, he described one of his business units as "a perfectly tuned engine, but stuck in the wrong vehicle." That metaphor sparked a full reorg, unlocking $6M in profit within six months.

What changed? His muscle memory. He stopped solving problems with the same mental tools and allowed another part of his leadership brain to take over.

Let me be clear, this isn't about becoming a new person. It's about reclaiming forgotten parts of yourself. Because most leaders didn't start out as narrow thinkers. You were once a builder, an improviser, a dreamer. But as the company grew, roles solidified, patterns formed, and soon the very consistency that helped you scale became the box that trapped your creativity.

The solution isn't to abandon your strengths. It's to complement them. To rotate your mental posture like an elite athlete who doesn't just train harder, but smarter, varying routines to avoid burnout, imbalance, and injury.

So what does a holistic innovation muscle actually look like in practice?

It looks like the ability to zoom out and ask, "What's the real problem here?" even when your team brings you a polished plan.

It looks like building a customer lab that tests radical ideas with real users before legal has even drafted a contract.

It looks like being the kind of leader who listens, not just to answers, but to the silences between them, and who can tell when a team is managing up instead of surfacing risk.

It looks like being able to sit with discomfort, with half-baked ideas, with friction between departments, and not rushing to fix it, but instead using it as a space to spark innovation.

Ultimately, it looks like this: a leader who doesn't just reflect, but evolves.

And that evolution doesn't happen by accident. It happens through practice, through intention, through strategic cadence. By engaging multiple parts of your leadership intelligence, analytical, emotional, visionary, operational, you develop the reflexes to adapt faster than your market, to spot disruption before it becomes decline, and to lead people through complexity instead of around it.

Remember, in a world where change compounds, so must your capacity. And the most adaptive leaders are not those with the most answers. They're the ones who built the widest range of ways to think.

So as you wrap up this section and prepare for the next, ask yourself not just "What did I learn?" but "What muscle did I stretch?"

Because innovation isn't a department. It's a discipline. And your ability to lead it depends on how holistically you train.

The Deep Dive Mirror: Uncovering Hidden Assumptions

There's a moment in every leader's life when the reflection looking back feels a little too familiar. Not because the answers are all right, but because the questions have stopped evolving. That's the danger. When your reflection becomes routine, it stops being revealing.

That's why I developed the Deep Dive Mirror, not for routine check-ins, but for those rare, uncomfortable pauses when you sense something big is being missed, but you can't quite name it yet. This isn't a daily journaling prompt. It's the mental equivalent of locking the boardroom door, rolling up your sleeves, and interrogating your beliefs under the spotlight.

Let me take you back to a moment when I had to use it on myself.

I was working with a £90M retail company in London. The CEO, Hamid, had grown it over 25 years, steady, profitable, admired. But something was off. Growth had plateaued. Talent was leaving. And innovation? Dead quiet.

We'd tried the usual playbook: strategy offsite, reorgs, culture workshops. Nothing stuck.

So I asked him to sit down with me. No slides. No agenda. Just a pen, a whiteboard, and a copy of the Deep Dive Mirror.

He resisted at first. "We've asked these questions before," he said. But that's the thing. It's not about the questions. It's about *what they expose the second time around.*

I asked him, "What's something you believe about your business that you haven't challenged in five years?"

Silence.

Then he said, "That our customers trust us."

I leaned in. "Why do you think that?"

"Because they've been with us a long time."

"So longevity equals trust?"

That's when the gears started grinding. Not just in the business. In Hamid. Over the next hour, we dismantled that one assumption, and uncovered a dozen others built on top of it.

That's the power of the Deep Dive Mirror. It doesn't hand you answers. It shines a light on the invisible scaffolding holding up your strategy, and asks if it still serves you.

Here are a few of the prompts I use with CEOs and their leadership teams when it's time to go deeper:

- What is something we've always believed to be true about our market that might be outdated?
- Which business unit or revenue stream would we *never* question, and why?
- What do I personally fear would happen if I challenged one of our sacred cows?
- What problem are we still trying to solve with an old definition of success?
- Where have we settled for efficiency at the expense of relevance?

This isn't surface-level stuff. It's meant to make you pause. Sweat. Maybe even feel defensive. That's the point.

But let's be honest, few leaders have the courage to sit in front of these questions alone. That's why I recommend doing this with at least one strategic partner who will call your bluff when you flinch. Someone who isn't invested in your comfort, but in your clarity.

For Hamid, that led to a redefinition of his core value proposition. He stopped selling reliability and started delivering relevance. Within six months, they launched a customer co-creation platform and brought in over 1,200 innovation ideas from their most loyal customers, none of which the executive team had ever considered.

All from one question.

So, here's your challenge. Before moving to the next section of this book, carve out 90 minutes. Find a quiet space. Take the five questions above, or write your own, and go deep. Not as a CEO. Not as a strategist. But as a human with blind spots like the rest of us.

Write down your answers. Then ask yourself one more:

Which of these assumptions, if proven false, would threaten everything I've built?

That's the one you need to wrestle with next.

Because the future doesn't reward certainty. It rewards those who keep questioning even their own best thinking.

The Future-Proofing Mirror: Your Business in 5 Years

Most CEOs I meet think in quarters. Some stretch into years. Few think in half-decades. Fewer still make today's decisions through the lens of who they *must become* in five years.

But the market doesn't care about your planning horizon. It rewards those who act as if the future is already here, because, in most ways, it is.

This is where the Future-Proofing Mirror comes in. Not as a fantasy projection or a five-year plan. But as a strategic interrogation of what your business is *becoming*, by design or by drift.

The Innovator's Paradox 2.0

Let me tell you a story.

I once met with Ayesha, the CEO of a £70M beauty manufacturing company based in Leeds. A powerhouse of a leader. Product margins were strong, and private label deals were flowing. On the surface, everything looked solid.

But she was uneasy.

AI was creeping into her category. Synthetic formulation. Predictive consumer trends. Even automated brand creation.

She wasn't losing market share, yet. But she could feel it.

"I'm not worried about next year," she said. "I'm worried about being irrelevant in five."

So, we stepped into the Future-Proofing Mirror.

I asked her to project forward. "It's five years from today. What does your most loyal customer expect of you now?"

She paused. "More personalisation. Zero waste. Instant delivery."

"Now," I said, "what part of your current business model makes that *impossible*?"

She looked down. "Our manufacturing partners. Our supply chain. Our packaging formats. All of it, really."

That's when the real work began.

The Future-Proofing Mirror isn't about vision statements. It's about surfacing the friction between today's decisions and tomorrow's demands.

It's about asking yourself:

- What systems, people, and beliefs are we investing in today that might actively work against us five years from now?

- What do our customers *not* complain about today that they'll *expect by default* in five years?

- Where are we doubling down on scale when we should be redesigning for speed or relevance?

One of the most dangerous myths in leadership is the illusion of "not yet." We tell ourselves we'll digitize next year. Automate after the next round. Enter new markets when the core is solid.

But the future doesn't arrive on your schedule. It arrives disguised as small shifts, until they're seismic.

For Ayesha, this meant launching a shadow supply chain pilot. A fully localised, AI-forecasted production model serving only 5% of her SKU line. Low risk. High insight.

Three years later, that 5% accounted for 38% of total profit. And the original chain? It's being phased out.

All because she stopped asking, "How do we optimise what's working?" and started asking, "What must work five years from now?"

Now, it's your turn.

Set aside time. Bring your leadership team, or go alone if you must. Ask:

1. **What does "winning" look like in your industry five years from now, and what would make your current business model obsolete in that world?**

2. **Which roles in your company will be replaced, enhanced, or irrelevant due to AI, automation, or customer empowerment?**

3. **Which competitors are already behaving like it's 2029, and what are they seeing that you're not?**

4. **What would your successor cut, build, or pivot the day after you resign?**

These are not just questions. They're provocations. They don't confirm your confidence, they challenge it.

Too often, I see leaders preparing their businesses for the *future they want*, not the one that's coming. But innovation isn't romantic. It's honest. Brutally so.

Here's the final challenge I gave Ayesha. I'll give it to you too:

Write your business obituary from five years in the future.

Be clinical. What did you ignore? What assumptions hardened into dogma? Who overtook you, and why?

Then, flip the page.

Now write your legacy letter. A vision of how you evolved. What you burned down. What you built. Who you became in the process.

This is the power of the Future-Proofing Mirror. It doesn't tell you what to do next. It reminds you what's at stake if you don't.

You don't need to predict the future perfectly. But you do need to *prepare your leadership posture* for it, starting now.

Because five years from now, your only regret won't be what you tried. It'll be what you postponed.

And by then, the mirror may no longer show your reflection, it'll show your replacement.

The Legacy Mirror: What Will You Leave Behind?

Legacy isn't a speech they write about you when you're gone. It's the residue of every decision you've made when no one was watching.

The Innovator's Paradox 2.0

It's how people felt after meetings with you. It's the processes that either outlived you, or died the moment you stepped away. It's what your leadership taught others to accept, reject, build, or destroy.

And here's the uncomfortable truth: you're building that legacy right now, whether you're aware of it or not.

Every policy you delay.
Every conversation you avoid.
Every innovation you sidestep in the name of "later."

These are not neutral acts. They are the architecture of your legacy.

I once sat across from a 9-figure founder, Rafiq, in a quiet lounge at The Shard. He looked tired. Not from lack of sleep, but from years of sustained effort that had started to feel... hollow.

"I built this company for freedom," he said. "But now I'm the bottleneck. Everyone still waits for me to make the big calls. And if I step away, the machine slows down."

He wasn't looking for a growth hack. He was looking for meaning. For permanence. For peace of mind that what he built would stand after he no longer could.

That's when I handed him the Legacy Mirror.

Not literally, of course. But I asked him a set of questions that rarely get asked at board level.

Questions like:

- If your business shut down today, what part of it would the world miss most?
- What values have you embedded so deeply into your culture that they could survive a hostile takeover?
- Who in your organisation is more courageous because you led them?

- Which decisions bought profit, and which bought principles?

These are legacy questions. They force us to look beyond quarterly earnings or media headlines. They force us to see our leadership through the lens of permanence.

What struck Rafiq most was this:

He'd built a company admired for its scale, but not remembered for its substance.

His culture was efficient, but not inspiring.
His profits were strong, but not transformative.
His people were loyal, but not unleashed.

Legacy, he realised, wasn't about empire. It was about imprint.

The conversations you encourage.
The kinds of risks you endorse.
The way you handle crisis, and whether your calm becomes theirs.

Now ask yourself: what story will your team tell about you when you're no longer in the room?

Will they speak about a leader who clung to power, or one who cultivated power in others?

Will they say you fought for innovation when it was hard, or that you tolerated mediocrity because it was comfortable?

Will they describe a culture that lived in fear of being wrong, or one obsessed with learning how to be better?

These aren't just philosophical questions. They're strategic ones.

Because legacy doesn't just shape your reputation. It shapes your business valuation, your succession planning, your ability to attract and retain top-tier talent. It defines whether what you built can endure.

And in an age of rapid disruption, where AI rewrites the rules faster than most CEOs can react, legacy isn't about stability anymore. It's about *renewability*.

That means leaving behind more than systems. You need to leave behind a mindset, one that expects change, rewards challenge, and doesn't confuse comfort with competence.

Let me offer you a framework I call **The Three Marks of Enduring Legacy**:

1. **Principle Over Preference**
   Your people should be able to predict how you'd respond to ethical dilemmas, not because you're rigid, but because you're consistent. What principles have you made non-negotiable?

2. **Empowerment Over Dependency**
   True legacy means the organisation can function, *and evolve*, without you. Are you building lieutenants or followers?

3. **Momentum Over Maintenance**
   The systems you leave behind should accelerate innovation, not just preserve what exists. Is your business still breathing once you're not the lungs?

When I reconnected with Rafiq a year later, things had shifted. He'd restructured his executive team. Instituted an innovation council with budgetary autonomy. Brought in AI-powered role players, "Zara," the client insights analyst, and "Amir," the supply chain optimiser, so the company's progress no longer depended on his daily input.

But the most telling change?

He'd started mentoring three younger founders in his industry, not because he needed more work, but because he realised legacy is also about what you give away freely, not just what you own.

That's the mirror he chose to look into. Now, it's your turn.

Take ten minutes today, no slides, no distractions. Just you and a blank page.

Write this prompt at the top:
"What do I want my leadership to make possible for others, even after I'm gone?"

Write the first answer that comes. Then the second. Then the one you didn't want to admit. That last one is where your real legacy begins.

Don't wait for retirement to think about it. The most powerful legacies aren't written at the end. They're forged in every uncomfortable decision you make today.

In the end, legacy isn't what you *leave behind*. It's what you *leave within*.

And the good news?

You still have time to decide what that will be.

The Action Integration Mirror: Bridging Thought and Execution

Insight is seductive. It can make you feel wise, enlightened even. But insight, on its own, doesn't build companies. Insight is sterile until it touches a decision, until it shapes a team, until it changes what happens on a random Tuesday morning.

This final mirror is different from the others. It's not about asking the hard questions. It's about *what you do after you've answered them.*

I want to introduce you to Arjun, the managing director of a mid-sized car parts and spares business based in Stuttgart, Germany. We met during a private roundtable I was hosting at a hotel suite in Mayfair. He was the kind of leader you notice straight away. Quietly confident. Controlled. The kind who carries the pressure of being the calm in every storm. After the session, Arjun waited until most of the room had emptied. Then he stepped closer, lowered his voice, and said, "Moe, I've got about a dozen pages of notes from today, but I still don't know what the hell to do on Monday."

He wasn't being dramatic. He was being honest.

He had a lot of insight already. He knew his company was reactive, not proactive, when it came to data. He had begun to suspect that much of their decision-making was built on tribal knowledge, not transparent process. And he admitted, somewhat reluctantly, that their lean image was mostly illusion. Behind the curtain, it was bloated, especially in middle management and operations.

But as he admitted all this, he sighed. "We've had these same conversations for over a year. Nothing's really changed. Why?"

I leaned in and asked him the only question that mattered: "What decision have you made because of that insight?"

That's where the room went quiet.

You see, there's a moment every CEO faces, when reflection isn't the hard part anymore. It's action. Translating thought into motion. That's what this mirror is for.

So I told Arjun, "Let's take one of those insights and run it through, end to end."

He picked the issue of bloated processes.

I asked, "What's one visible thing you'll do this week to show your team that this matters to you?"

He said he'd shadow the parts dispatch team in the warehouse, walk with them, observe, take notes. Not just review a report. Be physically present. Not next month. Not when it's convenient. This Friday.

That small shift changed everything. His behavior became a signal.

Then I pushed him further: "What decision have you been avoiding because it's politically messy or emotionally uncomfortable?"

He looked away for a second, then said, "We've been throwing good money after bad into a CRM integration project that's three months late and three times over budget. Everyone knows it's dead, but no one's saying it."

He cancelled the project the next day.

Once the behavior and the decision were clear, we turned to permanence. "What rhythm will make this a habit?" I asked.

He decided every department would run a 'waste audit' sprint every 60 days. Small, focused teams would use AI-powered task mapping tools to identify redundant workflows. They'd present findings directly to him and his COO. No filtering. No slide decks. Just clarity and speed.

Finally, I asked him, "How will you know this isn't just noise?"

That's when he decided to track how many fulfillment tasks were completed each month *without* human involvement. That one metric told a deeper story about tech adoption, efficiency, and cultural shift.

Two months later, Arjun sent me a voice message from the warehouse. He was walking, breathless with energy, narrating what had changed. "We cancelled two legacy projects. That freed up about €220k. Instead of replacing a retiring operations manager, we hired our first AI workflow engineer. Her name's Elina," he said, laughing. "Well, that's what the team calls her. She's not human, of course, but she's already cut down quote processing time by 30%.

The team's a little nervous, but they're also alive again. It feels like momentum, finally."

That's the bridge, when thought becomes action, and culture shifts around it.

Now it's your turn.

You've likely had more insights reading this book than you can count. But which ones are *alive*? Which ones have shaped your decisions, changed your systems, impacted your team's behavior?

Pick five that matter most. Not just intellectually, but emotionally. The ones that made you pause, that made you uncomfortable, that felt too true to ignore.

For each one, ask yourself:

What will I *do* to make this real in front of my team?

What hard decision have I been avoiding because it would signal that I'm no longer who I used to be?

What ongoing rhythm will anchor this shift so it survives my attention span?

And what result, tangible, visible, will show me it's working?

This is not theory. This is your leadership becoming operational.

You don't need another framework.

You need one move. One conversation. One week of focused change.

This mirror doesn't want more thinking from you.

It wants your next bold action.

CHAPTER 5:
The Post-Book Blueprint: From Insight to Unstoppable Momentum

SECTION 1: The 90-Day Innovation Sprint Template

Phase 1: Assess & Align (Days 1–15)

The final page is turned, the last insight digested, and now you're staring at the space between ideas and execution. That space, however small it looks, is where most leaders lose momentum. Not because they don't care. Not because they don't believe. But because they underestimate how heavy inertia is, especially when camouflaged as routine success.

This is where we start: not with action, but with alignment.

I want you to imagine walking into your next leadership meeting not as the operator you've always been, but as the architect of a new system. You're not there to manage performance or review last month's numbers. You're there to take stock, deep stock, of what your business is still built on. The first fifteen days of this 90-day sprint are not about fixing problems. They're about exposing assumptions.

And it begins with a brutally honest audit.

One CEO I worked with in Toronto told me his company was "lean, agile, and innovation-driven." By all external measures, he was right. Revenue was climbing, brand reputation was strong, and his team spoke fluent startup lingo. But when we peeled back the layers, what we found was a machine optimized for yesterday's challenges. Decisions were being made on outdated data, risk was being managed rather than explored, and AI was being "looked into" by an intern who barely had access to a budget. That's not innovation. That's maintenance with a new coat of paint.

So I asked him a question I now pose to you: if your entire executive team resigned tomorrow, would the business still be building the future, or would it be stuck protecting the past?

This audit is not about shaming. It's about illuminating.

In these first two weeks, I want you to map out three truths:

1. What are you currently optimizing for?
2. Where is your leadership team still playing defense?
3. And what decisions are being delayed, disguised as "strategic patience"?

You won't do this alone. Bring your core team into the room, not to present decks, but to hold a mirror. Ask them where they feel constrained, where they see opportunity being lost, and what parts of the business haven't evolved in the last three years. Then shut up. Let them talk. You'll hear things you don't want to hear. That's the point.

Once the fog of the audit starts to clear, the second part of this phase begins, alignment.

If the last few years have taught us anything, it's that fragmentation at the top is a silent killer. I've seen companies with brilliant products, talented teams, and robust funding collapse, not because they lacked potential, but because their leadership was misaligned on what "innovation" actually meant.

Some were chasing AI adoption like a shiny toy. Others were scared of touching the core business model. Some departments wanted speed. Others wanted control. And none of them were rowing in the same direction.

So, in this window of days 1 to 15, your job is to create a shared language.

Not slogans. Not strategy posters. A shared language that makes it clear what your sprint is designed to do.

This language should live inside three to five objectives that matter deeply, and that demand change. Objectives like: "Reinvent customer onboarding through AI." Or "Launch one internal team-led disruption pilot." Or "Automate 30% of operational reporting to free up strategic capacity." These aren't stretch goals. These are stakes in the ground.

You'll notice something else during this alignment period, resistance.

That's good. Resistance is the friction of change rubbing against comfort. When a CFO questions why the sprint diverts attention from quarterly metrics, that's your chance to lead. When a department head argues that "we've always done it this way," that's your moment to challenge. You are not here to protect the status quo. You are here to create a new one.

In one of the early WarRoom sprints, a member, let's call him Zain, a CEO of a Dubai-based marine tech firm, was deeply frustrated by his leadership team. They were capable but cautious. Every suggestion he made about shifting from legacy software to AI-driven fleet intelligence was met with "later." So I challenged him: What if you stopped convincing them, and started inviting them to co-create the objective?

The next day, he brought them into the room and laid out a single prompt: "If we were starting this company from scratch today, what would we do differently?" That changed everything. Within 72 hours, the same team who had blocked him were proposing pilots and restructuring meetings around AI data reviews. All it took was ownership.

That's what alignment looks like, not agreement, but ownership.

So by day 15, your team should not just know what the sprint is about, they should feel it. They should see their fingerprints on the outcomes. Because people don't resist change when they've had a hand in shaping it.

And you? You'll have moved from ideation to ignition. From leader of a business to leader of momentum.

Let's keep going.

Phase 2: Experiment & Iterate (Days 16–75)

If Phase 1 was about ripping the blindfold off, Phase 2 is about moving, fast, messy, uncomfortable movement that breaks things gently enough to learn, but firmly enough to never go back.

This is where most leaders hesitate. After the clarity of alignment, there's a strange, deceptive lull, like the eye of a storm. Meetings feel sharper, intentions clearer, energy higher. But clarity without movement is just another form of stagnation.

So we move. Quickly.

You're now entering the longest and most volatile stretch of the sprint: Days 16 to 75. These 60 days are not for planning. They are for proving. You're going to shift your culture from PowerPoint to prototype. From speculation to simulation.

The first step is creating your **cross-functional innovation pods**, small, deliberately mixed teams built to collide with friction and still deliver results. Not built for comfort. Built for creativity.

Let me tell you about a moment that made this clear to me.

The Innovator's Paradox 2.0

A few years ago, I was working with a high-end hospitality group in Austria that wanted to "digitize the guest experience." That was the vague mandate. Everyone nodded in meetings, but nothing happened. Why? Because the tech team didn't understand luxury, and the front-of-house team didn't trust code.

So, we built a pod. Three people from operations, two from tech, and one guest experience director who'd never opened Excel in her life. Their job? Create one experiment to improve the guest journey using predictive tools.

They came back 12 days later with a working AI-driven concierge interface built on WhatsApp that offered restaurant suggestions based on previous stays, weather, and dietary habits. Zero dev budget. Full implementation within a month. Hotel satisfaction scores went up 14%.

Not because the pod was brilliant. But because it was real. Fast. Imperfect. Aligned.

Now back to you.

Your role in this phase is not to micromanage these teams. It's to frame their challenge, protect their space, and hold them accountable to velocity, not perfection.

Each pod should have a single mandate. Not ten. Not five. One.

It might be: "Rebuild the onboarding journey using automation and predictive insights." Or: "Develop a revenue stream from unused data assets." Or even: "Cut a recurring manual task in finance by 70% using AI."

Keep it sharp. Keep it measurable.

The pods should be empowered with three freedoms: the freedom to try, the freedom to be wrong, and the freedom to talk directly to customers, users, or data, without waiting for permission.

That last one is crucial.

Too many innovation attempts fail not because the idea was weak, but because someone was waiting on approval, access, or authority. We don't have time for that. This is not about building bulletproof strategies. This is about building the muscle of iteration.

And that means iteration loops.

Every pod should be working in 7–10 day cycles. Build something small. Test it. Show it. Learn from it. And go again. These are **feedback-fueled sprints**, not passion projects. You don't get to fall in love with your solution. You fall in love with what the data tells you.

One of my clients, Maria, who runs a food processing company in Madrid, got this exactly right. Her team was experimenting with reducing packaging waste through real-time inventory tracking. The first dashboard was a mess. Too many variables. Poor visibility. She could have pulled the plug, but she didn't.

Instead, she asked a simple question: "What did you learn that you didn't expect?"

Turns out, one of the lesser-used sensors had been generating cleaner signals than the core tracker. They rebuilt around that. By week six, packaging efficiency had improved by 11%. Small signal, big shift. That's the power of iteration.

This phase is also where you learn what your culture actually rewards.

Does your team celebrate speed of learning or just final results? Are experiments being shared or hidden? Are mistakes used to shame or to sharpen?

You'll need to be vigilant here.

Publicly celebrate lessons, not just wins. Share failures that reveal truth. Make it clear that this isn't about status. It's about systems improvement.

There's something almost spiritual about watching a team start to believe in their own agility. I've seen risk-averse middle managers light up when they realize they don't need ten sign-offs to try something new. I've seen engineers who've spent their careers under task lists suddenly proposing bold product pivots. Not because someone told them to, but because someone finally removed the brakes.

That's your job here: remove the brakes.

By day 75, each pod should have at least two to three working prototypes, decision-ready insights, or live experiments in progress. Some will fail. Some will underwhelm. One or two might hint at something big.

What matters is this: your organization will have moved. Not in theory. Not in intent. But in action.

You will have transformed rooms of well-meaning professionals into teams of adaptive, empowered innovators.

And the question won't be "How do we keep this going?" The question will be, "Why didn't we do this sooner?"

Phase 3: Scale & Sustain (Days 76–90)

By now, you've earned more than progress, you've earned momentum.

But here's the danger of momentum: it can trick you into thinking you've already won.

Most organizations that run sprints fall into the same trap after the 60-day mark. They mistake prototypes for progress. They clap for early results. They write case studies. They send out internal newsletters and then... nothing changes.

Why?

Because nobody plans for what happens after the applause.

That's what Phase 3 is for. These final 15 days are about building permanence from progress. It's not the most exciting part, but it's the most important.

This is where you begin to ask the hard questions:

- What did we actually learn?
- What's worth scaling?
- What failed for good reason, and what failed because we quit too early?

Let me take you into a boardroom in Düsseldorf. I was working with a specialty automotive parts supplier, family-owned, €200M turnover, generations deep. They ran three pods during their sprint. One of the pods had built an AI-driven order prioritization engine that cut down fulfillment errors by 60%. The room lit up when the numbers came in.

Then I asked the CEO, Markus, "What are you doing with it?"

He paused.

Because he didn't know.

He hadn't built the runway.

That pod had done brilliant work. But there was no plan to integrate it into the wider ERP system. No owner. No training. No budget allocation.

In those last 15 days, we fixed that.

And that's what you need to do now.

The first step is to **evaluate your sprint outcomes like a portfolio**, not a pitch session. You're not looking for shiny ideas. You're looking for traction, repeatability, and alignment with your long-term strategy.

You're also assessing *energy*. Which pods thrived? Which leaders emerged? Where did bottlenecks still show up? These questions tell you as much about your culture as your output.

Then, it's time to choose.

You're going to select a small number of experiments to take forward, two or three at most. If you choose more, you'll dilute the focus and kill the rhythm. You're looking for experiments that hit three marks: validated in the field, scalable across teams, and strategically significant.

You assign owners.

You build 30–60–90 day roadmaps.

You fund them, not with wishful thinking, but with budget and resource.

This is the moment when sprints become systems.

But scaling alone isn't enough. You also need to **design for rhythm.** Because innovation that spikes and vanishes is just adrenaline. What you want is *cadence.*

That means planning your next sprint *before* this one ends.

Not necessarily another 90-day initiative, but something.

Maybe it's a mini-sprint focused on customer journey pain points.

Maybe it's a 45-day experiment on AI-driven pricing.

Maybe it's rotating the innovation pod members to seed capability elsewhere.

Whatever it is, schedule it. Fund it. Name it. Make it real.

This is how you institutionalize movement.

I call this the "Second Sprint Principle." If you don't define your second sprint before the first ends, you will revert to inertia. You will lose the culture shift you just sparked.

And don't forget the most underappreciated piece of this phase: **the story.**

You need to document the journey. Capture the friction, not just the wins. Interview your pod members. Film retrospectives. Turn lessons into internal playbooks. Why? Because stories scale belief. The next group that takes on a sprint will need courage, and courage comes from seeing others like them make it work.

One last story.

A team in South Africa ran a sprint focused on automating procurement reporting. Midway through, their lead analyst left the company. Everyone assumed the project would stall.

But the pod pressed on. They rebuilt their model using a new AI dashboard and finished on time. When they presented it, they didn't show a polished slide deck. They showed a video timeline of every mistake, every pivot, every conversation that got them to the finish line.

The CFO stood up after watching it and said, "This was better than our last million-euro transformation project. And it cost less than a long weekend in Cape Town."

That sprint changed how the whole company approached change.

That's what Phase 3 can do when done right.

It's not just about what got built. It's about what got *unlocked*.

You now have the opportunity to turn this 90-day window into a permanent operating shift. Not by scaling everything, but by *scaling the system that builds everything*.

By Day 90, you want your organization asking a new kind of question:

Not "Can we do it?"

But "What sprint are we launching next?"

That's when you know you've done it right.

Ready for what comes next? Let's talk about how to make this sprint part of something bigger, your **Disruption Council**.

SECTION 2: Building Your Disruption Council

Who Belongs on Your Council?

Most CEOs don't need more ideas, they need sharper people around them to test those ideas before the market does.

And that's exactly what your **Disruption Council** is for. Not another committee, not another title-heavy talking shop. This is your inner circle of strategic provocation. The people you call when the old way feels too safe, and the new way feels too raw.

Let me tell you how this all started for me.

Years ago, I was mentoring a manufacturing CEO, deep in the Midlands, whose company had grown comfortably stale. His board was polished but passive. They nodded at slides. They reviewed reports. But they never challenged the deeper assumptions. One day I asked him, "Who on your team would risk offending you to save the company?"

He stared at the wall for a long time.

Then said, "I don't think I have that person."

That was the day we built his first Disruption Council.

The first thing to understand is this: your council isn't your leadership team. It may include some of them, but not all. And certainly not by default. Position doesn't earn a seat, *perspective* does.

You want three types of people in that room:

1. The Challenger:
This is the one who never takes anything at face value. They're the person who constantly asks "why" and "what if." They might frustrate you. They might disagree with you in front of others. Good. You need them. Their job isn't to be liked. It's to be honest.

Take Sahar, for instance, a head of customer experience at a Middle Eastern telco I worked with. She didn't come from a tech background. She wasn't the most senior. But she saw friction before the analysts did. She sensed shifting sentiment before the data caught up. She challenged assumptions with a kind of quiet, persistent force that couldn't be ignored. She became the voice of the customer in every council meeting. And her insights eventually led the company to shut down a legacy product line that was slowly poisoning its NPS.

2. The Connector:
This is the one who sees patterns others miss. They're your bridge-builder. Your sense-maker. They may come from finance, strategy, operations, but they think in systems. They can take a loose idea and show how it could run through your entire org. They're the one who hears about a change in your product and instantly asks how it affects pricing, support, onboarding, and compliance.

In one London-based fintech, that person was Tom, their regulatory compliance officer. On paper, not the obvious choice for an innovation council. But Tom had this rare ability to map ripple effects, how a simple UX change could cascade into audit risks, partner queries, and legal friction. Without him, their "brilliant" innovations would've created chaos. With him, they were airtight.

3. The Wildcard:
Yes, you need one. Someone from outside your industry. Maybe even outside your company. A voice that doesn't think like you, talk like you, or plan like you. Their role is to pull you out of your echo chamber and stretch your aperture.

In my own council, I've had artists, AI ethicists, ex-military strategists, and even a poet. Why? Because disruption doesn't just come from your competitors. It comes from adjacent inspiration. From perspectives that challenge your fundamental definitions of value, risk, time, and trust.

Now here's what your council is *not*:

- It's not a boardroom. Leave the suits and showmanship outside.

- It's not about quarterly numbers. This is about long bets, dangerous truths, and early signals.

- It's not about agreement. If everyone nods, you've failed.

You also want diversity, not as a buzzword, but as a necessity. Diversity of thinking, background, and experience is the *fuel* of foresight. If your council all went to the same schools, worked in the same verticals, and read the same newsletters, you're not future-proofing anything. You're just recycling comfort.

Let's go deeper with an example.

In Copenhagen, I worked with a 9-figure clean energy firm. Their CEO, Liv, was visionary but isolated. Her executive team worshipped her, too much. Every initiative she floated became gospel. So, we built her Disruption Council in secret. She selected three internal voices known for their skepticism. We added an external AI researcher from Stockholm, a retired diplomat who now focused on resource geopolitics, and a Gen Z activist who'd criticized the company on LinkedIn.

At the first meeting, Liv was rattled. She said afterward, "I've never felt so uncomfortable, or so alive, in a conversation."

That council didn't just generate ideas. It shifted how she saw risk. It redefined what the company owed its future customers. And when new ESG regulations hit, they were already ahead of the curve.

That's the power of the right people in the right room.

So, who are yours?

Start with this question: Who tells you the truth when it's inconvenient?
Now ask: Who sees the future through a lens you don't yet understand?

If you can name them, invite them.
If you can't, go find them.

This isn't a luxury. It's leadership insurance.

In the next section, we'll explore how to give your council rhythm, relevance, and teeth.

Defining the Council's Mandate & Rhythm

Bringing the right people into the room is only the first move. What you do with them, how you use their minds, manage the energy, and give their voices real weight, is what makes the Disruption Council more than a talking circle.

I've seen too many advisory boards formed with good intent and then slowly decay into corporate theatre. They become ceremonial. The same people say the same things. The notes get typed, filed, and forgotten. Leaders nod, smile, and do exactly what they were going to do anyway.

So here's the hard truth: If your Council doesn't have a clear mandate, and a drumbeat to act on that mandate, it becomes a placebo. A clever-sounding way to pretend you're being challenged.

Let me show you how we fix that.

It starts with a **core purpose**. Every council needs a reason to exist that transcends vague "innovation" or "big-picture thinking." One of the first things I ask CEOs is: *What are you afraid your exec team is too close to see?* That usually leads us to the real mission.

For example, in Dublin, I worked with the founder of a B2B software firm scaling across Europe. He had loyal senior staff, most of whom had been with him for over a decade. But they were trained on the old map. When we formed his Disruption Council, its mandate wasn't "support growth", it was *challenge the sacred assumptions that built the company but may now be holding it back.*

That kind of clarity changes everything.

We gave them three standing questions they had to answer at each meeting:

1. What are we not seeing?

2. What are we pretending not to know?

3. What has changed outside, that we haven't changed inside?

These weren't casual prompts. They were interrogation lights. And over time, they led to real breakthroughs, like sunsetting a product that still drove 40% of revenue but had become strategically irrelevant, and launching a new platform that leveraged generative AI to reduce client onboarding time by 60%.

But purpose alone isn't enough. A council without rhythm dies. Which brings us to **cadence.**

I recommend most councils meet once every 30 days, strictly time-boxed to 90 minutes. Why monthly? Because strategy can't live on the same timeline as operations. Quarterly is too slow. Weekly is too reactive. Monthly forces a rhythm of reflection, without letting urgency smother insight.

Here's the format that's worked best across multiple WarRoom companies:

- **15 minutes: The Shift Signal**
  One member shares a signal of change, a new tech, policy, trend, or behavior shift they've observed. The focus isn't accuracy, it's provocation. They're not reporting news, they're scanning the horizon for asymmetries. We've had everything from TikTok algorithm changes to whispers about supplier contracts being AI-audited in Asia.

- **45 minutes: The Focus Challenge**
  A rotating topic or decision is brought to the table. Maybe it's "Do we enter this market?" or "Should we kill this feature?" The presenter makes the case in five minutes. Then the rest of the time is a brutal, no-fluff, no-politics interrogation. This is where the council earns its stripes.

- **30 minutes: The Mirror Round**
  We close with a reflection. Each member answers: "What assumption did you challenge today?" and "What should we take back to the leadership team?" This prevents drift. It keeps every conversation anchored to change.

Now here's the secret that keeps it alive: **decision traceability**.

Every quarter, the CEO meets with the council, not to debate, but to *report back* on what was acted on, what wasn't, and why. This flips the usual power dynamic. It holds *you*, the CEO, accountable to your own council. And it ensures this isn't theatre. It's transformation.

That's what we did with Elin, the CEO of a Norwegian healthtech company who invited me in last year. Her first council meeting left her reeling. They questioned her GTM assumptions. Tore apart her pricing. And called out a cultural blind spot in the way her team recruited from the same three universities.

"I've never been challenged like that," she said. "And it's exactly what I needed."

By the third meeting, she wasn't just listening, she was reconfiguring how her company made decisions. Her Head of People was now piloting a new DEI recruiting initiative. Her CFO had re-forecasted using variable pricing simulations from their AI engine. And her product lead had shifted roadmap priorities based on frontline feedback.

None of that came from a consultant's deck. It came from the council's rhythm. A drumbeat that echoed through the organisation.

One final point: this council doesn't exist to *vote*. It exists to *clarify*. It doesn't make decisions, it sharpens them. It doesn't replace your judgment, it upgrades it.

And that's what real leadership looks like: building a room where you're not the smartest voice, just the most open one.

In the next section, we'll dive into how to ensure this council actually drives *impact*, and doesn't become a sideline think tank. It's time to translate sharp dialogue into decisive action.

Leveraging Your Council for Impact

Forming a council is easy. Extracting real value from it is not.

I've seen too many leaders fall into the trap of what I call *"advisory board theatre."* The room looks impressive. The names on the list are credible. The conversations feel deep. But nothing actually changes. And no one is held responsible when it doesn't.

The Innovator's Paradox 2.0

Let's be blunt, most advisory boards are ornaments, not instruments.

But yours doesn't have to be.

To ensure your Disruption Council drives meaningful action, you need to anchor it around two things: *real challenges* and *clear consequences*.

When I was working with Jamal, the CEO of a UAE-based construction technology firm, his biggest complaint about his existing board was this: "They agree with whatever I say. Or they just give me ideas I could have Googled."

He didn't need a cheer squad or an echo chamber. He needed sharp insight, delivered with courage, by people who weren't afraid to disagree with him in public.

So we changed the game. Every quarter, Jamal had to bring **three unresolved business tensions** to the table. Not projects. Not updates. Tensions. Strategic knots he couldn't untie.

One quarter, he brought up a tough one, whether to open a new arm of the business focused on predictive maintenance, or double down on digitizing their current workflow systems.

The council didn't waste time theorizing. One member, a fintech founder, reframed the conversation entirely: "You're asking a build question. But what if this is a *partner* question? Who already owns the customer relationship you want, and what would it take to license them your tech?"

That insight didn't just unlock the dilemma. It shaved nine months off his roadmap.

But here's what made it *stick*.

Every recommendation from the council was tracked. Not just noted. Tracked. Jamal's team logged each piece of advice into a shared dashboard with three columns:

- Was this acted on?
- If yes, what happened?
- If no, why not?

Then, in the next meeting, they reviewed it. In front of everyone. No defensiveness. No excuses. Just honest feedback loops.

That created *accountability in both directions.* Jamal didn't waste their time. And they didn't offer throwaway ideas.

It also bred seriousness. When members saw that what they said mattered, that it changed resourcing, priorities, headcount, even market strategy, they stepped up. They researched harder. They challenged deeper. They started arriving with their own data.

This is the difference between *input* and *influence.*

If your council is going to drive real impact, you have to **earn their best thinking**, and then show them it mattered.

But this also requires you to become a different kind of leader.

You need to bring your mess, not your mask.

I worked with a CEO in Stockholm who struggled with this. Every meeting, he showed up polished. Every slide deck was immaculate. But his council saw through it. One finally said, "You want a sounding board, not a scalpel. If you're not willing to bleed a little here, this doesn't work."

That moment changed everything. He started bringing live challenges. Things he hadn't resolved. Fears he hadn't voiced. The trust went up. So did the intensity. The impact followed.

Within three quarters, his company had restructured product and engineering to work in parallel instead of sequence, cutting time-to-release by 40%. That idea came from a council member who ran a robotics company in Estonia.

Again, this wasn't generic advice. It was **contextual, lived wisdom** shared at just the right time.

One final lesson: You must **protect the edge.**

Over time, even great councils drift toward safety. People get comfortable. The tension dulls. The challenges soften.

Don't let that happen.

You protect the edge by rotating provocateurs. Bring in new members. Invite temporary guests with wildly different perspectives, a behavioural economist, a retired military strategist, a Gen Z founder. Use them to spike the energy. Disrupt the groupthink.

You also protect the edge by doing what few leaders dare to: **call it out.**

At one WarRoom in London, a member once said to the group, "We've gotten too polite. Last year, we were pulling each other apart, in the best way. Now we're tiptoeing."

He was right. And that honesty reset the tone. The next 60 minutes were brutal. One founder got told his new 'customer engagement strategy' was really just an apology tour for bad service. He didn't like it. But he needed it. And he came back three months later with a product experience that had churn cut in half.

That's impact.

That's what happens when your council becomes your crucible.

Not a decorative circle of trust, but a pressure chamber for growth.

Not a think tank, but a challenge engine.

And the only way it works… is if you *let it work on you.*

SECTION 3: The Digital Toolkit

Strategic Activation Guide
The Internal Toolkit You Didn't Know You Had

By now, you've read the frameworks, dissected the case studies, and likely had a few uncomfortable but necessary realizations. But insight without action is wasted potential. You don't need another download, dashboard, or digital course to start. What you need is activation, and that begins with a strategic self-interrogation.

This isn't about busywork or box-ticking. It's a conscious pause. A mental war room moment where you step back and ask: "What game am I really playing? And who's playing it for me?"

Let's begin.

Are You Treating AI as a Tool, or a Team Member?
If you're still talking about "AI tools," you're playing small. The companies rewriting their markets don't just plug in ChatGPT or automate a few processes. They assign names, roles, and expectations to AI like they would for a new executive hire.

In my own advisory work, I've helped leaders bring on AI roles like Sallay, their always-on receptionist, or Robert, the outbound sales manager who never sleeps. The moment they started treating AI as staff, not software, the mindset, and results, shifted.

Ask yourself:

- Which roles in your business could be reimagined with AI ownership?

- Where is AI assisting today, that it should be leading tomorrow?

Is Your Business Playing Offense or Defense?
Be honest. Are you reacting to threats, or designing moves that scare your competitors? Are you waiting for budget approvals to

explore innovation, or are you already reallocating resources from outdated wins to future-proof experiments?

Defense looks like quarterly reviews and comfort metrics. Offense looks like 30-day sprints, new category bets, and uncomfortable decisions that unlock new margins.

Run a gut check:

- What percentage of your current roadmap feels bold versus safe?
- Where are you trying to protect the past rather than build the future?

Which Strategic Pillar Is Cracking First?
Every high-performing business has its breaking point. For some, it's Systemization, they're scaling chaos. For others, it's Staffability, too many roles depend on heroic effort. Sometimes it's Sellability, a business that thrives only with the founder present.

Look at the Five Strategic Pillars and ask:

- Which one, if left unaddressed, would prevent you from exiting, scaling, or sleeping at night?
- What's your current blind spot, and what happens if it breaks in six months?

Are You Leading for Legacy, or for Love of Control?
Here's the hard one. Many CEOs claim they're building legacy, but what they're really building is a monument to their own decisions. If your team can't innovate without your sign-off, if your systems break without your presence, you haven't scaled, you've stalled.

This book wasn't designed to flatter you. It's here to challenge you.

So ask:

- If you stepped away for 90 days, what would your business forget to do?

- Who on your team would step up, or would it collapse under silence?

How Will You Measure the Next 90 Days?
Forget the usual metrics for a moment. What if your KPIs included:

- How many "sacred cows" you challenged

- How often your team told you the truth you didn't want to hear

- How many decisions your AI team made without you

This isn't about dashboards. It's about direction.

Final Note: This Is Your Launchpad
Don't close this book and wait. Use this activation checklist as your bridge from insight to movement. Share it with your team. Debate it with your board. Journal it yourself if you must.

But whatever you do, don't let this be just another great book on your shelf.

The next chapter isn't written in these pages. It's written in your calendar, your decisions, and the people (human or AI) you empower starting now.

2. Seven-Day Application Sprints
Build Momentum Before Monday Comes Around Again

You don't need a 90-day roadmap or a war chest of tools to begin transforming your business. What you need is one focused week, seven days of deliberate, uncomfortable, high-leverage action. This isn't theory. This is ignition.

Each of the next seven days invites you to take one targeted, no-excuses step toward systemic innovation. No team meetings required. No budgets to wait on. Just you, a notebook, and the discipline to act.

Let's begin.

Day 1: Kill a Sacred Cow
Every business has them. Old assumptions. Pet projects. Unquestioned norms that once served you, but now strangle growth.

Maybe it's a product line that "still makes money" but blocks innovation. Maybe it's a legacy hire protected by loyalty instead of performance. Or a process that everyone hates, but no one dares to change.

Today, identify one sacred cow in your business and write its obituary. Then take the first step toward phasing it out.

Ask yourself:
What would a new CEO do if they took over today? Now, be that person.

Day 2: Audit a Decision You've Delayed
You already know the decision. It's the one that's been haunting your whiteboard, dodging every meeting, and quietly draining your attention. It could be a hire, a pivot, a partnership, or a shutdown.

Grab a pen. Write out the cost of *not* deciding. Then block 20 minutes on your calendar and make the call, send the message, or set the wheels in motion.

You're not waiting for clarity. You're creating it.

Day 3: Appoint Your First AI Staff Member
If you're still calling it "a tool," you're missing the shift. AI isn't just software, it's talent, waiting to be assigned.

Today, give one role in your business to an AI teammate. Name them. Define their job description. For example:

Sallay – Virtual Receptionist
Answers FAQs on our website, routes messages to the right human, and logs patterns in client inquiries for product team review.

Robert – Outbound Sales Development Manager
Scrapes relevant leads from LinkedIn, writes custom cold outreach using our tone of voice, and auto-schedules qualified responses.

Once you assign the role, document what success looks like, and review it weekly like any other staff member.

Day 4: Find a Hidden Bottleneck in Your Leadership

Your business is constrained by what you won't delegate, what you don't know you control, or what people are too afraid to challenge.

Today, run a quiet diagnostic. Ask your team, or yourself:

- What decisions am I still approving that someone else could own?

- What meetings only exist because I haven't empowered the right person?

- Where does information stop flowing up, or challenge stop flowing down?

Name one bottleneck. Break it this week.

Day 5: Run a One-Hour Innovation Sprint

Pick a thorny challenge: falling margins, slow onboarding, inconsistent delivery, stagnant product. Set a 60-minute timer. Work solo or with one team member.

In that time, generate 10 ideas using the format "What if we…?"

- What if we rebuilt onboarding with AI and skipped the PDF manuals?

- What if we stopped serving this segment entirely?

- What if we charged based on outcomes?

Then pick one idea, just one, and commit to testing it in the next 30 days.

Day 6: Write a Strategic Memo to Your Future Self

Today, write a letter to the version of you 18 months from now. Be clear, be strategic, and don't self-censor. Start with:

"It's June 20XX, and here's what's true now about my company, my team, and my leadership..."

Describe what you've let go of. What you've built. Who's now leading beside you. What AI roles have been normalized. How much time you spend *on* the business, not in it.

Then seal it in your notes and revisit it in 90 days. You'll be surprised how fast you can catch up to it, or fall short.

Day 7: Give Power Away

You want autonomy-driven teams? Start by transferring power, real, consequential power.

Today, identify one meaningful decision that you've historically made alone. Hand it to a trusted team member. Tell them, "This is yours now. I'll support the outcome, but I won't override it."

Give them constraints if needed. But then get out of the way.

Innovation doesn't come from micromanagement. It comes from trust exercised under pressure.

Final Note: These Seven Days Aren't a Checklist. They're a Catalyst.

This sprint isn't about perfection. It's about proof, that you're ready to move from insight to offense. And that you're no longer mistaking thinking for leading.

By this time next week, your business will have made its first irreversible shifts. Small, maybe. But irreversible.

You'll have broken one sacred cow. Made one overdue decision. Given one AI a job. Handed one team member real authority. And created a new rhythm.

That's not a sprint. That's a signal, to your team, your board, and your future self.

Now go again.

3. Strategic Solitude Practices: Where Clarity Begins

In a world obsessed with connectivity, leadership clarity is becoming a casualty of constant noise. Meetings pile up, notifications intrude, and every moment is saturated with inputs. Yet, the most defining inflection points in business, and in leadership, rarely come during a boardroom discussion or Zoom call. They arrive in silence, when the noise finally dies down.

That's why, instead of directing you to another library of templates or downloadable content, I invite you into a more uncomfortable but far more potent arena: intentional solitude.

Strategic solitude is not about escape. It's not a digital detox or a wellness retreat. It's a recurring, structured practice where you deliberately remove yourself from operational gravity in order to access deeper levels of decision-making. Not reactively. Proactively.

Solitude as Strategy, Not Luxury

Most CEOs don't take time alone because they feel they can't afford it. But the truth is, they can't afford not to.

Solitude isn't a break from the work. It is the work. When you stop answering emails, your mind starts answering questions you've been avoiding. When you silence the noise of your team, you start hearing the signal of your own insight.

I've watched 9-figure CEOs rebuild entire companies from a single day of solitude. Not because they found a new framework, but because they finally saw the one they were too busy to notice.

The 6-Hour CEO Reset

Here's a simple practice you can implement right now, without a single download or dependency. I call it the 6-Hour CEO Reset:

1. **Find a space away from your team and your home.** Not a hotel lobby, not a WeWork. Somewhere private, ideally surrounded by nature or stillness. Bring a notebook, nothing else.

2. **Block 6 hours. No meetings, no calls.** Tell your team you're unreachable. If you can't do that, you've already found your biggest leadership weakness.

3. **Use a three-part structure:**
    - **Hour 1–2: Audit.** What are the 3 biggest unspoken assumptions you've been operating under? What parts of your strategy have gone unchallenged for too long?
    - **Hour 3–4: Imagine.** If your business burned down tomorrow, what would you rebuild, change, or eliminate?
    - **Hour 5–6: Decide.** What one hard, strategic choice are you avoiding? What would your future self thank you for doing right now?

You don't need a toolkit to ask those questions. You need space.

Strategic Silence in the Calendar

The most effective leaders I work with don't leave solitude to chance. They schedule it.

Some block one day a month. Others carve out one weekend per quarter. A few go further, creating "quiet weeks" each year to think, plan, and reset without meetings or demands.

The more complex your business becomes, the more simplicity you'll need in your own thinking. Strategic solitude is how you engineer that simplicity.

What Solitude Reveals

What usually surfaces during these sessions isn't more to do, it's what not to do.

One CEO in Berlin came out of his solitude reset realizing that 60% of his company's growth was coming from just one product line. Within a month, he shut down five others, slashed overhead by 22%, and doubled team focus.

Another founder I work with in Toronto built an entire new AI-led division during a silent weekend retreat after realizing his best engineer had been underutilized for over a year. "The idea was always there," he said. "I just couldn't hear it until I stopped talking."

Solitude doesn't generate ideas. It clears the space for the right ones to show up.

Your Leadership Rhythm

If you've followed this book closely, you already understand that growth is not linear. Neither is clarity.

Some days, you need collaboration. Others, confrontation. But often, what you need most is quiet.

Not because it's peaceful, but because it's powerful.

So as you prepare your post-book journey, ask yourself:

- When was the last time I thought deeply without interruption?

- What parts of my leadership need fewer opinions and more ownership?

- What truth has been trying to surface, but I haven't been still enough to receive it?

You won't find those answers in another PDF. You'll find them where you've likely been avoiding: in the pause.

The Directors WarRoom: Elite Peer Learning

The Problem Most Leaders Don't Admit

I've sat in rooms with CEOs whose companies turn over £100 million a year. I've shared tables with founders who have personally banked more in a quarter than most make in a lifetime. And yet, behind the bravado, behind the polished pitches and perfectly rehearsed answers, there's often a silence that says more than words ever could.

It's the silence of pressure. Of knowing the board expects clarity while you're still wrestling with chaos. Of having to appear visionary when your team has stopped challenging your thinking. Of walking into rooms where no one will tell you the truth, not because they don't see it, but because your success has made you untouchable.

This is the emotional truth of high-level leadership: isolation.

It's not spoken about at conferences. It doesn't show up in earnings reports. But I've heard it behind closed doors, late at night in the hotel bar after the awards dinner, in the side conversations during "strategy days," or whispered during one-to-one strategy calls when the mask briefly slips.

The Innovator's Paradox 2.0

You're expected to have the answers, but who's helping you ask better questions?

You know things must change, but who's strong enough to challenge you without fear or favour?

In one particular boardroom I walked into recently, a CEO had just approved a £2.2 million strategic plan. It was flawless, on paper. But no one in the room dared to point out the obvious flaw: the market had moved, and the plan was rooted in assumptions that were already 18 months old. When I asked, "Who here would bet their own bonus this works?" the silence was damning. Not one hand was raised.

That's the cost of unchecked leadership: brilliant people tiptoeing around the truth.

Not out of incompetence, but out of fear. Fear of rocking the boat. Fear of questioning someone who hasn't been questioned in years.

And that's why the WarRoom exists, not as another mastermind, but as a crucible where leaders are challenged, sharpened, and made dangerous again.

Why I Built the WarRoom

It didn't start with a whiteboard. It started with frustration.

I'd spent years being invited to elite mastermind groups. Rooms full of high-performers, great branding, Michelin-starred lunches... but beneath the surface? Safe conversations. Fluff dressed up as strategy. Leaders walking out with notebooks full of "insights" they'd never act on.

One day, after watching a billionaire founder nod politely through another well-meaning but shallow session, I snapped. Not outwardly. Just inside. I thought to myself, *this is a waste of time.* Not just mine, but his. And that's far worse.

The problem wasn't the people. It was the format. Too polite. Too passive. Too performative.

So I built the opposite.

Not a mastermind, but a crucible. A place where leaders couldn't hide behind their wins or their titles. Where we cut through ego, challenged blind spots, and demanded measurable transformation. Where showing up without clarity wasn't met with sympathy, but strategy.

The WarRoom was born from that fire, and shaped by it.

I didn't want a group that shared ideas. I wanted a group that demanded outcomes.

That's when the Five Strategic Pillars emerged, not from theory, but from necessity. Systemization. Staffability. Scalability. Sustainability. Sellability. These weren't buzzwords. They were survival. Every member had to benchmark their business across these five filters. No hiding. No excuses.

Because in the WarRoom, growth isn't celebrated unless it's replicable. Strategy isn't respected unless it's operational. And leadership? Leadership is judged by results, not rhetoric.

This isn't a place for dabblers. It's for leaders ready to put themselves under the same scrutiny they put their businesses through. It's a discipline. A practice. A test.

And it works.

How It Works Behind Closed Doors

Imagine walking into a room where nobody cares about your title, but everyone's invested in your results.

That's the WarRoom. No fancy intros. No ego-fluffing. You're paired with another high-level leader the moment you join, and that person becomes your mirror. Every month, you face each other in

The Innovator's Paradox 2.0

peer accountability, reporting on the promises you made and what actually happened. There's nowhere to hide.

Every 90 days, I personally review your ROI. Not theoretical progress, real, measurable outcomes based on the Strategic Pillars. If you're falling behind, the group rallies around you. But if you're not showing up or executing? You're removed. Not out of punishment, but out of respect, for the room, for the mission, for the standard.

We use diagnostic tools like the Kolbe 'A' Index to understand your cognitive strengths, and the Mastery Traits framework to reveal where you sabotage your own growth. But tools are secondary to culture. And the WarRoom culture is simple: No prisoners. No fluff. No passengers.

One CEO, I remember vividly, let's call him Harish, came in from Mumbai. He ran a group of manufacturing firms turning over £80M annually. Brilliant operator, high EQ, strong reputation. But too comfortable. In his first session, I pressed him on his team's repeated delays. He deflected. When I asked him to name the real bottleneck, he froze. The silence was thick.

By the end of the session, he admitted it: he'd been the bottleneck. He hadn't fired two underperformers because he feared destabilising morale. That week, he made the changes. Three months later, his operational efficiency had increased by 17 percent. He's still in the WarRoom. But he walks in sharper, lighter, and far more dangerous as a leader.

This isn't a group that pats your back. It sharpens your edge.

Because real transformation isn't about more information. It's about more confrontation, of your habits, your assumptions, your blind spots.

And that's exactly what happens behind those closed doors.

What They're Building Together

The magic of the WarRoom isn't just in the meetings, it's in what happens between them.

Members come in thinking they need more growth. What they actually need is more courage. More clarity. More confrontation. And once they get that, they start building companies that look nothing like the ones they walked in with.

Take Kareem, a logistics CEO from Frankfurt. His team was overwhelmed, payroll was bloated, and margins were thinning every quarter. Inside the WarRoom, we helped him restructure core functions by assigning AI team members. "Sallay," their virtual receptionist, replaced a rotating door of front desk staff. "Robert," an AI-powered outbound prospecting manager, delivered 28 percent more leads in his first two weeks than the human team did in a month. Within six months, Kareem had grown 26 percent while cutting operational costs by nearly 40 percent.

Then there's Alisha, a consumer goods CEO in Dubai. She was entrenched in wholesale and retail distribution models that no longer worked post-COVID. With WarRoom pressure behind her, she launched an AI-driven direct-to-consumer engine. No agencies. No gurus. Just experimentation, iteration, and relentless execution. She doubled her net margin in four months.

Or consider Tomás, a second-generation auto parts manufacturer in São Paulo. He came in clutching the legacy of his father's company. Sacred cows were everywhere. We helped him exit two legacy divisions, redirect capital into AI prototyping, and re-skill his workforce around predictive maintenance tech. His company didn't just survive. It became a category innovator.

This isn't about hacks or trends. This is about making irreversible shifts in how you build, lead, and scale.

WarRoom members kill sacred cows. They name their AI teammates. They cleanly exit what no longer serves. They restructure for scale or sale, and they do it with ruthless precision.

Because they're not just building better businesses.

They're becoming better leaders.

Why It's Not for Everyone

Let's be honest, most leaders aren't ready for this.

They say they want transformation, but they still crave comfort. They join groups looking for inspiration, not interrogation. And they cling to patterns that once made them, but are now quietly breaking them.

The WarRoom is different. It isn't inclusive. It's earned.

This room doesn't care how successful you've been. It cares how far you're willing to go. To confront what's no longer working. To hear what your board won't say. To let go of the status you've built for the sake of the scale you're capable of.

You'll be challenged. You'll be held accountable. You'll be forced to decide whether you want safety, or legacy.

This isn't for those who fear conflict, protect ego, or avoid hard conversations.

It's for the few willing to face them head-on.

Because you don't join the WarRoom because you're successful.

You join because you're no longer willing to succeed the old way.

Strategic Disruption Circle: Bespoke Advisory

Some leaders don't need a group. They need a mirror, a scalpel, and someone who won't blink.

That's where the Strategic Disruption Circle comes in. This isn't a coaching program. It's not advisory theatre. It's direct, bespoke, and often uncomfortable work, designed for CEOs and founders who are ready to rebuild their company while still steering the ship.

Every engagement begins with a ruthless diagnostic. We strip away the fluff and dig into the five core strategic pillars: Systemisation, Staffability, Scalability, Sustainability, and Sellability. This isn't theory. It's surgery.

Take Rafiq, a second-generation family business owner in Qatar. His retail empire had strong top-line growth but no real scalability. Staff churn was rising. Cash was stuck in stock. We tore down the structure, rewired his leadership team, replaced three departments with AI roles (including "Sallay," his always-on virtual operations manager), and introduced a remote-first governance model. Twelve months later, he was operating in two new markets, with 40% fewer human resources.

Or consider Nicola, a fintech founder in Oslo. She'd grown from £0 to £30 million in 4 years but hit a wall. Every new hire slowed her down. Every meeting drained energy. Together, we didn't scale her business, we dismantled it and rebuilt it as a product-led growth engine with AI at the center. Her headcount shrank, margins doubled, and, most importantly, she got her time and clarity back.

This work isn't scalable, and it's not for everyone. It's for the few leaders who are ready to burn the playbook and write a new one.

Speaking Engagements & Workshops

The ideas in this book don't belong in pages. They belong in rooms, on whiteboards, in heated debates, and at the center of real business reinvention.

That's why I speak. Not to inspire, but to provoke.

Whether it's a closed-door board session, a leadership offsite, or a main stage keynote, every engagement is custom-built around the strategic needs of the audience. I don't show up with slides. I show up to change how leaders think.

My workshops are built around the Five Strategic Pillars and can be delivered as half-day, full-day, or multi-session formats. They're not motivational fluff. They're frameworks that shift behavior, on the spot.

In the past 18 months alone, I've led private CEO intensives in London, family office roundtables in Dubai, and global strategy retreats in Singapore. Each one designed not to teach, but to help decision-makers unlearn what's no longer working.

If your board, leadership team, or portfolio company is at a turning point, this work creates the space and pressure to move from status quo to strategic offense.

Closing Lines: Your Next Strategic Challenge

You didn't read this book just to feel informed. You read it because, deep down, you know your current strategy won't be enough for the future you're trying to build.

Maybe you're already leading a successful company, but something's missing. The wins are there, but they feel slower. Safer. Less transformative. You know what your five-year goal is, but getting there in three? That takes something more. It takes a different kind of environment. One where you're not just encouraged to think bigger, you're expected to.

That's the environment we've built inside the Directors WaRoom.

In *Mastermind Groups: The Fastest & Safest Way To Grow Your Business – The Directors WaRoom Edition* (available now on Amazon.com), I unpacked exactly how we engineered this peer environment for 8- and 9-figure leaders who were done with surface-level advice and wanted real, ruthless accountability. Most of our members stay for 3 to 5 years. Why? Because what we do works. They're not waiting five years to hit their five-year goals, most of them are doing it in three. And what's more telling? The same goals take outsiders seven years to accomplish.

Now ask yourself:

Where do you go for real strategic confrontation, not comfort?
Who challenges your certainty when no one else dares to?
What part of your company are you defending, even though you know it's already rotting from the inside?

You don't need more theory. You need a crucible.

If this book opened your eyes, the WarRoom will sharpen your edge.

Because the WarRoom doesn't hand you answers. It pushes you to ask the questions no one else will, and then do something about them.

If you're serious about that, grab your copy of *Mastermind Groups* on Amazon, get under the skin of what elite growth really looks like, and when you're ready, come find us.

We'll be waiting in the WarRoom.

Moe's Mirror

1. The Legacy You're Building Today

Leadership is not measured in quarters, but in questions. The kind that echo long after you've left the boardroom. When your team speaks about you a decade from now, what will they say you stood for? What will remain because of the way you chose to lead?

Most CEOs don't realise they're building a legacy until they're already neck-deep in one. But every policy you sign off, every product you prioritise, every person you promote, it all stacks up into the architecture of your influence. That influence won't just define your company. It will ripple into your industry, your peers, your successors, your competitors. Whether you intend it or not, you are setting a tone.

Right now, you have a choice. You can default to the legacy of convenience, preserving the status quo, extracting a few more quarters of safe returns, resisting the discomfort of reinvention. Or you can build the legacy of transformation, one that challenges the norms, embraces strategic offense, and leaves your company more adaptable, more courageous, and more intelligent than when you took the helm.

You don't need to predict the future to shape it. But you do need to act like someone else is already building it while you're still thinking. The legacy of the coming decade won't belong to the cautious. It will belong to the architect, the disruptor, the one who refused to let today's comfort define tomorrow's limitations.

Your name might not be on the building one day. But your fingerprints will be in every decision it makes, if you start leading like your legacy depends on it. Because it does.

2. Your Next Bold Move

Reading this book was never the endgame. If you've made it this far, you already understand that. What matters now is what you do in the next 24 hours.

So here's your final challenge: choose one bold move. Not a "strategic consideration." Not another meeting. One real action, visible, measurable, and a little uncomfortable.

Will you assign your first AI team member and name them as part of your leadership toolkit? Will you shut down that legacy initiative that's been draining resources and dodging hard truths? Will you gather your executive team and run a brutal 90-minute audit on your current innovation bottlenecks? Or will you finally ask your board the question you've avoided: "What are we protecting that's already rotting?"

Don't wait for the perfect timing. That's the excuse of the defensive leader. Offensive leadership starts now, with imperfect data, partial buy-in, and the willingness to face the unknown.

You don't need more information. You need to move.

Pick your moment. Make the call. And remember, comfort is the enemy of legacy. But boldness? That's the start of everything.

3. The Continuous Journey Ahead

This book was never meant to be a conclusion. It was built to be a beginning.

Innovation isn't a one-off project, a quarterly goal, or a post-it on the strategy wall. It's a discipline, a muscle, a lens that must sharpen with use. And like any high-performing system, it needs rhythm. Reflection. Tension. And above all, commitment.

The work doesn't end here. In fact, the real work begins now, when there's no chapter to guide you, no diagram to reference, and no reassuring page break ahead. It begins when you walk into your next leadership meeting and choose to ask the harder question. When you pause before signing off on an old strategy and consider, "What would a disruptor do instead?"

You've now seen what's possible: AI not as a tool, but as a teammate. Peer groups not as echo chambers, but as crucibles. Systems not for efficiency alone, but for exponential evolution. The frameworks you've encountered are not boxes to tick, they are mirrors, maps, and momentum builders.

But here's the truth: you will be tempted to drift back. To return to what's familiar. To slow the pace, protect your status, and preserve your comfort.

Don't.

Instead, revisit the sprints. Re-enter the reflection cycles. Reengage your team in the hard, hopeful work of becoming truly future-ready.

Innovation isn't an event. It's a way of leading. And if you keep moving forward, even when no one's watching, you won't just keep pace with change. You'll become its author.

CHAPTER 6:
The Market's Roar: External Pressures and Competitive Disruption

SECTION 1: The Unseen Attackers: Who's Eating Your Lunch (and How)?

You didn't see them coming. Most companies don't.

They weren't the big-name competitors you'd studied for years. They weren't on your radar during strategic offsites. They didn't show up on traditional SWOT analyses. But when the numbers dipped and your best people started leaving for them, you realised you weren't fighting the old giants anymore.

You were being eaten alive by something smaller, faster, and hungrier.

Take the case of a traditional medical equipment supplier in Switzerland. For nearly two decades, they dominated hospital procurement across the DACH region. Their reps had relationships in every major hospital. Their catalogue was thick, their brand respected. And then... silence.

Within a year, orders dropped. Renewal rates evaporated. Long-standing clients were suddenly "reviewing other options." The intruder? A Polish AI-first startup that didn't even exist three years ago. They didn't bother with relationships. They used procurement data scraped from public sources to build real-time dynamic pricing.

The Innovator's Paradox 2.0

They offered instant fulfilment on 80 percent of items and personalised dashboards for every buyer.

The Swiss CEO told me over coffee in Geneva, "We had the trust. But they had the interface." And that was enough to swing the market.

This is the new predator: not necessarily bigger, but smarter, faster, and more aligned to modern buyer behavior. They weaponise things incumbents overlook, frictionless user experience, embedded AI, usage-based pricing, decentralised sales motions, influencer distribution, even community-led support.

One of the reasons these threats remain invisible until it's too late is because most leadership teams look for competitors in the mirror, not in the margins. They compare their strategy to other companies like them. They miss the companies unlike them.

Uber didn't come from the taxi industry. Netflix didn't emerge from Blockbuster. Canva didn't spin out of Adobe. In each case, the predator redefined the category by rethinking the value delivery model, not just the product.

And here's the sting: they rarely play by your rules. While you're preparing a five-year roadmap, they're testing five new offers this month. While your procurement team is reviewing three vendors, they've built a tool that replaces all three. While you debate which market to expand into, they're already there, with a viral TikTok campaign and 10,000 beta users.

The real danger isn't the disruptor's product. It's their tempo. Their willingness to move with imperfect information, to launch scrappy, to learn fast and double down hard. And unless you start hearing the market's roar, feeling that pressure on your margins, your talent, your positioning, you won't evolve fast enough.

So the question becomes: who's eating your lunch?

Not who you're watching. Who you're not watching.

Start with this prompt: if your top three revenue streams disappeared overnight, who would benefit the most, and why?

Now go a level deeper: which startups are serving your customers with a radically different cost model? Which tools are automating the tasks your team is still billing hours for? Which founder in a WeWork somewhere is asking, "Why hasn't anyone fixed this yet?", and actually building it?

Because in today's market, being the prey isn't about being weak. It's about being unaware.

The predators aren't knocking. They're already inside your house.

Let's look next at how you map this battlefield, and what to do when the attack has already started.

The Incumbent's Dilemma: Defend, Adapt, or Transform?

Disruption rarely knocks on the front door. It slips in through the cracks, unexpected competitors, adjacent markets, new technologies, or changing customer expectations. But the question isn't whether it arrives. It's how the incumbent responds when it does.

Across every industry, the same three patterns emerge. Some defend. Some adapt. A rare few transform.

The Default Reflex: Defense

The first instinct of many incumbents is to double down, protect what already works. They tighten up core operations, squeeze margins, fire off PR campaigns, and reassure stakeholders that the newcomer "doesn't understand the industry." They tell themselves it's just a fad. That customers value the reliability of a known brand. That they've seen hype cycles before.

This defensive posture buys time, but not much else.

A legacy bank in Ireland once dismissed fintech startups as "unregulated toys." Within 24 months, three of those "toys" had siphoned off their millennial customer base with sleek apps, zero-fee accounts, and instant credit decisions. The bank responded by rebranding, investing in a glossy mobile interface, and launching a modest innovation hub. It wasn't enough. Their new tech felt bolted on, not baked in. Trust, once lost, didn't return.

Defending can work, but only when paired with reinvention. When it's just a barricade, not a blueprint, defense becomes slow-motion defeat.

The Safer Path: Incremental Adaptation

Some incumbents try to evolve. They introduce pilot projects, acquire a tech firm or two, sprinkle AI across operations, and form "innovation task forces." These are good moves, but often too shallow to shift the core.

Incrementalism is where transformation goes to die, not because it lacks effort, but because it lacks intent.

A German auto parts supplier, with over €1B in annual revenue, found itself lagging behind newer entrants building direct-to-consumer supply chains powered by predictive AI. In response, they digitized order processing, upgraded their ERP system, and launched a new "digital strategy" division.

Internally, these changes felt seismic. Externally, they barely registered. Procurement managers still complained about slow response times. Newer competitors were offering predictive inventory matching and same-day delivery while the incumbent still operated on a 72-hour lag. They mistook movement for momentum.

Adapting around the edges isn't transformation. It's like repainting the walls while the foundation shifts underneath you.

The Rare Move: Full-Scale Transformation

And then, occasionally, a company rewrites its own DNA.

Not a pivot. Not a product launch. A full-blown reinvention.

In 2017, a leading South African publishing group saw the writing on the wall. Ad revenue was drying up. Print readership was collapsing. Their core business model was disintegrating. But instead of clinging to legacy, they asked a different question: "If we started from scratch today, how would we build value for this audience?"

They shut down two flagship print magazines. They spun up a digital product lab and recruited journalists with coding backgrounds. They partnered with edtech platforms to turn their content into accredited microlearning. Within two years, content that once filled newsstands was driving 8-figure B2B licensing deals in online learning ecosystems. They didn't "save the business." They built a new one, using the same mission, but a different model.

True transformation doesn't happen because leaders are bold. It happens because they're honest.

Honest about where the market is going. Honest about what the company is not built to survive. Honest enough to risk cannibalizing their current advantage before someone else does it for them.

The Psychological Cost of Change

What makes this transformation rare isn't just strategic complexity. It's identity trauma.

For many incumbents, the hardest part of transformation isn't the technology or investment, it's letting go of what made them successful in the first place. There's an invisible emotional contract between a business and its legacy. The founders, the leadership team, even the customers, they all carry assumptions about what the company *is*.

When that identity is threatened, fear masquerades as rational caution.

That's why disruption often wins long before the metrics show decline. The competitor isn't just cheaper or faster. They're unburdened by old definitions.

So, What Now?

Every incumbent faces this choice:

1. **Defend** and hope the storm passes.
2. **Adapt** and hope it slows down.
3. **Transform** and become the storm.

The first two paths feel safer. But the third one rewrites the game.

And here's the uncomfortable truth: by the time you realize you're being disrupted, the hardest decision is already behind you.

It wasn't whether to transform.

It was whether to see it coming, and still choose comfort.

Case Study: The Battle for the Legal Industry – How One AI-First Firm Shook the Foundations of Traditional Law

I remember the first time I met Aryan. A former M&A lawyer in Mumbai turned founder, he walked into our London office with a calm confidence and a single-minded goal: to disrupt the very industry he once served.

Aryan's frustration with the legal world had been building for years. Hours billed didn't always reflect value delivered. Clients were forced to choose between slow expertise and fast guesswork. Innovation was scarce, protected by tradition. And no one, absolutely no one, wanted to challenge the sacred cow of hourly billing.

Until Aryan did.

He launched **LexNova**, a hybrid legal services firm built around AI from day one. No mahogany desks. No towering libraries. Just two things: a lean legal team of sharp commercial minds, and a custom AI engine he called "Praavak," trained on thousands of contracts, case law precedents, and industry-specific clauses.

LexNova's promise wasn't lower cost. It was **faster thinking, deeper precision, and guaranteed outcomes**. Clients didn't just get a lawyer, they got an AI-backed legal strategist with the speed of a machine and the context of a seasoned dealmaker.

The first battleground? Real estate developers and mid-sized private equity firms in the UAE and Singapore, sectors where speed kills deals and standardization is a superpower.

Here's where it got interesting.

While traditional firms took 5 to 7 days to deliver contract markups, LexNova promised same-day turnaround. Where old-school partners argued over retainer fees, Aryan offered fixed-fee packages with SLA-backed delivery. His pitch was simple: "If my AI can't do it better, we don't deserve your business."

The incumbents didn't see the threat. They dismissed him as a novelty. Until he started eating their lunch, quietly and aggressively.

One Dubai-based client moved 60% of their transactional work to LexNova within six months. Not because they were cheaper, but because they were faster, clearer, and results-focused. Aryan's team embedded AI into the client's deal pipeline, flagging risks *before* they reached the negotiating table.

Traditional firms scrambled. Some tried to license white-label AI tools. Others spun up internal innovation teams, most without clear roadmaps. A few simply tightened retainers and reassured their long-term clients with legacy loyalty.

But one by one, the cracks widened. General Counsels were under pressure to deliver more with less. Boards started asking why AI wasn't being used to reduce legal spend. And as younger, tech-savvy founders took over client companies, the expectation shifted from "Who's your firm?" to "How fast can they deliver?"

LexNova didn't win by being flashy. They won by being *designed for scale*. Every engagement fed Praavak more intelligence. Every clause reviewed taught the system nuance. Every feedback loop made the next client delivery sharper.

By year three, Aryan had not only captured market share, he was licensing Praavak to boutique firms across India, Australia, and the Middle East.

What's the lesson here?

Disruption rarely starts with loud moves. It begins with a better way, one the market can't ignore once they taste it. LexNova didn't attack law firms with ads or headlines. They attacked with **efficiency, intelligence, and trust**, three things many traditional firms assumed they already owned.

But in a world where trust is earned by outcome, not heritage, the predator no longer looks like a partner in a three-piece suit. It looks like Aryan, with a trained AI model, a lean team, and the courage to challenge what everyone else assumed was untouchable.

And the prey?

They're still clinging to their hourly rates, hoping the storm passes.

But the market has already moved.

SECTION 2: The Speed of the Market

The Exponential Curve of Change

It doesn't happen gradually. It happens all at once.

That's the uncomfortable truth about exponential change. One year, your competitors are fiddling with automation in back-office functions. The next, they've replaced entire departments, slashed costs by 40%, and launched two new AI-powered services that your board hasn't even heard of.

Technological acceleration doesn't knock politely. It breaks down the door.

For decades, we lived in linear markets. Change occurred, but it was relatively predictable. Business models evolved over years, not quarters. Innovation was something you could benchmark annually, react to thoughtfully, and maybe catch up with if you moved fast enough. That world is gone.

Moore's Law was just the beginning.

When Gordon Moore observed in 1965 that computing power doubled roughly every two years, few realized he was laying down the first rule of disruption. What he described for semiconductors now applies broadly across digital domains: AI capabilities, data processing speed, storage efficiency, and even the pace of AI model training all follow exponential curves. These aren't just engineering marvels, they're strategic threats.

In practical terms, this means the tools that feel novel today will be standard (and possibly commoditized) within 12 to 18 months. The AI that gives you a competitive edge this year may be your undoing next year, because someone else used it better, faster, or smarter.

And while most leaders *think* they're planning for the future, they're really preparing for a version of today, just with better graphics.

The Compression of Business Cycles

What used to take a decade now takes five years. What took five now takes one.

Entire business models rise and fall within a single market cycle. Look at retail. E-commerce once ate at the edges of traditional storefronts. Then, in less than a decade, it flipped the whole sector inside out. Same with media. Newspapers had centuries to build trust. Platforms like YouTube and TikTok disrupted them in under five years with zero physical infrastructure, just speed, algorithmic intelligence, and creator-led content.

These are not isolated cases. From banking to healthcare to manufacturing, incumbents are being outpaced not because they lacked resources, but because they couldn't move at exponential speed. Their decision-making cadence, board meetings, annual plans, cautious rollouts, was built for a linear world. But disruption doesn't wait for the next strategy offsite.

Why Volatility is the New Normal

When acceleration increases, volatility becomes standard.

Technologies emerge, compete, and collapse in tighter intervals. Consumer expectations evolve in real-time. Entire ecosystems, supply chains, marketing channels, distribution platforms, get disintermediated by a single API.

We've seen this repeatedly: Kodak fell not because digital cameras arrived, but because the pace of adoption shocked their planning horizon. Nokia didn't misjudge the smartphone, it misjudged the exponential nature of what "smart" would become. Blackberry had market share. But Apple had Moore's Law on its side, and a relentless cadence of improvement to match.

The same is now true for AI.

If your competitor builds an intelligent agent that closes deals, updates your CRM, and adapts to customer behavior faster than your sales team can, you won't feel that threat gradually. You'll feel it all at once, when your best customers no longer return your calls, and don't tell you why.

What This Demands of You

The implication is simple, yet devastating for those stuck in linear thinking: strategy must operate on exponential terms.

You cannot lead at yesterday's speed. You must rewire your assumptions around time, investment, and competitive advantage. The three-year product roadmap? Irrelevant if your competitor launches an AI-powered version in three months. The "pilot, pause, review" mindset? Fatal when the market shifts quarterly.

The most resilient companies now operate with compressed feedback loops. They test, learn, adapt, and deploy in 30 days. They embed AI agents that surface market shifts before humans notice. They run live simulations, not annual plans. And most critically, they don't just watch the curve, they ride it.

Shifting Sands: Consumer Behavior & Expectations

The market no longer waits.

In the past, consumer behavior evolved in slow arcs, generational preferences, gradual tech adoption, predictable demand curves. Today, the ground beneath your business shifts in real-time. And those who fail to track the tremors are swallowed by the quake.

Digital natives, those who grew up with smartphones, streaming, and instant everything, have become the dominant force in the market. But this is not a generational issue. Their behaviors have infected the rest of us. We are all digital natives now.

We expect immediacy. We expect personalization. We expect that the companies we buy from will know us, serve us, and adapt to us without delay.

Think about it: A customer who gets same-day delivery from Amazon won't tolerate a 7-day shipping window from your business. A client who uses ChatGPT to get instant answers will not sit patiently for a reply from your support team 48 hours later. These are not isolated experiences. They are setting a new baseline of expectation, one that keeps rising.

And it's not just speed. It's context.

Consumers now expect businesses to anticipate their needs before they even articulate them. They want offers that feel like recommendations, not ads. They want experiences that feel tailored, not templated.

This shift has been accelerated by AI. Tools like recommendation engines, predictive search, AI-powered customer service agents, and dynamic pricing models have rewired consumer psychology. People don't just want to be served. They want to be *understood*.

Consider Spotify. It doesn't just let users pick songs, it curates entire listening experiences based on past behavior, mood, and even time of day. The algorithm has become the DJ. The same principle applies across industries. Whether it's Netflix, Duolingo, or Uber Eats, the bar is no longer set by your direct competitors, it's set by the best digital experience your customer had last.

This is where most incumbents go wrong. They benchmark themselves against industry peers instead of the best in class, regardless of industry. But customers don't compartmentalize. They carry expectations from Apple into your retail experience. From Tesla into your customer service. From Google into your user interface.

The Innovator's Paradox 2.0

So when your product onboarding takes 12 steps and three password resets, it doesn't just feel inefficient. It feels *outdated.*

This shift has made brand loyalty more fragile. Trust is earned and re-earned at every interaction. The companies that win are those who obsess over the *entire* customer journey, from discovery to post-sale support.

In today's market, "good enough" is gone.

What's needed is frictionless design, proactive support, and a constant feedback loop that evolves the experience in real-time. This is where traditional businesses struggle. Their systems were built for scale, not intimacy. For control, not adaptation.

To thrive in this new environment, you must make three strategic pivots:

1. **From Transaction to Relationship**
   Stop focusing on the sale. Start focusing on the lifecycle. Map your customer's journey not just through your funnel, but through their world. Where do they feel stuck? Where do they need guidance, not just goods? Build trust in those moments.

2. **From Data Collection to Data Application**
   Most companies collect mountains of data but never act on it. Use your data to fuel decisions in real time. If a customer drops out of a purchase flow, trigger a smart re-engagement. If their behavior shifts, offer new products before they ask. AI tools make this scalable, but only if the intent is strategic.

3. **From Standardization to Personalization**
   Legacy systems thrive on sameness. The future thrives on difference. Your systems must evolve to serve the *individual,* not the average. Whether it's through dynamic

pricing, customizable interfaces, or AI-driven content, the one-size-fits-all model is no longer viable.

Let's be clear: You don't need a Silicon Valley budget to do this. You need a Silicon Valley *mindset*. Start by listening better. Embed feedback mechanisms at every touchpoint. Use lightweight tools like Typeform, Hotjar, or sentiment analysis dashboards. Identify pain points. Iterate relentlessly.

And most importantly, shift your perspective. Your customers aren't just buying a product or service. They're choosing a *relationship*. A digital handshake. An ongoing dialogue. If you go silent, they will too, and someone else will take your place.

In this new era, experience is the differentiator. Not features. Not price. Not location.

Ask yourself:

- Are we designing for today's expectations, or yesterday's capabilities?
- Are we building systems that adapt, or systems that defend?
- Are we learning from every customer interaction, or just measuring conversions?

Because while you're optimizing your quarterly metrics, someone else is optimizing your customer's *loyalty*.

And the market doesn't wait.

The Network Effect of Disruption

In the age of digital dominance, the old rules of competition are not just outdated, they're obsolete. Today's giants are built not merely on better products or lower costs but on superior networks. And once those networks take root, they don't just grow, they multiply. Welcome to the era of the *network effect*, where each new user adds value to the system, making it exponentially harder for anyone outside the ecosystem to catch up.

Let's take a step back.

Historically, scale came from owning infrastructure, factories, fleets, staff. But now, the most dominant companies don't own the assets. They orchestrate them. Think Uber. Think Airbnb. Think Amazon Marketplace. Their secret weapon? Platforms powered by network dynamics.

Here's the simple logic: when more users join a platform, be they customers, creators, or collaborators, the value for everyone increases. For example, a freelancer joins Upwork because clients are there. Clients come because freelancers are there. The more that join, the more efficient, valuable, and sticky the platform becomes. This feedback loop is what locks competitors out.

But it's not just Silicon Valley. Network effects are bleeding into every industry.

In real estate, data-rich platforms like Zillow are becoming more influential than legacy brokers. In supply chains, digital ecosystems connect manufacturers, vendors, and logistics providers in real time, leaving disconnected firms gasping for relevance. Even in pharmaceuticals, open research platforms and AI-enabled molecule databases are leapfrogging the traditional R&D timelines.

And then there's AI.

When AI is added to the mix, the network effect takes on a whole new scale. AI systems trained on more data, across more user interactions, get better faster. This compounds the advantage. It's why Google Search or ChatGPT becomes exponentially more useful over time, the more we use it, the smarter it becomes.

What's most alarming for legacy businesses is this: network effects don't just shift market share. They collapse it.

The Innovator's Paradox 2.0

Once a dominant network is established, competitors find themselves playing a game they didn't sign up for. They might have better service or a stronger brand, but it doesn't matter, because the market now values access, interoperability, and data flow over isolated excellence.

Let's bring this to your doorstep.

Ask yourself:

- Are you building a product or a platform?
- Are you capturing one customer at a time, or enabling a system where each customer brings five more?
- Are you connected to the value networks of your industry, or standing outside them, hoping to catch up?

One of my private clients in the automotive aftermarket parts sector learned this the hard way. They had a world-class distribution model, stellar customer service, and three decades of market loyalty. But they were slow to join the emerging digital parts platforms that garages and dealerships were moving toward.

Within 18 months, their direct orders dropped by 42 percent. Not because they got worse, but because their competitors got networked. Mechanics preferred ordering through a platform that cross-referenced parts, offered live chat support, integrated inventory, and automatically updated pricing. Once a few garages switched over, others followed, because it became easier, faster, and smarter. The client was not defeated on product. They were shut out of the network.

The lesson?

You don't beat a network with a better brochure. You beat it, or join it, by thinking in systems. By turning your business into a connector, not just a provider. By designing interactions that compound value with every new user, supplier, or partner.

Some ways leaders are adapting:

- Building customer communities where feedback fuels development in real time.

- Creating APIs and plug-ins so third-party players can extend and enrich their platform.

- Partnering with AI firms to create learning loops where data from every transaction improves the experience for the next one.

But most important of all?

They're acting now. Because the most dangerous moment isn't when a network begins. It's when it hits escape velocity, when its value becomes self-sustaining, and no amount of brilliance from the outside can break in.

So, ask yourself again:

Are you building something that scales linearly, or something that scales exponentially with every new participant?

Because in the world of disruption, you don't just need a better strategy.

You need a network.

SECTION 3: Competitive Intelligence in the Age of AI

Beyond Google Alerts: AI-Powered Market Sensing

In a world of accelerating change, traditional methods of competitive intelligence, monthly reports, static dashboards, Google Alerts, are simply not fast enough. By the time a new entrant becomes visible on your radar, they may have already begun to siphon your customers, undercut your pricing, or redefine your

The Innovator's Paradox 2.0

market. AI is changing that. Done right, it turns your competitor awareness from a static snapshot into a living, breathing pulse.

Let's begin with a distinction: market sensing is not market research. It's not about asking questions. It's about listening, continuously and systematically, to the signals that your competitors, and your customers, are giving off every single day. Signals that reveal direction, movement, and intent. When paired with the right tools, AI enables this kind of listening at scale, in real-time.

Take funding rounds. When a rival startup raises Series B capital, it's not just financial news, it's a clue. With AI scraping thousands of venture databases and news outlets, you can be alerted the moment a potential disruptor gets a cash injection. Combine that with natural language processing (NLP) to analyze press releases, and the picture becomes sharper: are they moving into your territory, or just reinforcing their core?

Patent filings offer another overlooked goldmine. While your product team is focused on next quarter's roadmap, your future competitor may already be laying legal groundwork for technologies that won't hit the market for 12 to 24 months. AI tools like The Lens, Quant IP, or even custom-trained models on patent databases can surface not just who is filing, but the thematic clusters of innovation that are emerging. Are they doubling down on AI-driven diagnostics? Supply chain automation? Precision agriculture? That's not just IP. That's intention.

Then there's sentiment analysis. While most companies still rely on customer surveys and net promoter scores, AI-driven listening tools scan social platforms, Reddit threads, and customer forums to surface what real users are saying about your competitors' offerings. And crucially, how those perceptions are shifting over time. Are customers excited, frustrated, bored? Are influencers beginning to talk about a new player in your field with increasing reverence?

But the real power lies in connecting the dots. An early-stage competitor hiring aggressively in your region. A spike in LinkedIn posts from their team about a new feature. An uptick in forum discussions and a fresh wave of glowing reviews. These aren't isolated data points. They're a storm front building. AI doesn't just gather them, it contextualizes, patterns, and prioritizes. It shows you where the next punch might land.

And yet, many leaders still default to anecdote or intuition. "We're fine, no one's touching our core customer." Until someone is. Because their business model makes yours obsolete. Or their onboarding experience redefines ease. Or their AI-driven backend makes them 40% more efficient.

Consider what it means to move from reactive to anticipatory. Not quarterly competitor slides, but daily intelligence feeds. Not gut-based decision-making, but data-backed sensing. Not Google Alerts, but an intelligent radar scanning the market's edge for signs of a coming wave.

In the chapters ahead, we'll explore how to act on this intelligence. But here's where it begins, with awareness. The kind that never sleeps. The kind your competitors hope you'll ignore.

If you're not building an AI-powered market sensing capability, you're not just flying blind. You're surrendering the high ground in a battlefield that punishes delay.

Wake up. The signals are all around you. Start listening.

Predictive Analytics for Competitive Advantage

Most leaders think of analytics as something you do to explain the past. But predictive analytics flips that logic, using past and present signals to make accurate forecasts about what's coming next. And in today's volatile, AI-fueled landscape, predictive power is no longer a luxury. It's a strategic necessity.

Consider this: a company that knows where the market is going, even just 10% sooner than the competition, can outmaneuver rivals in pricing, product development, hiring, and resource allocation. That time advantage compounds. It becomes a wedge. And eventually, a moat.

AI supercharges this ability.

Instead of waiting for quarterly reports, you can now train models on a blend of structured data (sales performance, market indices, weather, logistics) and unstructured data (earnings call transcripts, social media chatter, online reviews). These models uncover patterns that humans can't perceive, then forecast what's likely to happen across key variables like customer churn, product adoption, or competitor aggression.

Let's break that down.

1. Forecasting Market Trends Before They Peak

Traditionally, trend spotting relied on gut instinct, anecdotal evidence, or lagging indicators. Today, predictive models scan millions of consumer touchpoints, search volume, e-commerce activity, content engagement, keyword spikes, to detect early signs of emerging demand.

For example, one high-end appliance brand began noticing a quiet uptick in voice-search queries for "silent dishwashers" across German and Nordic markets. Their predictive system flagged it. Two weeks later, a surge in YouTube and TikTok content echoed the trend. The team greenlit a fast-track R&D sprint and beat the market by five months. Sales outpaced forecasts by 27%.

That kind of foresight doesn't happen with gut alone.

2. Predicting Competitor Moves

Think of your competitors not as mysterious black boxes but as systems governed by inputs, constraints, and patterns. AI helps decode them.

By feeding models with competitor hiring data (from LinkedIn), new patent applications, executive interviews, website changes, and product release cycles, AI can forecast:

- What new markets they're entering
- Whether they're prepping for a price war
- Which customer segment they're pivoting toward

One B2B SaaS company we worked with noticed a rival aggressively recruiting AI engineers and filing several machine learning patents. Their model predicted an AI-based product rollout in Q2. The insight allowed them to shift their roadmap and position their own AI module months earlier, owning the category narrative before their rival even launched.

3. Identifying Untapped Customer Segments

Many businesses segment customers using the usual suspects: geography, age, income. But predictive models often surface non-obvious clusters based on behavioral signals.

One retailer discovered a surprisingly lucrative segment: first-time dads aged 30–40 who were previously tech-focused consumers now searching for family-friendly smart home devices. AI didn't just spot them, it projected the lifetime value of targeting them early. The company created a dedicated campaign and saw a 38% higher conversion rate compared to their core demo.

Prediction reveals invisible markets.

4. From Reactive to Proactive Strategy

The final shift is psychological.

Too many leaders operate in "reaction mode." They chase KPIs. They respond to fires. They optimize what's already happening. But predictive analytics enables strategy that moves *before* the market.

Proactive leaders:

- Launch products in sync with nascent trends, not mature ones
- Set pricing strategy based on predicted demand elasticity, not historical norms
- Build supply chain flexibility around expected shifts, not known bottlenecks

This shift from reactive to predictive is what separates the disrupted from the disruptors.

Implementation Notes

You don't need a 20-person data science team to begin. Start with:

- A clear question: What do we want to forecast?
- A reliable data pipeline (internal + external sources)
- A lightweight tool or platform (many plug-and-play options exist)
- A team leader with strategic curiosity, not just technical skill

Most importantly, tie predictions to *decisions*. Insight without action is trivia.

As one of our clients said: "Our forecasts don't live in a dashboard, they live in boardroom decisions."

When your organization begins treating predictions as pathways, not just probabilities, you'll know you're on the right track.

War Gaming with AI: Simulating Future Scenarios

In a world of constant volatility, planning for a single future is a liability. The most resilient companies don't guess, they simulate.

AI-powered war gaming takes strategic planning from hypothetical to high fidelity. It allows leadership teams to model competitive scenarios, stress-test assumptions, and pre-play the market's next moves.

The premise is simple: Don't just ask "What could go wrong?" Ask "What are the top 3 moves our competitors might make?" and "How would we respond if the market shifts faster than expected?"

How It Works

AI simulations begin with input variables, market data, customer trends, competitor activity, internal performance metrics. These inputs are run through scenario engines, many of which use reinforcement learning and agent-based modeling to simulate behavior.

Each agent in the model, your company, your competitor, your customer, acts according to predefined rules, incentives, or predictive data.

The result? You don't just get linear forecasts. You get complex, adaptive simulations that reflect how real-world players would react under pressure.

Applications in Strategy

1. **Competitive Countermoves**: One UK retail chain simulated three likely moves of a dominant e-commerce rival, aggressive price cuts, same-day delivery expansion, and private label product launches. The AI model helped

them identify the most probable path (delivery expansion) and pre-invest in logistics. When the shift came, they were ready.

2. **M&A Scenario Testing**: A mid-cap software firm used war gaming to test post-acquisition integration risks. It ran hundreds of simulations around team attrition, brand dilution, and cross-sell velocity. This led to better onboarding plans and prevented three high-risk hires from derailing synergy.

3. **Policy and Regulation Impact**: One EU-based fintech firm tested the downstream effects of a potential crypto tax law. The AI engine revealed unexpected second-order effects, clients would switch platforms en masse unless communication was proactively managed. They launched a trust-building campaign and retained 92% of affected users.

Why It Matters

Most strategy sessions are built around confidence theater, linear plans, fixed assumptions, and a hope that the future will cooperate. But AI war gaming replaces confidence with preparedness.

It's not about predicting a single outcome. It's about preparing for many.

From Fragile to Agile

Companies that simulate:

- Spot vulnerabilities before competitors exploit them
- Reduce strategic blind spots
- Build optionality into their plans

They become anti-fragile, not just surviving shocks but gaining strength from them.

Getting Started

You don't need a defense-grade AI lab to begin. Start with:

- One high-stakes decision or initiative (M&A, pricing change, market entry)
- A set of known variables and assumptions
- A partner tool or advisor to build a lightweight simulation

The power lies not in perfection, but iteration. Each war game improves your playbook.

As one CEO told us, "Before war gaming, our strategy was polished. Afterward, it was battle-tested."

SECTION 4: Moe's Mirror

Your Top 3 Agile Competitors: A Deep Dive

Let me ask you something direct.

Who scares you?

Not the loudest player in your space. Not the legacy brand with deep pockets. I mean the competitor who moves like smoke, fast, formless, hard to contain. The one who somehow keeps showing up in your deals, your customer conversations, your boardroom debates. The one who isn't supposed to win… but keeps doing it anyway.

That's your agile competitor.

In this exercise, we're going to do what most leaders avoid. Not benchmark the biggest, but dissect the fastest. Because in today's market, speed and adaptability often trump scale and history. And if you're not studying your most agile rivals, you're training for a war that's already changed.

Step 1: Identify Your Top 3 Agile Competitors

Don't default to the usual suspects. This list isn't about headcount or market cap. It's about behavior:

- Who has launched the most products in the past 12 months?
- Who has pivoted fastest in response to market shifts?
- Who has adopted AI or automation at scale while you're still piloting?
- Who's gaining mindshare among your customers?

Write their names down. Be brutally honest. It might sting a little, good.

Step 2: Analyze Their Speed Profile

Look at their last 3 moves. For each, ask:

- What triggered it (e.g., market data, customer demand, competitor pressure)?
- How quickly did they act?
- How long would it have taken us to do the same?

Now zoom out. What's the pattern? Are they reacting fast, or are they setting the tempo? If they're setting the tempo, they're not playing your game. You're playing theirs.

Step 3: Dissect Their AI Adoption

Agile companies treat AI like a team member, not a tool.

- Have they named internal AI agents or systems publicly?
- Are they using AI in customer service, operations, product development?

- Have they redesigned roles or org structures around AI capabilities?

You don't need their org chart to find out. Look at their job postings. Their press releases. Their investor briefings. Look for phrases like "AI-first," "intelligent automation," "co-pilot," or "generative workflows."

If they're speaking in that language and you're not, you're not just behind. You're invisible to the next wave of buyers.

Step 4: Understand Their Customer Acquisition Strategy

Agility isn't just operational, it's also how quickly a company learns from the market.

Ask:

- Are they experimenting with new channels or platforms?
- Are they using AI to personalize offers, funnels, or outreach?
- Have they built communities or ecosystems that feed growth?

You might notice that while your team is still split-testing ad copy, your competitor is launching micro-offers using AI to create 50 versions in an afternoon. That's not luck. That's systemized experimentation.

Step 5: Map the Threat Landscape

For each competitor, build a simple profile:

- **Primary Edge:** What is their unfair advantage?
- **Vulnerability:** Where are they weakest?
- **Trajectory:** Are they gaining or losing momentum?

- **Your Exposure:** Where could they steal your market?

This isn't paranoia. It's pattern recognition. And once you see their pattern, you can break it.

From Admiration to Action

You don't study these competitors to admire them. You study them to sharpen yourself.

Remember: The real threat isn't being worse. It's being slower.

The next subsection will walk you through how to close those gaps, before your customers do it for you.

The 'Gap' Analysis: What Are They Doing That You're Not?

Let's shift from observation to execution. Now that you've mapped your top agile competitors, it's time to ask the harder question:

What are they doing that you're not, and why?

This isn't a blame game. It's a wake-up call.

Step 1: Capability Inventory

For each competitor, list specific capabilities they've demonstrated that you currently lack. These might include:

- Advanced AI deployment (e.g., predictive models, co-pilot tools, autonomous workflows)
- Hyper-personalized customer experiences (e.g., dynamic pricing, AI chat agents)
- Speed-to-market mechanisms (e.g., agile pods, no-code prototyping, innovation sprints)
- Data infrastructure and insight loops (e.g., unified data lakes, real-time dashboards)

Then ask: Are these capabilities unavailable to you, or have you simply not prioritized them?

Often the gap isn't technology, it's attention.

Step 2: Cultural Contrasts

Agility isn't just structural. It's cultural.

What behaviors do your competitors embrace that you suppress?

- Are they faster to test and fail?
- Do they reward experimentation more than perfection?
- Are their teams empowered to make real-time decisions without layers of approvals?

Map the culture gap. Then ask: What are you defending that's actually dragging you down?

Step 3: Strategic Posture Gap

Every company signals how it sees the future. What strategic bets are your competitors making?

- Are they investing ahead of the curve in green tech, AI, Web3, or decentralized systems?
- Are they building ecosystems while you're still selling stand-alone products?
- Are they recruiting for roles you haven't even imagined yet?

Their job listings, partnerships, and public statements will tell you. Don't just watch them, decode them.

Step 4: Narrative and Positioning Gap

Perception creates momentum. How are they telling their story differently?

- Do they sound future-facing while you sound feature-focused?
- Have they claimed a thought leadership space that you abandoned or never occupied?
- Are customers repeating their language in public forums, Reddit, Trustpilot, LinkedIn?

This is a silent but powerful edge. A company that owns the narrative often wins the category.

Step 5: Gap Prioritization Framework

Not all gaps are worth closing. Some are noise. Some are existential. Use a simple matrix to evaluate each:

- **Impact:** Would closing this gap unlock growth, margin, or defensibility?
- **Feasibility:** Can it be closed within 90 days or 12 months?
- **Urgency:** Is this gap widening with each quarter?

Focus on the gaps that rank high on all three. Then commit.

Closing the Loop

Choose one high-impact, high-feasibility gap. Assign ownership. Tie it to a specific revenue or efficiency goal. Review weekly.

The goal isn't to become your competitor, it's to become uncatchable by building your own edge.

And that starts by knowing exactly where you're behind, and doing something about it.

In the next and final step of this Moe's Mirror section, we'll translate this clarity into a 90-day counter-offensive plan you can act on immediately.

The 90-Day Counter-Offensive Plan

You've done the hard diagnostic work. Now it's time to move.

This isn't a strategy session for next quarter. This is a 90-day counter-offensive.

Step 1: Choose the Strategic Focus

From your gap analysis, select one needle-moving opportunity:

- Launch a new AI-enabled product feature.
- Rebuild a broken part of your customer journey using automation.
- Overhaul your internal decision cadence to increase speed.
- Shift your marketing narrative to match where the market is heading.

One focus. Not five. The tighter the target, the more brutal the execution.

Step 2: Assign the Offensive Unit

Don't run this like a cross-functional committee. Create a small, empowered strike team.

- No more than five people.
- Clear decision rights.
- Direct access to data, customers, and capital.

Name a leader. Give them air cover. Eliminate bureaucracy.

Step 3: Set the 30-60-90 Day Milestones

Break down the next 90 days into three distinct phases:

- **30 Days:** Proof of momentum. Is the thing real? Are we seeing friction or traction?
- **60 Days:** Visible progress. What has been shipped, tested, or restructured?
- **90 Days:** Tangible outcome. What changed for the customer, the team, or the bottom line?

Tie every phase to outcomes, not activities. A milestone without a metric is just a meeting.

Step 4: Declare the Win Condition

Before you begin, define success in concrete terms:

- "By day 90, this AI feature is live and has reduced handling time by 40%."
- "By day 90, we've shifted 25% of our marketing content to AI-generated workflows."
- "By day 90, customer NPS on onboarding rises by 15 points."

Declare it. Share it with your board or leadership team. Make it real.

Step 5: Build the War Map

Treat this like a campaign. Map:

- Key dependencies.
- Potential blockers.
- Communication cadence.

- Feedback loops.

Use tools like real-time dashboards, weekly stand-ups, and automated progress trackers.

Step 6: Run the War Room

Host a weekly 30-minute check-in. Same time, same agenda:

- What did we accomplish?
- What got in the way?
- What's next?

Celebrate traction. Kill what's stalling. Keep it ruthless and fast.

Step 7: Document the Learnings

At the end of the 90 days, conduct a retro:

- What worked that we can repeat?
- What assumptions did we prove wrong?
- What surprised us?

Package the learnings. Turn them into templates for the next sprint.

Final Thought: Offense as a Habit

This counter-offensive isn't a one-off. It's a prototype for a new rhythm.

When you make strategic offense a recurring discipline, not a last resort, you stop chasing the competition and start building the playbook they'll copy next year.

That's the power of Moe's Mirror.

What you just built is clarity. What comes next is commitment.

CHAPTER 7:
The Disruptor's Blueprint: Building Your Legacy as an Industry Shaper

SECTION 1: The Offensive Mindset

Beyond Survival: The Drive to Dominate

Most business books stop at defense. How to survive. How to adapt. How to avoid becoming the next cautionary tale. And while that's useful for companies hanging on by their fingernails, you didn't build a nine-figure business to "hang on." You're not here to survive disruption, you're here to cause it.

That changes everything.

The psychology of a true disruptor isn't rooted in fear. It's not about dodging decline or protecting turf. It's driven by something deeper and far more dangerous to the status quo: **a hunger to dominate.** To define the game, not just play it better.

Let's be blunt. Most companies, even good ones, are still playing not to lose. Their strategies are defensive, even when dressed up as innovation. They monitor the competition, react to market signals, refine what already exists, and call that progress. And it works... until it doesn't. Until someone comes along who isn't trying to improve the game, they're trying to **rewrite it** entirely.

That someone should be you.

The Psychology of the Offensive Leader

There's a fundamental difference in the mental architecture of leaders who play offense. They don't start with "What might go wrong?" They start with "What could be possible if we stopped asking permission?"

These are leaders who:

- Prioritize velocity over validation.
- See uncertainty as leverage, not liability.
- View market conventions not as boundaries, but as invitations to redraw the map.
- Don't obsess over benchmarks, they *set* them.

This mindset isn't reckless. It's calculated aggression. It's the difference between a general defending their border and one expanding their empire. The first tries not to lose ground. The second rewrites the map and moves the front line forward.

You don't disrupt by being careful. You disrupt by being correct, early.

That's what this chapter is about.

Not how to survive in a world of change.

But how to **shape** that world. How to move first. Signal differently. And become the company others have to respond to, not the one reacting.

"Playing Not to Lose" vs. "Playing to Win Big"

Let me paint a picture.

In the same year, two companies in the industrial safety sector approached me. Both did £100M+ in annual revenue. Both had legacy contracts with blue-chip firms. And both saw the AI wave coming.

The first wanted to "integrate AI where appropriate." They built a task force, scoped use cases, ran pilot programs, and waited for the results.

The second asked a different question: "If we were launching this business from scratch today, using AI from day one, what would we build, and how fast can we kill our current model to do it?"

Twelve months later, the first company had a slightly faster procurement system. The second launched a spin-off platform that captured 18% market share from both competitors and itself, before the rest of the industry even noticed.

That's the delta between "not to lose" and "to win big."

It's not just mindset. It's motive.

The Hidden Cost of Playing It Safe

Here's what most CEOs don't realise: conservatism compounds, negatively.

Every quarter spent optimizing yesterday's model is a quarter someone else is inventing tomorrow's. Every budget round where R&D is seen as overhead, not oxygen, is a missed opportunity to build the future before the customer even asks for it.

I once asked a board member of a global construction supplier why they hadn't moved more aggressively into prefab AI-designed modules, despite having the tech in beta.

He shrugged and said, "We don't want to cannibalize our current business."

And there it was again, **fear dressed up as logic.**

But let's be clear: you don't get disrupted because you tried something new. You get disrupted because you *didn't.*

The market doesn't wait for your comfort. It rewards your courage.

You're Already Qualified

One of the myths I see in rooms like yours, the £100M boardrooms, the family offices, the private equity halls, is this quiet assumption that disruption is something done by 25-year-old founders in hoodies with a VC cheque.

That's nonsense.

Some of the greatest category creators I work with are seasoned operators. Not because they're reckless, but because they have something even more dangerous: **strategic memory and cash.** They know the game. They've built empires. And now they're ready to redesign the rules that made them rich.

If that's you, good.

Because no one's better positioned to break a market than the person who understands how it was built.

But to lead that charge, you have to give yourself permission.

To kill what still works.

To question what still sells.

To risk alienating the past to invent the future.

Because that's what real disruptors do. They don't wait for a trend to validate their next move.

They **make the move**, and let the market catch up.

First Principles Thinking: Deconstructing Your Industry

The most dangerous sentence in business is:
"That's how it's always been done."

Offensive disruptors don't just challenge competitors, they challenge the very **assumptions** their industry is built on. And to do that, they use one of the most potent mental tools in the strategist's arsenal: **first principles thinking.**

Borrowed from physics and popularised by Elon Musk, first principles thinking is the discipline of breaking down complex systems into their most fundamental truths, then rebuilding from scratch, without assumptions, analogies, or inherited models.

Most companies operate by analogy. They iterate. They copy. They make version 2.0 of something that worked before.

First principles thinkers ask:

> "If we were building this company, this product, this experience from the ground up today, with no legacy constraints, what would we do?"

This isn't a thought experiment. It's a weapon.

The Cost of Default Thinking

Default thinking is the enemy of innovation. It tells you:

- "Margins in our industry are always thin."
- "Customers won't pay a premium for this."
- "It takes years to scale in this market."
- "Regulators won't allow that."

- "Our buyers only respond to in-person sales."

Every one of these statements was once true. Until someone challenged it. And proved it wasn't.

Take Stripe, for example. Before they entered the scene, the default truth was that online payments were complex. You needed a merchant account. A developer. A legal department. Weeks of back-and-forth with banks.

Stripe asked a first principles question:

> "Why can't a developer start accepting payments in minutes, with just a few lines of code?"

That question dismantled an entire industry's assumption. And it gave birth to one of the most developer-loved APIs in history, and a business now worth over $50 billion.

Or look at Lemonade in the insurance space. Traditional assumption?
Insurance is sold, not bought. It's boring, slow, paperwork-heavy.

Lemonade rebuilt it around AI chatbots, behavioral economics, and real-time underwriting. They didn't just digitize the experience, they **reimagined** the product from scratch.

The result? A brand that feels more like Apple than Allstate.

The lesson? When you stop accepting your industry's defaults, you start seeing space to invent.

How to Deconstruct Your Industry with First Principles Thinking

To think from first principles, start by stripping everything back.

Here's a simple three-step approach I use with my private clients:

1. Identify Core Assumptions

List every assumption your business or industry holds to be true. Especially the "obvious" ones.

Examples:

- "It takes six weeks to deliver."
- "Service must be high-touch."
- "Price must stay below a certain point."
- "Customers expect this feature."
- "We need X people to operate this."

Now ask: **Is this a law of nature, or just a habit?**

2. Reduce to Fundamental Truths

Next, ask: *What is the real purpose of this function?*
What is the outcome we're trying to achieve?

Take delivery, for example. If the core purpose is to get goods into a customer's hands, what's the fastest, cheapest, most delightful way to do that **today**, with **today's** technology, partners, and expectations?

Not "what do we currently do," but **"what is possible now?"**

You'll start to see cracks. In pricing. In process. In roles.

Those cracks are your invitations to rebuild.

3. Reconstruct with a Blank Canvas

Now, if you were launching your company from zero today, using only the fundamental truths and none of the legacy constraints, **what would you design?**

This is where the breakthroughs happen.

I once ran this exercise with a high-end dental group. The assumption was that clients wouldn't pay more than £2,000 for a cosmetic smile package. Why? Because that's what competitors charged.

But when we stripped everything back, we realised the real value wasn't the procedure. It was confidence. Convenience. Privacy. Prestige.

So they rebuilt the offering, from branding, to environment, to post-treatment concierge. Same outcome, reimagined delivery. New pricing? £6,500, and fully booked six months in advance.

When you shift from "what's standard" to "what's essential," you stop making marginal improvements, and start making **category shifts.**

Why Most Leaders Resist This (and Why You Can't)

Here's the truth: deconstructing your own industry takes courage.

It means risking ridicule. It means questioning the foundation of what made you wealthy. It means being wrong, publicly, before you're right.

That's why most leaders stop short. They innovate around the edges. Polish the UX. Repackage the same thing with new messaging.

But you? You're here to **reshape the market.**

And reshaping requires destruction, strategically.

Because sometimes the only way to lead is to break what's working before someone else does.

And here's the upside: when you build from first principles, the moat isn't just deep, it's invisible. Because while your competitors are still trying to outprice or out-market you, they won't realise you've quietly **changed the physics** of the business underneath them.

The Visionary's Edge: Seeing What Others Miss

Every market has noise, forecasts, reports, competitor moves, analyst chatter. Most leaders swim in that data, chasing what's already visible. But disruptors operate differently. They see what others don't. Not because they have better information, but because they look for **what's missing**, not just what's present.

That's the visionary's edge.

It's not about guessing the future. It's about interpreting the present more precisely, and acting on signals while everyone else is still waiting for certainty.

Disruptors don't wait for trends to become trends. They act when the signal is faint, when the dots don't quite connect, when it still feels too early.

That's the paradox of foresight: by the time something feels obvious, it's already too late to lead it.

The Two Lenses: Intuition and Data

Vision isn't guesswork. But it's not pure analytics either. The best disruptors master **two lenses**, intuition and data, and they know how to move between them.

Intuition helps you sense the unsaid. The mood shift in your customers. The change in how your team talks about their work. The friction points your industry has accepted as "normal" but your gut tells you are ripe for reinvention.

It's the pattern recognition that comes from years in the trenches, not just reading reports, but reading people. Sensing where demand is evolving before spreadsheets catch up.

But intuition without evidence becomes ego. That's where **data** comes in. Not rear-view data, but predictive insight.

Today, you don't need to rely on gut instinct alone. AI can now surface micro-signals in consumer behavior, pricing elasticity, content engagement, even hiring patterns across competitors. And if you're not building those feedback loops into your leadership rhythm, you're not lacking vision, you're flying blind.

The real edge comes from combining the two:

> Using intuition to spot the opportunity,
> And data to validate it at speed.

One gives you direction. The other gives you precision.

How Visionaries Train Their Senses

Here's the truth most leaders won't admit: vision is trainable. It's not some mystical gift. It's a discipline. A daily decision to **see differently**.

Here are three ways offensive disruptors train their edge:

1. They Immerse in Adjacent Spaces

The best ideas rarely come from inside your own industry.

A logistics CEO might find their breakthrough in how Netflix uses recommendation algorithms. A manufacturer might spot opportunity by studying how gaming companies onboard new users. A legal tech founder might borrow from the hospitality world to redesign user experience.

Disruptors expose themselves to edge cases, fringe experiments, niche communities. Not because they plan to copy them, but because it expands their mental canvas.

If you're only benchmarking your peers, you're not visioning. You're mirroring.

2. They Ask Questions Others Ignore

Instead of asking, "What's working right now?" they ask:

- "What's frustrating the customer but no one's addressing?"
- "What do we do because we *have to*, not because we *should*?"
- "What would happen if a company with no legacy entered our space tomorrow?"

These questions aren't theoretical. They surface pressure points, cracks in the system, that visionaries use as entry points for disruption.

I once worked with a B2B SaaS founder who ignored the sales dashboard everyone else obsessed over, and instead studied customer service tickets. He found a recurring pain point around onboarding delays, then built a machine-learning model to preemptively trigger help flows based on user hesitation. Churn dropped 28%. It wasn't flashy, but it was surgical.

That's the visionary edge: solving the problem no one else is even framing yet.

3. They Tolerate the Fog Longer

Most executives want clarity before they commit. But disruptors act while things are still blurry.

They understand that **the early edge always lives in ambiguity**.

I call it "leading in the fog."

You move when others are frozen. You build when others are still drafting slide decks. You test when others are waiting for perfect conditions.

Because by the time the fog clears, the advantage is gone.

Vision Is Not Enough, You Must Act on It

Plenty of smart leaders see the future. Very few act on it.

Why? Because vision without courage is just fantasy.

Every visionary move feels premature at first. Releasing a product no one's asking for. Doubling down on a market others don't take seriously. Building infrastructure before demand has caught up.

But if it feels obvious, it's already too late to lead.

The companies that shape industries don't just see what's next. They **build it**, while others debate its viability.

That's your edge, not the ability to predict the future, but the will to create it before it's demanded.

And if you're willing to live in that uncomfortable space, between clarity and chaos, you'll find the blue oceans no one else has mapped yet.

SECTION 2: Category Creation Strategies

Uncovering White Space: The Art of Market Discovery

If disruption is the goal, **white space is the battlefield.**

This is where category creators thrive, not in existing lanes, but in the gaps between them. The unmet needs. The unexplored combinations. The customer frustrations no one has owned yet.

You don't dominate by fighting for market share. You dominate by **building a market no one else saw coming.**

What Is White Space, Really?

White space isn't just an empty market. It's an **under-imagined one.** A space where demand is forming, but no one has claimed it with precision. It's not always brand new, it's often a collision of the familiar and the forgotten.

Think about it this way:

- Uber didn't invent transportation. They redefined immediacy.

- Airbnb didn't invent lodging. They unlocked intimacy and flexibility.

- Peloton didn't invent fitness. They packaged community and convenience.

White space appears when a company sees the **underlying customer motivation** others have missed.

And in a noisy world full of competitors, being the best isn't enough. You have to be the **only.**

Where White Space Hides

Most companies look for growth in the same tired places:

- What are our competitors doing?

- What's our share of wallet?

- Where can we cross-sell or upsell?

Category creators ask different questions:

- What do our best customers hate about this industry, but tolerate?
- What would they pay for that no one offers?
- What are the conversations they're having that no one is listening to?

This is where the white space lives, not in the market data, but **in the margins.**

Some of the most powerful white space moves come from digging where others don't. For example:

- A legal tech startup found white space in family law by offering AI-powered divorce mediation tools, quietly carving out a $30M niche with zero marketing spend.
- A cosmetics company spotted a white space by combining DNA testing with skincare, offering personalised formulations and bypassing traditional segmentation entirely.
- A waste management firm created a new B2B category by using blockchain to audit environmental compliance, becoming the de facto standard for ESG reporting in regulated industries.

In each case, the company didn't "pivot." They discovered an invisible hunger, and served it with precision.

How to Hunt for White Space

There's a system to this. A process you can run with your team, or as a solo founder at the whiteboard. Here's a four-part white space discovery sprint I often run with private clients:

1. Find the Friction

Every industry has friction, slow processes, clunky interfaces, inconvenient pricing models, opaque systems.

List them. One by one. Not just in your company, but across your industry.

Then ask: **"What would this look like if it were effortless?"**

That single question has created billion-dollar companies.

2. Identify the Underserved Persona

Most companies focus on the 80% middle. Category creators focus on the edges:

- The non-consumer who doesn't buy because nothing quite fits.
- The premium buyer who wants exclusivity, speed, or status.
- The overlooked niche with urgent, complex, or emotional needs.

Ask: **"Who's being ignored, and why?"**

3. Follow the Workarounds

Customers always hack solutions before the market provides them.

- Spreadsheet workarounds.
- Manual integrations.

- Whisper networks and underground communities.

Where you see workaround, you see **unmet need**.

4. Run the "What If" Play

Take three forces, technology, regulation, culture, and run "What if?" scenarios.

- "What if regulation forced X tomorrow, who's prepared?"
- "What if Gen Z refuses to use Y?"
- "What if AI made this 80% cheaper, what would break?"

This stimulates lateral thinking and reveals where assumptions are vulnerable.

Leveraging AI for Demand Sensing and Trend Discovery

Ten years ago, white space discovery was mostly gut feel. Today, it's an **AI-powered exercise in precision.**

Here's how the best category creators are using AI to surface opportunity before it shows up in mainstream dashboards:

1. Predictive Search & Behavior Clusters

Tools like **Google Trends, Exploding Topics**, and proprietary AI scrapers can track **search velocity** and **emergent phrases** weeks before they become commercial categories.

Look not just for volume, but for acceleration. The **slope of interest** is often a stronger signal than the absolute size of demand.

2. Social Sentiment + Semantic Drift

AI can analyze millions of social conversations, not just what people are saying, but **how the language is shifting.**

Example: one B2B cybersecurity firm noticed "zero trust" was being used less in technical circles and more in boardroom conversations. That shift in context prompted them to reposition around **executive risk narrative**, not just IT security. Their pipeline doubled in three months.

3. AI-Powered Product Gaps

Using AI to ingest review data, yours and competitors', can reveal **patterns of dissatisfaction** across SKUs, industries, or buyer types.

One consumer electronics firm ran NLP analysis across 3,000 Amazon reviews and discovered that "setup confusion" was a recurring 2-star issue across their category. They built a plug-and-play onboarding app, then used that as a wedge to rebrand the entire company around **simplicity.**

The category? "Effortless Tech."

They didn't invent a product. They claimed a need no one else had owned.

White Space Is Only Valuable If You Own It Fast

There's one more truth about white space: **it doesn't stay white for long.**

Once you spot it, you must **name it, claim it**, and **move aggressively.** Delay, and someone else will define the narrative, and you'll be stuck playing catch-up in the market you should've owned.

White space discovery is not an academic exercise. It's a countdown clock.

And the leaders who win don't just explore it, they **build into it**, fast, before it becomes common ground.

The 'Blue Ocean' Playbook: Creating New Demand

Most companies are trapped in red oceans, crowded waters, saturated markets, and a race to the bottom on price, features, or speed. In red oceans, the goal is to beat the competition.

But **true disruptors don't fight over existing demand. They create new demand.**

They don't improve the value curve.
They redraw it.
That's the essence of a **blue ocean strategy**, and it's one of the most powerful tools in the disruptor's arsenal.

If white space is about spotting gaps, then blue ocean is about **creating new terrain altogether**, and inviting customers into a category they didn't know they needed.

What Is a Blue Ocean?

A blue ocean isn't defined by novelty. It's defined by **non-competition**.

You're not entering an industry to win by existing rules. You're changing the **basis of competition** entirely.

Examples:

- **Cirque du Soleil** didn't compete with circuses or theatre, they fused artistic performance with acrobatics and targeted adults at premium prices.
- **Tesla** didn't launch with a mass-market car, they created a luxury EV category infused with tech appeal and environmental status.

The Innovator's Paradox 2.0

- **Salesforce** didn't just offer a cheaper CRM, they created the category of *software-as-a-service*, removing infrastructure burdens from IT buyers.

Each of these companies made **competition irrelevant**, not by being better in familiar terms, but by offering **a different kind of value**.

Four Strategic Levers of Blue Ocean Creation

When I work with 8- and 9-figure founders looking to reshape their market, I guide them through four disruptive levers that underpin blue ocean creation:

1. Eliminate

What can you **remove** that the industry assumes is essential?

Cirque du Soleil eliminated animals and traveling tents, staples of the circus model. That didn't weaken the experience, it sharpened the brand for a completely new audience.

Ask:

- What features, departments, or traditions do we keep out of habit?

- What industry costs could we avoid entirely, and still deliver joy?

2. Reduce

What can you do **less** of, without compromising perceived value?

This isn't about cutting costs. It's about rebalancing expectations.

When Ryanair stripped customer service and luxury from flights, they weren't downgrading, they were **repositioning** the product for people who didn't want frills, just speed and savings.

Ask:

- What do customers overpay for that they don't really use?
- What effort are we making that doesn't meaningfully move the needle?

3. Raise

What could you **elevate** far above industry norms to create real differentiation?

Tesla raised performance, design, and over-the-air updates, taking the EV from compliance vehicle to aspirational machine.

Ask:

- Where can we overdeliver in a way that redefines what "quality" means?
- What expectations could we blow past to make the old category feel outdated?

4. Create

What new elements, experiences, or formats could you introduce that don't currently exist?

This is where the leap happens. You're not just remixing the old. You're building **new value dimensions** that reframe what the customer is even looking for.

Ask:

- What jobs are our customers doing **outside** of our category that we could integrate?
- What emotional drivers are being underserved in our space?

This four-lever framework is known as the **Eliminate-Reduce-Raise-Create Grid**, and it's a non-negotiable tool for any category creator. It forces deep, uncomfortable questions. But those questions are where category shifts begin.

Case Study: The Silent Headphones Company That Beat Bose

One of my clients in consumer electronics came to me with a radical idea:
Headphones with no sound.

Not silent, but no audio delivery at all. Just a lightweight, wearable product that measured brain activity and stress, then played tailored white noise or silence to help executives focus and decompress.

At first glance, it was ludicrous. Why would anyone buy headphones that don't play music?

But through the blue ocean lens, it made perfect sense.

- Eliminate: Audio features, playlists, speakers.
- Reduce: Hardware complexity, battery size.
- Raise: Focus, mental clarity, neurological feedback.
- Create: A wearable that wasn't for listening, but for thinking.

The product launched with one goal: **turn noise into an advantage.**

And it worked. In its first year, they sold 80,000 units in Europe, entirely through word of mouth, executive communities, and the neuro-performance niche. No ads. No audio. No competition.

Because no one else was even **playing that game.**

The Methodology Behind the Move

Here's how that move was structured:

1. **Discomfort First** – The idea sounded "wrong" to industry veterans. That's often a good sign you're entering blue ocean.

2. **Obsess Over Jobs-to-Be-Done** – Instead of focusing on features, we asked: "What is the executive trying to achieve in moments of fatigue, overwhelm, or cognitive noise?"

3. **Narrative Clarity** – We didn't pitch it as a gadget. We pitched it as "focus you can wear."

4. **Design for the New Buyer** – Not the audiophile. The strategist. The founder. The investor. A different audience with different desires.

Blue ocean success isn't about being outrageous. It's about **being precise with a different logic.**

If You're Not Creating Demand, You're Competing for It

Let me leave you with this:

In a saturated world, the most valuable companies aren't competing, they're creating. They're designing new meanings, new expectations, new behaviors.

And they're doing it not by playing harder, but by **playing differently.**

You don't need to invent a new product.
You need to **shift what the product *means*.**

That's what blue ocean strategy makes possible.

The Innovator's Paradox 2.0

And if you do it well, your competitors won't know what hit them.

Because they'll still be fighting over old metrics, in a market you've already rendered obsolete.

Naming & Framing Your New Category

If white space is where your opportunity lives, and blue ocean is how you claim it, then **naming and framing** is how you **own it**.

Disruptors don't just build new offerings. They **define the language** of a new market.
And the one who defines the language, defines the rules.

Because until you give your category a name, your prospects will mentally file you under something they already understand.
And if they can't tell the difference, they won't pay for one.

Why Language is Your Trojan Horse

The most powerful companies didn't just launch products, they **launched new conversations**.

- Salesforce didn't sell CRM software, they sold *cloud computing* before it was cool.

- HubSpot didn't just sell marketing tools, they evangelized *inbound marketing*.

- Gong didn't market sales call software, they introduced *revenue intelligence*.

Each of those phrases didn't just clarify what the product did, they redefined what the buyer should **want**.

That's the key.

Naming a category isn't about description. It's about **direction**. You're giving buyers a new lens, then positioning yourself as the only clear solution that fits it.

Done right, your category becomes a **movement**.
A flag people rally behind.
A mindset shift people want to be part of.

How to Name Your Category

There's no perfect formula, but there is a pattern. Category-defining phrases usually fall into one of three types:

1. The Function Frame

This tells people what the product *does*, but through a new lens. Think: Revenue Intelligence, Conversational Commerce, Predictive Hiring.

This works best when:

- The function is misunderstood or undervalued.

- You want to elevate a tactical solution into a strategic imperative.

Example: Instead of saying "AI call recording," Gong reframed it as *Revenue Intelligence*, turning a utility into a CEO-level insight platform.

2. The Identity Frame

This focuses on *who* the customer becomes by adopting your solution.
Think: Creator Economy, Solopreneur OS, AI-Native Companies.

This works best when:

- You're trying to rally a tribe.

- You want emotional resonance over technical specs.

Example: Notion isn't just a productivity app. It's a tool for *creators* and *second brains*. Their language reshapes identity, not just workflow.

3. The Impact Frame

This emphasizes the *outcome* or transformation.
Think: Effortless Tech, Frictionless Finance, Zero-Lag Logistics.

This works best when:

- Your solution is hard to explain technically.
- The end result matters more than the process.

Your goal is to anchor the category around a future state the buyer desires, but hasn't seen clearly articulated until now.

Category Framing: The Story You Must Own

Once you name the category, you must **frame it.** And that means answering three implicit questions in the buyer's mind:

1. **Why this?** (Why does this category need to exist now?)
2. **Why now?** (What changed in the world to make this urgent?)
3. **Why you?** (Why are you the one to lead it?)

Your website, your decks, your sales conversations, all of it must reinforce this narrative.

You're not just selling a product.
You're inviting people into a **new worldview.**

And every good worldview needs an enemy.

That enemy isn't always a competitor, it might be:

- Inefficiency.
- Complexity.
- Disconnected data.
- The old way of thinking.

You don't need to bash the competition. Just contrast your **future state** with the **present frustration**, and let the category sell itself.

Evangelizing the Vision

Once the narrative is clear, your job shifts from architect to evangelist.

Here's how category leaders evangelize with precision:

1. Publish Your Manifesto

Create a document, video, or keynote that declares the **problem** in bold terms, defines the **new rules**, and positions your solution as the logical next step.

It shouldn't read like a product pitch. It should feel like a rallying cry.

2. Seed the Language Everywhere

Use your category name and framing in:

- Your LinkedIn posts.
- Your founder story.
- Your investor updates.
- Your team culture.

Your goal is **linguistic saturation**, until prospects start using your terms in their own sentences.

3. Turn Early Adopters into Champions

Category creation isn't lonely when others preach for you.

Equip your early customers to spread the language:

- Give them metaphors to explain your solution.
- Co-brand case studies using the new terms.
- Build slack groups, closed-door events, or digital spaces where this language becomes *social proof*.

People want to be part of something before it becomes big. Your job is to make them feel like insiders, **not just users.**

You're Not Just Competing for Market Share, You're Competing for Mindshare

And mindshare follows language.

If you fail to name the category, the market will do it for you, and they'll anchor you to the very box you were trying to escape.

But if you **name it early, frame it clearly,** and **evangelize it relentlessly**, you're not just launching a product.

You're leading a movement.

And in the long run, movements always outperform features.

SECTION 3: The 'Musk' Mentality

Elon Musk: The Grand Vision & Relentless Execution

Few figures in modern business provoke more admiration, and controversy, than Elon Musk. But whether you view him as genius, maverick, or maniac, one fact remains: **he disrupts entire industries with repeatable consistency.**

From electric vehicles to private space travel, brain-computer interfaces to solar power, Musk doesn't just enter markets, he **rebuilds them from first principles.**

So what makes his style of disruption unique?
And more importantly, what parts of it can **you** adopt without needing to be Elon?

Let's break down the core elements of his approach, and extract what's actually transferable to your business.

The 'Impossible Problems' Filter

Most companies ask, *"What can we improve?"*

Musk starts with: *"What's broken in the world that no one else is willing to fix?"*

His greatest ventures, Tesla, SpaceX, Neuralink, Starlink, each began with **a mission that seemed absurd**, even laughable, by conventional standards:

- Build mass-market electric vehicles people actually want.
- Reduce the cost of space travel by 10X.

The Innovator's Paradox 2.0

- Enable direct communication between the human brain and machines.

- Provide global internet through low-orbit satellite networks.

The key insight isn't the ambition, it's the **filter**.

Musk looks for problems so large, so entrenched, and so complex that everyone else has already **decided not to try.**
Because that's where competition is weakest, and **impact is exponential.**

This mindset is transferable. Even in a B2B business or a traditional sector, ask yourself:

- *What problems do our competitors avoid because they seem too hard, too expensive, or too long-term?*

- *What constraints have we simply accepted, without re-evaluating them?*
  The moment you stop optimizing and start **redefining the problem**, you enter Musk territory.

First Principles Thinking at Scale

Musk's method of problem-solving comes from physics:
Break a system down to its **most fundamental truths**, then reason up from there, without assumptions.

For example, when building Tesla's battery packs, the team asked:
"What are the actual raw materials needed? Lithium, nickel, cobalt, etc. How much do they cost on the market?"
They discovered the total commodity cost was far lower than what the battery suppliers were charging.

Conclusion? Build it in-house.
This became the rationale for the Tesla Gigafactories, an investment most automotive CEOs wouldn't have dared consider.

The takeaway for you is this:
Don't inherit your supply chain, pricing models, or org charts. Deconstruct them.
Ask:

- *What is the most basic input we're working with?*

- *If we started this business today, would we design it the same way?*

Musk doesn't innovate by tweaking. He innovates by **starting from zero** and rebuilding the logic.

Vertical Integration as a Strategic Weapon

Most modern companies embrace outsourcing.
Musk does the opposite, **he vertically integrates with surgical focus.**

Tesla builds its own software, chips, batteries, charging infrastructure, even its own insurance product.
Why? Because the more of the value chain you own, the faster you can innovate.
No vendor delays. No coordination drag. No watered-down differentiation.

The logic is simple:

> If the experience matters, own the stack.
> If the customer notices it, control it.
> If it slows you down, eliminate the dependency.

You may not build rockets, but think:

- *Where is my company too dependent on third parties for speed, data, or experience?*

- *What parts of the process could we bring in-house to move faster or differentiate more deeply?*

Vertical integration isn't just an ops move, it's a **defensibility strategy.**

Speed Over Perfection

Musk doesn't wait for perfection, he launches early, iterates in public, and **lets the market pressure improve the product.**

SpaceX crashed early rockets. Tesla had years of production hell. Yet both companies improved faster **because they chose progress over polish.**

The underlying philosophy?

> *"If you're not embarrassed by version one, you launched too late."*

This is a critical lesson for legacy companies. Many 8- and 9-figure firms delay product evolution for months, sometimes years, because it's not "ready."

Meanwhile, the disruptors ship faster, gather data, and improve in weeks.

If you want to lead disruption, ask yourself:

- *What would we launch this quarter if we had to cut approval cycles in half?*
- *What experiments are we delaying out of fear of imperfection?*

Speed isn't a luxury, it's the **currency of innovation.**
And Musk trades it relentlessly.

Long-Term Thinking With Tactical Obsession

Musk is often framed as a big-picture visionary, but he's also obsessively tactical.

He doesn't just talk about colonizing Mars. He drills into **heat shielding, fuel composition,** and **supply chain delays for screws.**

That paradox, *macro vision, micro execution*, is a powerful model for any high-level CEO.

You need to think decades ahead.
But you also need to be able to drop into the detail when **leverage is at stake.**

In your business:

- Keep the 10-year narrative.
  But don't let that story become an excuse for avoiding **daily operational intensity.**

Vision is only credible if it's backed by visible execution.

Adopt the Mindset, Not the Persona

You don't need to tweet like Musk.
You don't need to gamble your company on Mars.

But you **do** need to:

- Hunt problems others avoid.
- Think from fundamentals, not frameworks.
- Move faster than feels comfortable.
- Control what matters most.
- Marry vision with execution.

That's the Musk mentality.
Not hype. Not ego. Not eccentricity.

Just relentless clarity, unreasonable ambition, and a refusal to play by inherited rules.

And that's what separates the disruptors from the disrupted.

Jeff Bezos: Customer Obsession & Day 1 Mentality

If Elon Musk is the disruptor of physics, **Jeff Bezos is the disruptor of patience.**
Where Musk breaks industries with raw force and ambition, Bezos reprograms them with relentless clarity, consistency, and time.

Amazon didn't become a trillion-dollar company by chasing quarterly wins or launching flashy features. It won by staying ruthlessly committed to a single principle:
Customer obsession.

Not customer satisfaction. Not customer focus.
Obsession.

It's a different mindset, one that most leaders claim, but few actually practice.

Let's unpack the Bezos playbook and explore how it can shape how you lead, build, and scale disruption with precision.

The Day 1 Philosophy

In every Amazon shareholder letter, Bezos reinforced one simple mantra:

> *"It's always Day 1."*

Day 1 means staying paranoid.
It means operating with the urgency, agility, and inventiveness of a startup, **even when you're the market leader.**

Why? Because Day 2, the alternative, is death.
Complacency. Bureaucracy. Irrelevance.

Bezos defined Day 2 as:

> "Stasis, followed by irrelevance, followed by excruciating, painful decline, followed by death."

That may sound dramatic. But for 8- and 9-figure business leaders, it's a warning worth tattooing on your boardroom wall.

The Day 1 mindset is a defense against what Bezos feared most, not competitors, but **internal stagnation.**

Ask yourself:

- Are our best people still challenged, or are they protecting what they've built?
- Are we moving faster this year than last?
- Where have we started sounding like incumbents?

If the answers make you uncomfortable, good.
That's the point. Day 1 is not a slogan. It's a discipline.

The Relentless Customer Flywheel

Bezos didn't just serve customers. He **designed the business around them**, at every level.

He believed customers were always **beautifully, wonderfully dissatisfied**, and that dissatisfaction was the most reliable source of innovation.

The Amazon Flywheel, now legendary, was built on this obsession:

- Lower prices → attract more customers → drive more traffic → attract more sellers → increase selection → improve customer experience → drive growth → lower prices further.

It's a loop. And it spins faster the more you remove friction for the customer.

But what's rarely discussed is how Bezos **institutionalized customer obsession.**

Amazon meetings don't start with financials. They start with the **customer perspective.**
Executives write six-page narrative memos instead of bullet-point decks, forcing deep thought about **what the customer truly needs.**

And perhaps most importantly, Bezos was willing to **delay profit** to create long-term customer loyalty.

This is the piece most leaders miss.

Long-Term Thinking as a Competitive Weapon

Bezos famously said:

> "If we have a good quarter, it's because of the work we did three, four, five years ago, not that quarter."

While the market demanded short-term gains, Amazon played a different game:

- Prime took years to become profitable, but permanently shifted customer expectations.

- AWS was mocked as a distraction, but is now Amazon's most profitable business.

- Alexa didn't start as a speaker, it started as a bet on voice as an interface.

Each move looked irrational in the moment.
But Bezos wasn't building for moments.
He was building **infrastructure for inevitability.**

This level of patience is rare, and brutally effective.

Because while competitors tried to win quarters, Amazon won **categories.**

The Power of Frictionless Thinking

Bezos didn't just ask, *"How do we serve the customer?"*
He asked, *"How do we remove everything that slows them down?"*

This led to:

- One-click checkout.
- Same-day delivery.
- Predictive shipping.
- Frictionless returns.
- WhisperSync for Kindle.
- Voice ordering via Alexa.

Every one of these innovations removed micro-points of friction, creating **cumulative delight.**

Bezos understood that convenience compounds.

And the companies that win are those who **remove more pain, more often, with less effort.**

For your business, that means asking:

- *What do our customers tolerate, but secretly hate?*

- *Where can we shave 10 seconds or 10 clicks or 10 doubts from the process?*

- *What would it take to make our product feel effortless, every single time?*

You don't need Amazon's scale to apply this.
You just need the courage to reorient around **removing pain**, not just adding polish.

Innovation Anchored in Principles

Amazon isn't innovative because it chases trends.
It's innovative because it **operates from principles.**

Bezos articulated several guiding ideas that shaped how teams made decisions, even in ambiguity:

- **Customer Obsession Over Competitor Focus**
- **Long-Term Thinking Over Short-Term Profit**
- **Willingness to Be Misunderstood**
- **High Standards and Operational Excellence**

These weren't poster values.
They were operational commitments. Used in hiring, in meetings, in product design.

And most critically, they were stable.

While the market panicked, Amazon stayed anchored.
And that calm, principle-driven consistency became one of its greatest weapons.

How to Apply the Bezos Playbook Today

You don't need to build the next Amazon.
But you **can** adopt the parts of the mindset that built it:

1. **Declare Your Day 1**
   Create a quarterly ritual where your team challenges assumptions, kills complacency, and asks, "What would a startup do differently here?"

2. **Write the Customer Backwards**
   Start your product planning from a customer-facing press release, then build to that future.

3. **Measure Time Differently**
   Ask: "What's a move we can make now that will compound value for the next five years, not the next five months?"

4. **Design a Friction Audit**
   Have every team document the top 5 friction points they create, for internal and external users. Then commit to removing them, fast.

5. **Institutionalize Long-Term Incentives**
   Tie performance bonuses, product roadmaps, and hiring decisions to **long-range customer impact**, not just quarterly outcomes.

Bezos didn't disrupt by shouting louder.
He disrupted by listening harder. Waiting longer. Moving quieter.

His obsession wasn't with the stock price, it was with **delivering so much value that the market couldn't ignore it.**

And that's a playbook every disruptive leader should steal.

Other Industry Shapers: Diverse Paths to Disruption

Not all disruptors look or lead the same.

Musk dominates with scale and first-principles reinvention. Bezos wins with patience and systems. But disruption isn't a single formula, it's a mindset expressed through wildly different leadership styles.

To round out this section, let's explore three more industry shapers, **Steve Jobs**, **Reed Hastings**, and **Sara Blakely**, each of whom rewrote their category in their own way. Then we'll extract what unites them beneath the surface.

Steve Jobs: Obsessive Design and Narrative Control

Jobs didn't invent the personal computer. Or the music player. Or the smartphone.
What he did was **reimagine their purpose**, and wrap each one in a narrative so emotionally resonant that customers didn't just buy the product, they bought the story.

His genius was in understanding that people don't buy features, they buy **identity, elegance, and emotion.**

- The iPod wasn't "5GB of storage." It was *1,000 songs in your pocket.*

- The iPhone wasn't a tech device. It was *a new way to live.*

He shaped behavior by shaping **language, context**, and **experience**, with fanatical attention to every interaction, from unboxing to interface.

Transferable principle:

> Disruption doesn't just solve problems. It **elevates expectations**.
> What your customer touches, sees, and hears, **it all speaks**. And Jobs made sure it all said the same thing.

For CEOs, the lesson is this:
If you're not crafting the narrative around your innovation, the market will fill in the gaps, and dilute your impact.

Reed Hastings: Reinventing Models, Not Just Products

Hastings didn't start by dreaming about streaming. He started with a late fee at Blockbuster.

Netflix's first disruption was logistical, a DVD-by-mail model that removed pain. But what made Hastings truly dangerous was his willingness to **destroy his own success.**

When the DVD business was thriving, he pivoted to streaming. When the content catalog became a liability, he moved into **original production.**
When binge-watching rewired viewer habits, he doubled down on releasing entire seasons at once.

Hastings wasn't loyal to the format. He was loyal to the **customer's evolving behavior.**

Transferable principle:

> True disruptors kill what still works, **before the market forces them to.**

Netflix has been disrupted multiple times, **by Netflix itself.**

For your company, ask:

- What would we shut down today if we weren't afraid of the revenue hit?

- What part of our model would we disrupt if we weren't the ones who built it?

If the answer makes you uncomfortable, you're on the right track.

Sara Blakely: Scrappiness, Simplicity, and Underdog Momentum

As the founder of Spanx, Blakely disrupted the rigid, male-dominated fashion and undergarment industry without outside funding, technical partners, or a blueprint. She had a problem (visible panty lines), a pair of scissors, and a willingness to embarrass herself in department store bathrooms until buyers paid attention.

She built not just a product, but a **movement**, with humor, relatability, and a direct appeal to real-world women.

What makes her style of disruption unique is its simplicity. No tech stack. No complex flywheel. Just **customer empathy** turned into product excellence, backed by sheer tenacity.

Transferable principle:

> You don't need complexity to be disruptive. You need **clarity, conviction, and persistence.**

Spanx didn't out-fund its competition. It **outfelt** them. And that's a lesson many high-revenue companies forget.

In your business, are you overengineering innovation?
Would your customers choose simplicity over scale, if someone finally offered it?

Common Threads of Disruptive Leaders

While their tools and tactics vary wildly, these leaders share a set of powerful traits:

1. Courage to Look Stupid

Jobs was mocked for caring about fonts. Hastings was ridiculed for abandoning DVDs. Blakely was laughed out of meetings for pitching underwear without seams.

But each of them stayed with the vision, even when others couldn't see it yet.

Disruption almost always looks premature, until it isn't.

2. Deep Empathy for the End User

Whether through technology, design, logistics, or humor, these leaders **obsessed over how the customer experienced the world.** They didn't just improve it. They reshaped it, by aligning with real, human needs better than anyone else.

3. Willingness to Cannibalize

They weren't loyal to the last win. They were loyal to the **next evolution**.

This is the discipline most 8- and 9-figure companies lack. The courage to build the thing that makes your current cash cow obsolete.

But disruption **rewards bravery, not preservation.**

Final Thought: Diverse Playbooks, Shared Psychology

You don't need to be Jobs, Hastings, or Blakely to be a disruptor.

But you do need to adopt the **psychological posture** they all shared:

- See what's missing.
- Say what others won't.
- Build it before anyone else dares.

Disruption isn't a job title.
It's a decision.
One you can make, today.

SECTION 4: Building an Ecosystem of Disruption

Strategic Partnerships for Exponential Growth

Disruption is rarely a solo act.

Behind every breakthrough company is an **ecosystem**, a network of allies, co-creators, and accelerants that allow ideas to scale faster than the founder ever could alone.

Musk has SpaceX powered in part by NASA contracts and Tesla superchargers embedded in hotel partnerships.

Bezos built Amazon Web Services with integrations across thousands of startups, APIs, and SaaS platforms.

Even Apple, a company famed for closed design, has quietly forged deep partnerships with content providers, chipset vendors, and manufacturers to support its global dominance.

The disruptors who scale don't just build products. They build ecosystems.

And at the core of those ecosystems?
Strategic partnerships.

Why Partnerships Accelerate Innovation

Startups and scale-stage businesses often treat partnerships as secondary, something to pursue after product-market fit. But for disruptors, partnerships can be **a primary driver of exponential value.**

Here's why:

1. **Speed to Market**
   Alliances with nimble startups, R&D teams, or technology labs can shortcut years of internal development.

2. **Credibility & Distribution**
   Established partners can provide instant market validation and access to networks that would otherwise take years to build.

3. **Risk-Sharing**
   Co-creating solutions or launching joint ventures allows you to test bolder innovations while distributing execution risk.

4. **Access to IP & Talent**
   Partnering with academic institutions or niche innovators gives you access to cutting-edge research and specialist talent without permanent overhead.

Who Should You Partner With?

Think beyond vendors or affiliates. You're looking for **alignment at the edge of possibility.**
The best partnerships tend to fall into three categories:

1. Startups & Emerging Tech Firms

These partners bring speed, risk tolerance, and breakthrough thinking. You bring scale, capital, and market access. It's a potent trade.

- Ideal for: Piloting new technologies, acquiring experimental IP, future M&A pipelines.

2. Academic & Research Institutions

Universities and research labs often have under-leveraged ideas sitting in limbo. With the right partnership model, you can commercialize innovations the public hasn't seen yet.

- Ideal for: Deep tech, sustainability, biotech, AI models, and intellectual property incubation.

3. Ecosystem-Oriented Corporates

Companies in adjacent industries that aren't direct competitors but serve a similar audience or value chain.

- Ideal for: Co-marketing, bundled services, platform plays, and infrastructure sharing.

The Co-Creation Model: From Supplier to Partner

To unlock true disruptive value, shift from procurement-based relationships to **co-creation frameworks**.

That means:

- Joint R&D roadmaps.
- Shared outcomes and risk.
- Embedded teams across organizational boundaries.
- Open APIs and mutual data access.

Open innovation models, where solutions are developed collaboratively between firms, are becoming the norm among disruptors.

For example:

- BMW and Nvidia co-created virtual factories using AI digital twins.
- Moderna partnered with the U.S. government and biotech labs to fast-track mRNA vaccines.
- L'Oréal collaborates with tech startups to develop AR-based beauty experiences.

These aren't bolt-on partnerships. They're **strategic fusions**.

A Final Litmus Test

When evaluating a partnership, ask:

- *Will this accelerate our disruption, faster, deeper, or more credibly?*
- *Are we learning something new, or just outsourcing convenience?*
- *Does this partner force us to grow in uncomfortable but strategic ways?*

If the answer is yes, move fast.
If it's just about ease or margin, walk away.

The goal isn't more partners.
It's the right partners, **at the edge of your ambition.**

Attracting & Retaining Disruptive Talent

You can't build a disruptive company with risk-averse people.

The Innovator's Paradox 2.0

Technologies change. Markets shift. But your true competitive advantage, your **only sustainable one**, is the **density of disruptive talent** on your team.

Not just smart people.
Not just experienced ones.
But those rare individuals who **see around corners, challenge assumptions, and execute fast**, even when there's no clear playbook.

So how do you attract them? How do you keep them?

You don't need ping-pong tables, pizza Fridays, or slick perks. You need to engineer a culture where **they can win.**

The Three Motivators of Disruptive Talent

Disruptors aren't motivated by hierarchy or predictability.
They're driven by three core currencies:

1. Purpose

Give them a mission that matters. Not a job description, but a **problem worth waking up for**.

Whether it's eliminating friction for millions of users, redefining a legacy industry, or solving an overlooked social problem, **meaning scales retention.**

If your company is still selling roles instead of missions, your best candidates have already tuned out.

2. Autonomy

Disruptive talent doesn't want to be micromanaged.
They want ownership. Room to experiment. Room to fail and learn fast.

Create clear guardrails, but give them the **freedom to roam within them.**

If every decision needs six approvals and three meetings, you're not building a team. You're building a cage.

3. Growth-Based Compensation

Disruptors want to feel the upside.
That doesn't mean throwing equity at everyone. It means **tying rewards to value creation**, not just tenure.

- Performance-linked equity.
- Project-based bonuses.
- Venture spinouts or internal founder paths.

These tools tell your innovators:

> *"When you grow the business, you grow with it."*

What They're Really Interviewing For

Remember, top-tier talent interviews **you** just as much as you interview them.

Here's what they're watching for:

- Do you tolerate mediocrity, or celebrate courage?
- Is this a culture of permission, or experimentation?
- Will they be empowered, or buried in politics?

Your answers don't come from your careers page.
They come from the **stories people tell about working with you.**

If your culture rewards safe choices, slow cycles, and politics over performance, **you've already repelled your best candidates.**

Designing for Talent Density

Talent density is not about how many smart people you hire.
It's about how few low-performers you tolerate.

Netflix's culture deck famously said:

> *"Adequate performance gets a generous severance package."*

It's harsh. But it's honest.

In high-velocity environments, **one misaligned hire slows ten great ones.**
Every meeting. Every sprint. Every big bet.

If you want to attract elite builders, your culture must say:

> *"We don't have room for passengers. Only drivers."*

Great talent isn't looking for comfort.
They're looking for **velocity, vision, and a tribe that gets it.**

Design for that, and they'll find you.

Funding Your Future: Beyond Traditional Capital

Disruption needs fuel.

Not just in the form of ideas or talent, but in the form of **capital that's willing to play the long game.**

The most dangerous mistake established leaders make is applying traditional funding models to non-traditional innovation.
They expect exponential outcomes, while enforcing linear budgeting.

That's how game-changing projects get killed in year two. Not because the idea failed, but because the **funding lens never fit the ambition.**

If you're serious about disruption, you need to **rethink how you finance it.**

The Limitations of Traditional Capital

Classic budgeting frameworks, quarterly ROI reviews, annual planning cycles, fixed cost allocations, can crush early-stage innovation.

Here's why:

- Disruptive bets often have **non-linear timelines**.
- Early returns may look weak compared to core business metrics.
- Success often comes from **unexpected pivots**, not rigid execution.

If you apply the same KPIs to a moonshot that you apply to a mature product line, you'll **starve the very thing that could leapfrog your company forward.**

Alternative Models for Funding Innovation

High-growth disruptors use a different toolkit. Here are three routes worth considering:

1. Corporate Venturing

Establish a dedicated innovation fund or internal VC arm to back early-stage ideas, both in-house and external.

- Allows you to de-risk big bets.

- Keeps experimental initiatives insulated from day-to-day politics.
- Creates optionality: successful ventures can be spun in or out.

Example: Google's parent company, Alphabet, incubates disruptive ventures (e.g., Waymo, Verily, X) through its "Other Bets" division, keeping them financially and culturally separate from the core.

2. Strategic Capital Partnerships

Rather than chasing traditional VC, consider co-funding with:

- Large suppliers
- Channel partners
- Sovereign innovation funds
- Academic research grants
- Customer co-creation agreements

These partners often care more about **strategic relevance than financial control**, making them ideal allies for shared-risk innovation.

3. Internal Innovation Allocation

Dedicate a percentage of annual revenue or EBITDA to a protected "future fund."
This pot doesn't answer to traditional business units, it reports directly to the CEO or strategy office.

Its job is singular:

> *"Make bets today that will look obvious in five years."*

The best organizations give this team permission to break internal norms, faster cycles, different metrics, even rogue talent structures.

Funding Is a Signal

How you fund disruption **signals how seriously you take it.**

If your innovation projects live on leftover budget scraps and require five signatures to spend £10,000, your team already knows it's just theatre.

But when you create capital structures that:

- Reward boldness over incrementalism,
- Protect risk-takers from premature judgment,
- And align funding timelines with innovation timelines,

You unleash real momentum.

Disruption doesn't wait for permission.
And it certainly doesn't wait for perfect cash flow projections.

If the future matters, **fund it like it does.**

SECTION 5: Moe's Mirror

1. Your Industry in 10 Years: A Visionary Exercise

Pause.

Forget your quarterly KPIs. Forget the board politics. Forget what your competitors are doing this week.

Now ask yourself a more dangerous question:

> **"If I could reinvent my entire industry from scratch, what would I build?"**

Not improve. Not increment. **Reinvent.**

What would you eliminate entirely?
What would you make possible that isn't yet?
What would you do if you weren't bound by legacy systems, staff politics, or investor expectations?

This is not fantasy.
It's a mirror.

Because the companies that reshape industries don't wait for permission.
They don't predict the future. **They design it.**

Step Into the Future, Now

Project forward ten years. Your market has changed beyond recognition.
Customer behaviors are unrecognizable. Competitors look like sci-fi versions of their old selves.

Now imagine you've stayed ahead of it all.

What does your company *actually* do?

Ask:

- Who are we serving that we don't serve today?

- What painful friction do we eliminate completely?

- What is our most profitable product, and does it even exist today?

- What does "winning" look like in this future?

- What are our customers saying about us that no one says now?

Strip away today's constraints.
Write the vision as if your board had already signed off.

This is not about prediction. It's about **permission.**

You're giving yourself the mental runway to imagine a version of your business that could lead, not just survive.

The Trap of Realism

The enemy of this exercise is realism.
Realism anchors you to what already exists.

But the leaders who redefine their industries **suspend realism long enough to explore radical alternatives.**

Steve Jobs envisioned a world where the phone, camera, music player, and computer became one seamless device.

Reed Hastings imagined television without broadcast schedules.

Sara Blakely envisioned undergarments designed for function and comfort, by someone who actually wore them.

All of them started with a radical "what if."
And then, step by step, they built it.

So now it's your turn.

Not to copy, not to tweak, but to **break the frame.**

Ask yourself:

> *"If someone smarter, faster, and bolder than me launched a new version of my industry today, what would it look like?"*

Then ask:

> *"Why shouldn't that be me?"*

Because if you can see it, you can start building toward it.
And once you take that first step, you're no longer reacting to the future.

You're shaping it.

The First Domino: Identifying Your Initial Action

Vision without motion is just imagination.

You've just outlined a radical future for your industry. But now comes the harder part, **beginning.**

Not the five-year roadmap.
Not the org chart redesign.
Just the **first domino.**

Because all disruption begins with a decision, a single, bold, irreversible step that sets everything else in motion.

What's Your First Domino?

Look at the vision you just painted.
Now ask yourself:

> **"What is the smallest, most powerful move I can make today that aligns with this future?"**

Not the biggest. Not the flashiest.
The one that removes the most inertia from your system.

It might be:

- Assigning one high-performer full-time to incubate a moonshot idea.

- Reallocating 3% of next quarter's budget to fund a pilot initiative.

- Killing a legacy product or process that no longer serves the vision.
- Calling a potential partner who could accelerate your speed to market.
- Writing and sending a one-page internal memo reframing your company's future.

The first domino doesn't build the empire.
It breaks the **momentum of the status quo.**

Why This Step Matters More Than Any Other

Most leaders overestimate what they need to launch disruption.
They imagine needing perfect timing, internal consensus, or a new round of funding.

But real change starts when someone with authority does something **slightly unreasonable and entirely non-reversible.**

Once the first domino falls, the psychology shifts:

- Your team sees that the vision isn't abstract, it's active.
- Your peers realize this isn't lip service, it's movement.
- And most importantly, you feel the friction of change begin to dissolve.

Progress loves motion.
And motion begins with **one bold step** that others can't ignore.

A Challenge for You

Take the visionary future you wrote down.
Now write a single sentence:

"The first domino I will push in the next 7 days is…"

Be honest. Be specific. Be courageous.

Because the difference between a disruptor and a dreamer isn't the quality of their vision.

It's **who moves first.**

Committing to the Uncomfortable

Disruption doesn't feel like a breakthrough when you're in it.
It feels like friction. Like resistance. Like doubt.

And that's exactly where most leaders retreat.

They prefer clean plans over messy progress.
They want certainty before movement.
They crave consensus before courage.

But here's the truth you already know deep down:

> **If it doesn't feel uncomfortable, it's not real change.**

The Anatomy of Discomfort in Innovation

When you push your first domino, discomfort shows up immediately:

- Legacy staff question your priorities.
- Comfortable performers resist the speed of change.
- Board members ask for metrics you don't yet have.

And that's before the market even notices.

But this is not a signal to slow down.
It's confirmation you've finally **left the safe zone.**

Discomfort means you're now leading where the map ends.
And **that's where disruption begins.**

From Tolerance to Commitment

The best leaders don't just tolerate discomfort.
They **train for it.** They embed it into the culture.
They model it so clearly that others stop looking for comfort and start chasing momentum.

Here's how to move from avoidance to ownership:

1. **Name It Publicly**
   Let your team know this next phase will be hard. Not polished. Not predictable. But necessary.
   When leaders name the tension, they remove the fear of failure.

2. **Reward the Risk-Takers**
   Make visible heroes out of those who act boldly, even when outcomes are uncertain.
   Disruption is emotional. Recognition is fuel.

3. **Reframe Resistance**
   When you hit obstacles, remind the team:

   *"If this felt easy, someone would've already done it.
   We're uncomfortable because we're ahead."*

That's not spin. It's strategy.

The Final Commitment

You've seen the future.
You've identified your first step.
Now ask yourself the hardest question:

> **"Am I willing to lead through discomfort long enough to see this through?"**

Because discomfort isn't a sign to stop.
It's the toll you pay to earn the right to disrupt.

Push through it, and you won't just change your company.
You'll reshape your industry.

And more importantly, you'll become the leader you were meant to be.

The Innovator's Paradox 2.0

Conclusion: The Continuous Innovation Journey

Innovation Is Not a Destination

Some books end with answers.
This one ends with a mirror.

Because if there's one truth that has echoed through every chapter, every case study, and every challenge, it's this:

> **Innovation is not a finish line. It is a habit. A posture. A way of operating, especially when there is no clear path ahead.**

The mistake most leaders make is treating innovation like a project. They plan it, budget for it, assign a team to it, and wait for a tidy outcome.

But real innovation doesn't work like that.

It's messy.
Non-linear.
Uncomfortable.
And, when done well, **never-ending.**

You're Not "Done" After This Book

Too many leaders read books like this one and say:
"That's exactly what we need."
They run a workshop. They rebrand a division. They appoint a head of innovation.

But within six months, the muscle atrophies.
Why?

Because they mistake **awareness for transformation.**

Understanding the innovator's paradox is not enough.
You must operationalize it, every quarter, every hire, every boardroom decision.

That means constantly asking:

- Are we preserving a model that deserves to be disrupted?
- Are we moving fast enough to make our own success obsolete?
- Are we leading with questions, or hiding behind old answers?

The moment you stop asking, you start decaying.

The Cost of Success Is Complacency

Ironically, the more successful your company becomes, the more vulnerable it gets.
Success builds infrastructure.
Infrastructure breeds process.
Process breeds comfort.
And comfort is the enemy of innovation.

This is the paradox at the heart of your journey:

> **The better you perform today, the less pressure you feel to innovate, and the more urgent innovation actually becomes.**

Your margin becomes your blindfold.
Your reputation becomes your resistance.

And your best people quietly begin to look elsewhere, for challenge, for change, for meaning.

The companies that avoid this trap are those who build discomfort into the culture.
They treat curiosity as a competency.
They celebrate pivots more than plans.

These companies don't chase disruption.
They **become** the disruptors, again and again.

Innovation Is Not an Act. It's a System.

You've already seen this theme throughout the book:

- **The Innovation Flywheel** isn't a one-time campaign. It's a compounding rhythm of reflection, action, and refinement.

- **The Five Strategic Pillars** aren't just checklists. They're how you build resilience into your DNA.

- **AI as a teammate**, not a tool, so the business grows even as your time becomes more valuable.

When these become embedded into your leadership operating system, innovation is no longer reactive.
It's routine.

Not easy.
But expected.

And over time, your organization builds a tolerance for uncertainty, a fluency in change that most competitors can't match.

You're Now the Architect

There is no "they" anymore. No external savior. No consultant with a silver bullet.

You are the architect of what happens next.

This is not a burden.
It's a privilege.

Because while most CEOs spend their time managing the past, **you now have the tools to create the future.**

So, what will you build?

- A more agile organization?
- A team that thinks in systems, not silos?
- A model that creates space for moonshots?
- A culture that rewards risk, not just results?

Whatever it is, don't wait for the perfect moment.
Disruption doesn't care about your calendar.
It moves at the speed of your courage.

One Final Truth

You will never feel fully ready.
You will never have all the data.
And your board may not applaud your boldest moves, at first.

But that's the cost of leadership at this level.

> Innovation isn't about what's safe.
> It's about what's next.

You've spent this book learning how to anticipate the future.
Now your job is simpler, and far harder.

Go create it.

The Innovation Flywheel: How to Keep Momentum After the Book

Finishing this book doesn't mark the end of your innovation journey.
It marks the **starting line of your second curve**.

Because the real danger facing successful leaders isn't failure, it's **momentum loss**.

You've rethought your model, questioned your market, and perhaps identified your first domino.
But what happens after that first bold step?

> You need rhythm.
> You need structure.
> You need a **flywheel**.

What Is the Innovation Flywheel?

A flywheel is a self-reinforcing cycle that gets easier the more it spins.
At first, it takes enormous effort to move. But with consistency, it begins to generate its own energy.

For innovation, your flywheel looks like this:

1. **Sense** – Ongoing observation of customer needs, market shifts, and emerging technologies.

2. **Reflect** – Strategic pause to reframe assumptions, identify opportunities, and challenge internal orthodoxy.

3. **Act** – Small, fast, low-risk experiments to test hypotheses and move forward.

4. **Learn** – Feedback loops that extract insights, regardless of outcome, and embed them into culture and systems.

5. **Adapt** – Apply what works at scale, and restart the cycle with higher clarity and confidence.

This loop becomes your organization's **metabolism for change**.

Step 1: Build a Culture That Senses

Most companies are blind to early signals because their culture is designed to **report the past**, not explore the edges.

Instead:

- Appoint "disruption scouts" across key divisions.
- Run monthly market sensing meetings with AI-powered insights.
- Reward those who surface customer friction or latent needs, not just solutions.

Your goal is to constantly expose your leadership team to **what's changing before it's obvious.**

Make sensing a strategic ritual, not a once-a-year retreat.

Step 2: Reflect with Strategic Cadence

This isn't casual brainstorming.
Reflection requires structure, timing, and psychological safety.

Schedule:

- Quarterly "break the model" reviews.
- Annual off-sites that ask: *"If we were launching today, what would we do differently?"*
- 90-day retrospectives on innovation experiments, not to punish, but to extract learning.

If your leadership team only reflects when the numbers are down, you're already too late.

Step 3: Take Fast, Focused Action

Every insight must lead to motion.

But not all motion is equal. You're not looking for grand transformation overnight, you're looking for **purposeful experiments** that feed the next iteration.

Use principles like:

- "Test before you scale."
- "Spend little to learn a lot."
- "Act fast, learn faster."

Assign a fixed innovation fund or reserve 10% of every product team's capacity for "next curve" initiatives.

Make speed and feedback, not perfection, your benchmark for progress.

Step 4: Learn Relentlessly

The best companies don't just win more, they **learn more per unit of action.**

Capture both successes and failures with discipline:

- Create "learning memos" after every pilot or launch.
- Hold post-mortems that ask: *"What would we do differently if we did this again tomorrow?"*
- Feed those lessons into onboarding, playbooks, and leadership development.

Knowledge hoarded by a few is a liability.
Knowledge shared across functions becomes **institutional momentum.**

Step 5: Adapt with Precision

This is where most innovation efforts collapse: they discover what works, but never make it **part of the core.**

Integration matters as much as invention.

When something proves valuable:

- Translate it into your operations, not just strategy decks.
- Automate it, templatize it, teach it.
- Protect it from regression to old norms.

Make change **real** by making it **repeatable.**

From One Flywheel to Many

Over time, you'll want to build parallel flywheels:

- A customer insight flywheel.
- A talent flywheel.
- A digital capability flywheel.

Each one reinforces the other, turning your company into a **self-disrupting ecosystem** that improves while operating.

That's when innovation stops being an initiative.
It becomes identity.

Ritualizing the Habit of Innovation

If you remember nothing else, remember this:

Innovation dies in the absence of structure.

It needs time on the calendar.
It needs line-item resources.
It needs your **attention, when things are going well**, not just when they're going wrong.

Here are five quick ways to ritualize the flywheel:

1. **Monthly Innovation Stand-ups** – Share wins, ideas, and lessons in 30 minutes.

2. **Quarterly Reimagination Workshops** – Pressure-test core assumptions.

3. **Annual Disruption Council Reviews** – Align big bets with market trends.

4. **Innovation Scorecard** – Track metrics like time-to-insight, time-to-test, and learning velocity.

5. **Culture Signals** – Celebrate speed, curiosity, and resilience as visibly as revenue or growth.

The Innovation Flywheel Is Not Optional

Markets are moving faster.
AI is collapsing timelines.
Competitors are being born out of nowhere, often with more speed, fewer constraints, and better funding than legacy players.

If you don't install a flywheel for innovation, **they will outpace you.**

But if you do?

You won't just keep up.
You'll shape what comes next.

Not once.
Not occasionally.

Continuously.

The Strategic Disruption Circle: Who You Surround Yourself With Shapes How Boldly You Move

You've come this far because you're not like most leaders.
You don't just want to survive disruption.
You want to *lead* it.

But here's the truth very few will tell you:

No disruptor does it alone.

The companies that win aren't just driven by great strategies. They're driven by leaders who surround themselves with **strategic pressure, high-trust feedback, and future-facing peers** who hold them to a higher standard.

Disruption isn't just technical. It's relational.
The quality of your circle shapes the size of your ambition.

And that's where I come in, not just as an author, but as a mentor, an ally, and, when necessary, a challenger.

Why Isolation Is the Silent Killer

Most leaders in scale-stage companies operate in isolation.
They have advisors, but not truth-tellers.
They have peers, but not equals.
They attend events, but rarely experience **strategic confrontation,**

the kind that forces deep rethinking, not just incremental improvement.

The higher up you go, the less candor you get.
And without candor, **your assumptions harden. Your blind spots expand. Your edges dull.**

That's why I built the *Directors WarRoom*.
And why I've spent over four decades sitting behind closed doors with FTSE 100 and Fortune 500 leaders, asking the questions nobody else dares to ask.

> *"What are you avoiding?"*
> *"What legacy thinking is holding your company hostage?"*
> *"If your top three competitors merged tomorrow, what would break first in your business?"*

This book was written to provoke new questions.
But books have limits.

You need people who **won't let you drift.**

The Role of Strategic Confrontation

There are two kinds of growth:

1. Growth you *pursue*, new products, new markets, new opportunities.

2. Growth you're *forced into*, after disruption hits and you're playing catch-up.

The difference often comes down to who's in your ear.
Who's challenging your assumptions.
Who's asking you, not how things are going, but **what you're not yet facing**.

This is the role I play for the leaders I work with.
Not just as a sounding board, but as a **mirror, a model, and a multiplier.**

A Mirror, a Model, a Multiplier

- **A Mirror** – To show you where your thinking needs refinement, not just reinforcement.

- **A Model** – To offer frameworks and real-world examples that keep you ahead of your industry.

- **A Multiplier** – To push you further, faster, so your five-year goals collapse into three.

That's not motivational fluff.
That's what happens when clarity meets pressure meets execution.

If you've resonated with the ideas in this book, then you're already thinking differently.
But don't stop at insight. **Surround yourself with people who won't let you stagnate.**

Because clarity fades.
Momentum decays.
Even great leaders drift, if left unchallenged.

Why This Is Personal

I didn't write this book to impress you.
I wrote it to **equip you**, and, if you're ready, to **partner with you**.

Disruption is in my DNA.
From boardrooms in London to scale-ups in Dubai, I've advised leaders navigating acquisitions, overhauls, reinventions, and exponential growth.

And if you've made it to the end of this book, it means you don't want average answers anymore.

You want **precision. Strategy. Pressure.**
Not just to win, but to **win on your terms.**

That's why I built platforms like *The Directors WarRoom*, and why I open up a few private mentorship seats per year, for CEOs and founders who aren't just managing companies, but **re-architecting industries.**

An Invitation

This isn't a sales pitch. It's a **strategic invitation**.

If something inside you has been stirred by these pages…
If you know that your next curve requires deeper reflection and sharper allies…

Then I want to hear from you.

You're not just a reader.
You're a leader on the brink of something far greater, if you choose to move.

Let's explore what's possible together.

Because the companies that reshape the future are led by people who **commit to environments that demand their best.**

And that's the circle I build.
With clarity.
With courage.
And with people who are done playing small.

The Innovator's Paradox 2.0

Moe's Final Mirror: Your Legacy, Designed Today

Let's end where all real innovation begins, not with more theory, but with a **decision.**

You've read the whole book.
You've explored frameworks, case studies, challenges, and confrontations.
You've reimagined your industry, identified your first domino, and reflected on what leadership at the edge truly demands.

But now comes the part that matters most.

> **Will you act, or will this become just another book on the shelf?**

You Don't Need More Ideas. You Need Momentum.

The business world doesn't reward clever thinking.
It rewards decisive action backed by strategic consistency.

At your level, the gap between potential and performance isn't knowledge.
It's **activation.**

And if you've come this far, you already know that something inside your business, your model, your role, maybe even your purpose, needs to evolve.

So the mirror turns to you now, with one last question:

> **What will your legacy look like, if you start leading like the disruptor you were born to be?**

Innovation Is Personal

Don't make the mistake of thinking innovation is just about product launches or AI models.

Real innovation is deeply personal.

It's how you choose to:

- Challenge assumptions that have protected your success.
- Lead teams through ambiguity with conviction.
- Build cultures that reward courage more than compliance.
- Take ownership of a future that nobody else can see, but you.

That's not just strategy.
That's **leadership.**

Why I Want to Hear From You

Here's the part most authors won't say:
I didn't write this book for volume.
I wrote it for **connection.**

Every time a founder, CEO, or board member reaches out to me with a story of what this book sparked, a question it raised, a bet it catalyzed, a business it forced them to rethink, I grow too.

Because innovation doesn't just scale through content.
It scales through **conversation.**

And I want to learn from *your* vantage point:

- What did you believe about innovation before you opened this book?
- What shifted for you as you read it?

- What conversations are you now ready to have with your board, your team, or even yourself?

So here's my request:
Message me on LinkedIn.

Introduce yourself.
Tell me you've read *The Innovator's Paradox 2.0*.
And share just one insight, one challenge, or one bold move you're now considering.

> I read every message. I respond personally.
> Because this book is not the end of the dialogue, it's the beginning.

Never Be Shy About Reaching Out

Some readers feel hesitant.
They think, *"He won't have time,"* or *"My business isn't big enough,"* or *"What if my thoughts don't sound smart enough?"*

Let me be clear.

If you've made it to this page, you are exactly the kind of leader I want to speak with:

- A thinker who doesn't settle for surface answers.
- A builder who's still hungry for better.
- A disruptor in progress, whether you've scaled to £10M or £1B.

So don't self-select out.
Don't assume I'm unreachable.
Reach out.

Whether you're leading a multinational, preparing for a strategic pivot, or just stepping into a new innovation role, I want to hear your lens on this work.

> I learn through listening.
> I refine through challenge.
> I grow by serving those who lead at the edge of uncertainty, people like you.

Visit My Website, Explore Further

If you're ready for a more structured next step, head to **www.MoeNawaz.com** or **www.TenXMentor.com**.

You'll find:

- Private mentoring options (for qualified leaders)

- Application-only mastermind circles like *The Directors WarRoom*

- Speaking, workshop, and strategic session formats for boards and leadership teams

- Complimentary resources, tools, and downloads to help you embed innovation into your organization's daily rhythm

My work exists at the intersection of ambition and accountability. If that's where you are, or want to be, let's talk.

Leave a Public Footprint

If this book challenged you, share it.

Not because I need the marketing.
But because somewhere in your network is a leader who's still running on outdated assumptions.

Who's scaling a business that's already at risk.
Who's playing it safe, and doesn't realize the cost yet.

Post about it.
Leave a review on Amazon.
Tag me with your takeaways on LinkedIn.

Let the world know what changed for you, and invite others to rise with you.

Because transformation becomes contagious when one person decides to lead out loud.

Your Legacy Doesn't Start Later. It Starts Now.

You don't build a legacy when you retire.
You build it when you:

- Say the thing no one else in the room is willing to say.
- Kill a sacred cow that's stalling your company.
- Bet on talent that hasn't yet proved themselves, but will.
- Write the new playbook instead of clinging to the old one.

And you build it when you stop seeking safety, and start choosing **significance.**

So let's close with this:

What will your industry say about you in 20 years?

Not what products you launched.
Not what buildings carry your name.
But what **shift** you created.

If you've made it this far, you're not just a business leader.
You're a disruptor-in-waiting.

And the only thing between you and that legacy?

Action.

Let this book be the final permission you needed.
And the first step you took, toward everything that comes next.

**With deep respect and relentless belief in your potential,
Moe Nawaz**

Mentor & Strategic Advisor to FTSE 100 and Fortune 500 Leaders
www.MoeNawaz.com   LinkedIn: @MoeNawaz

www.ingramcontent.com/pod-product-compliance
Lightning Source LLC
Chambersburg PA
CBHW052140220526
45471CB00004B/1452